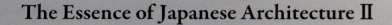

The Essence of Japanese Architecture II

First published in Japan on April 17, 2017
TOTO Publishing (TOTO LTD.)   TOTO Nogizaka Bldg. 2F
1–24–3, Minami-Aoyama, Minato-ku
Tokyo 107-0062, Japan
[Sales] Telephone: +81-3-3402-7138 Facsimile: +81-3-3402-7187
[Editorial] Telephone: +81-3-3497-1010
URL: http://www.toto.co.jp/publishing/

Copyright	©2017 Yutaka Saito
Photograph Copyright	©2017 Yutaka Saito
Author	Yutaka Saito
Publisher	Toru Kato
Editor	Naomi Miwa
Book Designer	Tsuyokatsu Kudo
Printing	TOSHO Printing Co., Ltd.

This book may not be reproduced, in whole or in part, in any form or by any means, including photocopying, scanning, digitizing, or otherwise, without prior permission. Scanning or digitizing this book through a third party, even for personal or home use, is also strictly prohibited.
The list price is indicated on the cover.

ISBN978-4-88706-363-1

The Essence of
Japanese Architecture
Text and Photographs by Yutaka Saito
II

日本建築の形

著・写真 齋藤 裕

TOTO出版

日本建築の形 II　The Essence of Japanese Architecture II

目次　Contents

008　**日本建築の形──交わりの空間**　文：齋藤 裕
The Essence of Japanese Architecture: Spaces of Society　Essay by Yutaka Saito

022　**円覚寺 舎利殿**
Engakuji Temple Shariden (Reliquary Hall)

038　**東福寺 三門・禅堂**
Tofukuji Temple Sanmon Gate and Zendo Hall

060　**鹿苑寺 金閣**
Rokuonji Temple Kinkaku Pavilion

088　**慈照寺 銀閣・東求堂**
Jishoji Temple Ginkaku Pavilion and Togudo Hall

116　**相國寺 鐘楼**
Shokokuji Temple Bell Tower

124　**龍安寺 方丈庭園**
Ryoanji Temple *Hojo* Garden

136　**園城寺光浄院 客殿**
Onjoji Temple Kojoin Guest Hall

150　**高台寺 霊屋**
Kodaiji Temple Otamaya Sanctuary

160　**姫路城**
Himeji Castle

178　**妙喜庵 待庵**
Myokian Temple Taian Tea Room

192　**有楽苑 如庵**
Urakuen Jo-an Tea Room

212	**真珠庵通僊院 庭玉軒**	
	Shinjuan Temple Teigyokuken Tea Room	
222	**西翁院 澱看席**	
	Saioin Temple Yodomi-no-seki Tea Room	
232	**桂離宮**	
	Katsura Imperial Villa	
292	**孤篷庵 忘筌**	
	Kohoan Temple Bosen Tea Room	
310	**三溪園 聴秋閣**	
	Sankeien Garden Choshukaku Tea Pavilion	
326	**江沼神社 長流亭**	
	Enuma Shrine Choryu-tei Pavilion	
336	**角屋**	
	Sumiya *Ageya* House	
350	**旧閑谷学校**	
	Former Shizutani School	
364	**吉村家住宅**	
	Yoshimura House	
378	**吉島家住宅**	
	Yoshijima House	
392	**主要建造物データ**	
	Data of the Buildings	
394	**注・主要参考文献**	
	Notes/References	
396	**謝辞**	
	Acknowledgements	
397	**著者紹介**	
	About the Author	

Book Design: Tsuyokatsu Kudo

日本建築の形——交わりの空間

齋藤 裕

禅宗が吹きこんだ活力——楼閣と庭

　古来、建築の形が変わるとき、そこにはかならず新たな人の流れがあった。異国の人々が渡来し、日本人が海を往来する。権力者が交替する。既存の社会階層が崩壊し、新興層が台頭する。時代の過渡期、社会の変動とともに新たな建築が誕生した。力や富を有する者が、その象徴として、これまでとは異なる建築の形、清新な空間を求めたからである。建築は新しい思想や信仰、美学を展開する舞台であった。

　鎌倉時代に入り、武家政権の誕生とともに、中国の南宋より禅宗が本格的にもたらされたことは、その後の日本の歴史と文化に計り知れない影響を与えた。奈良や京都とは遠く隔たる鎌倉で、新たな支配階層が全面的に庇護した宗教は禅宗であった。その基盤をつくったのは、栄西（1141-1215）をはじめとする留学僧であったが、同時に、13世紀後半に起きた南宋の政治的混乱により、日本の為政者の招請を受けて高僧が海を渡り、禅宗を直接的に移入できた背景があった。当初、鎌倉の建長寺（1253年創建）や円覚寺（1282年創建）ではそのような禅僧を開山に迎え、建物の種類、配置、構法、形態からディテールのすみずみにいたるまで、南宋の禅宗寺院を直写して伽藍が建造された。現代人の目には、日本各地にある禅宗様建築のなかに異国性を強く感じ取るのはもはや容易ではないが、当時の人々にとっては、そこはさながら異国であり、新鮮な空気に満ちた場所であっただろう。

　また、禅寺を拠点に中国大陸の文物が流入し、禅宗は新たな文化を生み出す源泉となった。喫茶の習慣や精進料理をはじめ、墨蹟や水墨画といった書画、花器や茶碗に代表される美術品の輸入により、日本文化の原形といえるものの形成が、禅宗の摂取を契機に触発された。その舞台となった建築では、貴重な舶来品（唐物）を飾る違棚や押板、床の間、書院をしつらえた座敷飾りの装置がつくられ、連歌会や茶会

鎌倉時代創建の禅宗寺院・東福寺
Tofukuji, a Zen temple established in the Kamakura period

The Essence of Japanese Architecture: Spaces of Society

Yutaka Saito

Since antiquity, it was movements of people or leaders that ushered in changes in Japanese architecture—the influx of people from other countries, the comings and goings of Japanese abroad, the rise of new elements of society to positions of power. The emergence of new styles of architecture invariably accompanied such times of transition and social upheaval. Leaders with power and wealth sought distinct forms of architecture and fresh ideas of space to symbolize their ascendancy. Architecture provided the stage upon which new ideas, beliefs, and art made their appearance.

The Zen Dynamic
With the advent of the Kamakura period (1185–1332), when warlords based in the eastern stronghold of that name consolidated a military regime with extensive power, Zen Buddhism was introduced from Southern Song-dynasty China. The impact of Zen on both the course of Japanese history and the culture of the entire country was tremendous. The new ruling class based in Kamakura, far from the old Buddhist centers in Nara and Kyoto, gave its complete support to Zen. The new school of Buddhism flourished partly because of foundations established by Japanese priests who had gone to study in China like Eisai (1141–1215), but also because of the presence of Chinese priests who, perhaps because of political turmoil in China at the time, were persuaded by Japanese rulers to come across the ocean to directly transmit their teachings in Japan. In the early days, it was these Chinese Zen priests who were invited as founders of temples like Kenchoji (1253) and Engakuji (1282), and the types, layout, structure, and all manner of shapes and details of the buildings were designed and built in direct imitation of Southern Song Zen temples. People today may not think of the Zen architecture they see in various parts of the country as in any way alien, but from the viewpoint of people of those times, the temples were like foreign lands, places that exuded a new and exotic atmosphere.

The Zen temples also became the centers of the import of books and other products of culture from the continent, and Zen became the vehicle of a new influx of culture. The temples introduced the custom of drinking tea and of eating vegetarian *shojin* fare as well as the practice of *bokuseki* and *suibokuga* calligraphic arts, along with many flower vases, tea bowls, and other works of fine art. The advent of Zen thus stimulated the emergence of what were to become the prototypes of Japanese culture. The architectural backdrops of that culture included the private quarters of aristocratic residences. In the elegantly appointed sitting rooms of these buildings, built-in staggered shelves, alcoves, wall recesses, and broad window sills were used to display valuable ceramics and other curios

などの新興の遊芸や接待に使われる会所、茶の湯専用の座敷、草庵の囲い、さらに対面の場としての書院造、数寄屋造にいたる日本独自の空間へと展開していった。

禅宗様建築が日本建築の発展に寄与した点は多々あるが、意匠面では火灯窓や木鼻の繰形といった装飾性、構造面では貫の多用による軸組の強化や、大梁と束を組み合わせた構造による柱の省略などが挙げられる。なかでも、禅宗様が垂直の空間領域を日本建築にもたらした点を重視したい。それは楼閣（重層）建築である。

元来、日本の空間は水平志向であり、中核となる身舎のまわりに庇や孫庇を加えつつ屋根をつなげ、縁をまわし、空間を水平に拡げていく。高さのある建築は、五重塔にしろ、東大寺の南大門にしろ、「仰ぎ見る」ためにあった。一方、禅宗様の建築においては、上層は実際に「使う」ためにつくられた。ここで、日本人は垂直的に重層する空間を初めて体験した。鎌倉末から室町初期（14世紀前半）の禅宗寺院の様子は、「三聖寺古図」（東福寺蔵）を通して推察することができるが、そのなかには2階建ての方丈や法堂が描かれており、上階が現・東福寺三門（15世紀前半）の2階（pp. 50-51参照）のように、仏堂として使われていたことを示唆する。上階はまた、伽藍を一望する視点を提供する場所でもあった。そこからは南北軸に立ち並ぶ仏殿・法堂をはじめ、伽藍全体の景観を眺める視点が得られたのである。

将軍・足利義満（1358-1408）が建てた北山殿（のちの鹿苑寺）の金閣（1398年・1955年再建）と、その孫・義政（1436-1490）が建てた東山殿（のちの慈照寺）の銀閣（1489年上棟）は、禅宗様がもたらした楼閣建築の流れを引くものである。両者ともにその構想は、禅僧・夢窓疎石（1275-1351）が14世紀前半に西芳寺に築いた苑地と庭園建築の組み立てに倣ったものであった。禅宗は社会の上層部に浸透することで、造形面で新たな日本的展開をうながしたが、その最たるものに、庭園芸術があった。中国の水墨山水画に描かれた世界は日本の庭づくりに影響を与え、庭は禅の境致や理想郷を表現する一つの術となる。その先駆者であり、第一人者でもあったのが夢窓疎石であった。自然のランドスケープと、人工の池や島、築山、植物、石を用いた象徴的表現とを一体化し、日本の庭は芸術として高められた。金閣や銀閣は、庭の深化とともに形成されたものである。

義満の金閣も、義政の銀閣も、上層は火灯窓を開けた禅宗様とし、前者は舎利殿、後者は観音殿として宗教性を存在理由としながらも、下層は人の使用を想定した住宅風の空間であり、垂直に重層する建物のなかに仏（上）と人（下）の空間が共存している。どちらも外から

典型的な禅宗様式で建てられた円覚寺・舎利殿
Typical Zenshuyo-style details of the Engakuji Shariden

鏡湖池のほとりに立つ三層の楼閣建築・鹿苑寺金閣
The three-storied Kinkaku Pavilion overlooks the "Mirror" Pond.

慈照寺銀閣・広縁からの庭の眺め
The veranda of the Ginkaku Pavilion commands the view of the garden.

imported from the continent. In other settings, there were also banquet halls used for entertainment and practice of poetry writing, and tea drinking as well as indoor rooms or rustic-style enclosures built exclusively for performance of the tea ceremony. Spaces of society and exchange among people began with the large and sturdy *shoin-zukuri*-style halls of the medieval-era warrior lifestyle. The more refined and intimate *sukiya*-style sitting rooms that evolved thereafter paved the way for the development of spaces that could be defined as distinctively Japanese.

The contributions of the Zenshuyo style to the development of Japanese architecture were numerous, among them decorative molding elements as seen in the bell-shaped *katomado* window frames and post and beam nosings. The strengthening of building frameworks through the generous use of penetrating members and the reduction of the number of posts through structures combining large beams and struts are structural elements of Zenshuyo. Especially important among these contributions in terms of the typology of architecture was that it opened the way for the development of vertical space as seen in multi-story pavilion buildings.

Space had long been oriented to the horizontal in Japan, being expanded outward by means of eaves and additional eaves extending over encircling aisles or verandas added on around the central core. Until then, height in architecture was aimed mainly at creating a sense of awe and grandeur, as in the five-storied pagodas and the Nandaimon south gate at Todaiji. In Zenshuyo buildings, upper levels were made not so much to look imposing as for practical use. With this style of structure, Japanese came to experience verticality in space for the first time. We can get an idea of what Zen temple architecture of the early fourteenth century looked like from a diagram of Sanshoji temple preserved at Tofukuji temple. There we find that the abbot's residence (*hojo*) and lecture hall (*hatto*) were both two-story buildings and that the upper floors might have been used to house Buddhist statues, as seen in the second floor of the Tofukuji Sanmon gate (see pp. 50–51) extant today. The upper story also afforded a full view of the entire compound. Its vantage point made it possible to gaze out over the whole temple laid out on the north-south axis with its Buddha hall, lecture hall and other structures.

The Kinkaku reliquary hall or Golden Pavilion (1398; rebuilt 1955) built by shogun Ashikaga Yoshimitsu (1358–1408) at his Kitayama villa (later Rokuonji temple) and the Ginkaku Kannon hall or Silver Pavilion (ridge raised 1489) of his grandson Yoshimasa (1436–1490) built at the latter's Higashiyama villa (later Jishoji temple) are examples of the multi-storied architecture introduced by the Zenshuyo style. The schemes for both villas imitated the combination of garden design and garden architecture pioneered at Saihoji temple in the early fourteenth century by the priest Muso Soseki (1275–1351). As Zen gradually spread through the upper class of society, it brought forth new developments in architecture, at the pinnacle of which were to be the garden arts. Garden building was influenced by the worlds portrayed in Chinese landscape paintings and became a way of expressing the Zen state of mind or utopia, and in these arts Muso Soseki was preeminent. Japan's gardens became an increasingly sophisticated art through the unity of the natural landscape with symbolic expressions using artificial ponds, islands, hills, plants, and rocks. The Kinkaku and Ginkaku pavilions came into being as part of this refinement of the garden-building arts.

Both Yoshimitsu's Kinkaku and Yoshimasa's Ginkaku have Zenshuyo-style *katomado* windows on their upper stories. In the case of the former, the upper story was a *shariden*, used to enshrine a relic of the Buddha, and in the latter, was built as a hall to enshrine the Bodhisattva Kannon (Skt.

見ると庭の中心的な構成要素となっており、さらに内部からは、理想郷を表わした、小さな宇宙とでもいうべき完璧な庭の眺望が得られるように計画されている。このような庭園建築の系譜は、のちに数寄屋建築の源流となる。

庇の下の洗練──縁と建具

　金閣と銀閣の間には、約100年の隔たりがある。両者の間には共通点も多いが、相違点もある。その一つに、建具がある。金閣の池に面する2階正面には引違いの舞良戸（板戸）が入り、1階正面には寝殿造で使われてきた平安時代以来の建具である蔀戸が全面に吊られている。一方、銀閣の池に面する1階正面には、腰高明り障子だけが入っている。この建具は、軒の深さが充分にあれば舞良戸の上半分は雨に濡れることがないので、その部分を紙張とし、いわば舞良戸と明り障子を合体して一つの建具にしたものである。従来の形式よりもはるかに軽く、動かしやすく、また、閉めたまま内部を明るくするとともに、外観を軽快にする。

　日本の建具の歴史は、可動化と軽量化を求めるなかで発達した。建具は開閉方法により、吊戸、開き戸、引き戸の三つに分けられ、吊戸は蔀戸、開き戸は妻戸や板扉、引き戸は遣戸（厚板戸）や格子戸、舞良戸、襖、明り障子を指す。

　平安以来使われてきた蔀戸は、一枚のものもあるが、扱いやすいように上下に分かれているもの（半蔀）が多く、上部を吊り上げ、下部を取り外してしまえば、内部と縁との境には柱しか残らない。空間は大きく開放され、外と内の空気が流動する。空間の呼吸度は大きい。しかし、蔀戸は重いのが難点で、気軽に開閉できない。しかも閉じてしまえば光は入らず、空気の流れも遮断される。

　一方、平安末から鎌倉時代に使われるようになった遣戸や舞良戸といった引き戸は、引違いによる開閉の自在性や軽量化の要求を満たす建具であった。これは、壁の一部が可動式になったと考えればイメージしやすいだろう。操作しやすいために出入りの利便性が高まり、動線の多様化がうながされた。さらにこれに付随して、引き違い戸の2本溝から、内側にもう1本溝を彫り、明り障子を組み合わせた3本溝形式が開発された。日本建築は、木と土と紙でできているとよくいわれるが、紙の要素がここでようやく表に登場する。その過程のなかには、東福寺塔頭・龍吟庵（14世紀・国宝）のように、縁との境に蔀戸を吊り、その内側に1本溝を彫って2枚の明り障子を立てた「子持ち障子」が考案されたりもしたし、あるいは、銀閣に見られるような腰高明り障子の

金閣・1階の蔀戸と2階の舞良戸
The first and second floors of the Kinkaku Pavilion

銀閣・1階の腰高明り障子
The waist-high shoji panels enclose the first floor of the Ginkaku Pavilion.

宇治上神社・拝殿（鎌倉時代）の半蔀
Latticed shutters of the Ujigami Shrine worship hall

Avalokiteshvara), even though the lower floor was built in residential style intended for human use—the spaces for human use (below) and for the deity (above) enclosed vertically in the same building. In both cases, when viewed from outside, the pavilion is the central factor in the composition of the garden, while from inside it was planned in such a way as to provide exquisite views of a garden conceived as a microcosm expressing paradise. This lineage of garden architecture was to give rise to later trends in *sukiya* architecture.

Veranda and Moveable Partition Refinements

About 100 years separate the building of the Kinkaku and Ginkaku pavilions. They have certain features in common, but in others are quite distinct, and one of those features is in the various kinds of sliding doors and partition panels collectively known as *tategu*. In the Kinkaku Pavilion, we find sets of *mairado* sliding board panels on the outside front of the second floor. The first floor has latticed wooden *shitomido* shutters, which swing open and closed vertically, the type that had been in use since the *shinden-zukuri* dwellings of the Heian period. The first floor of the Ginkaku Pavilion on the front side facing the pond, however, has only shoji panels with translucent paper in their upper half. These panels appear to be a merging of the *mairado* board door and the shoji panel, developed as partitions that could be used when a roof had extended eaves that would protect their upper parts against rain. The newly devised half translucent panels were much lighter than the older types of doors and easier to move; they both illuminated the interior and gave the exterior a brighter, more light-weight appearance.

The history of *tategu* is one of the pursuit of mobility and light weight. They are divided into three types by the way they open and close: hanging doors (*tsurido*) hinged along the top (this includes *shitomido*); swinging doors (*hirakido*) hinged on the sides (this includes *tsumado* and *ita-tobira* doors); and sliding doors (*hikido*), sliding in grooves in a frame (this includes thick *yarido* wooden doors, *koshido* latticed doors, *mairado*, *fusuma*, and translucent paper shoji).

The latticed shutters used for protection against rain called *shitomido* are in some cases one panel that fits into a bay from top lintel to sill, but most are "half-closing" *hajitomi*, with the top half suspended from the lintel and the bottom half made to be completely removable, so that the entire bay is opened with only the pillars between interior and veranda. This method allowed the space to be opened up wide for circulation of air between inside and out. The weight of *shitomido*, however, makes them difficult to maneuver. When they are closed, moreover, light is shut out and circulation of air, too, is slowed.

The sliding types of doors, which came into use from the late Heian period and into the Kamakura period, fulfilled the demand for more easily moved, lighter-weight partitions. They are essentially parts of the wall that are moveable. Their movability facilitated coming and going through the space and made possible more diverse lines of movement. The next convenience to appear was the addition of one more groove to the two-groove frames for sliding panels so that the use of a shoji panel covered with translucent paper running in the inside groove became possible. Traditional Japanese architecture is sometimes described as being made of wood, earth, and paper, and it was from around that time that paper came to the fore as an architectural material. In the process of these developments there were clever inventions like the *komochi* (nested) shoji panels set in a single groove on the inside of a bay fitted with *shitomido* panels. An example may be found at the late fourteenth-century Ryogin'an

単独使用は、舞良戸+明り障子形式のさらなる発展形といえる。また、江戸時代前期には、雨戸に新たな工夫があり、1本溝で可動させて戸袋に収める方式が普及した。このことで、側柱（外周の柱）に明り障子を立てこむことができるようになり、入側縁（畳敷きの縁）のような縁の室内化が一部の建築で採り入れられた。18世紀の改造部分となるが、桂離宮の中書院・新御殿（17世紀）の入側縁や、江沼神社・長流亭（1709年）の川にのぞんで四方にめぐらされた入側縁（p.335参照）にその例を見ることができる。

建具の進化は人々の生活の要求から引き起こされ、建築の形や空間の質に変化をおよぼしたが、なかでも薄くて破れにくい和紙を漉くことができるようになり、明り障子が開発されたことは画期的なことであった。外と内を仕切る半透明の建築の皮膜は、閉じたまま採光でき、室内にほどよい明るさを与える。しかも風や雨を遮りつつ、天候や時間の変化、人の気配、鳥や虫の鳴き声といった庭の様子を、室内にいながらにして、紙1枚隔てて感じることができる。軽々と開閉できる利便性は、室内と縁との連続感を強め、内部と庭との親和性を高めた。外と内をつなげる中間領域——庇の下の空間は、高い完成度を目指した庭とつねに対の関係となって洗練されていったのである。

角柱の美学——同仁齋の空間

日本建築にとって、柱は空間構成の要であり、部屋のつくりの中心をなす。空間が変われば、柱が変わる。あるいは、柱が変われば、空間が変わるともいえる。本書I巻では、古代以来の円柱がつくる建築を主要テーマとし、それを祈りの空間と定義し、円柱文化の建築として括った。本書II巻では、角柱と皮つき丸太や面皮柱で形づくられた建築が主要テーマとなる。そこは日常生活・社交・教養・趣味・宗教を混成した建築空間であり、人が住まい、交わり、学び、花鳥風月を愛で、茶を飲み、風流に遊ぶ空間であった。

鎌倉時代を境にして、室町以降は角柱の時代が到来する。金閣も銀閣も基本は仏堂でありながら、すでに古代的な身舎（円柱）と庇（角柱）の関係から脱し、両方とも角柱による空間となっている。屋根構造が桔木構法の定着と完成によって発展し、住まいや接客のための建築は、一つ屋根の下で使い方に応じて部屋を分化し、大小に仕切る空間構成法へと移行していった。それとともに、襖や明り障子といった間仕切りの発達に応じて、敷居や鴨居の溝を彫り、建具が納まる角柱が主流となったのである。

慈照寺・東求堂（1485年）のなかにつくられた義政の書斎・同仁齋

龍吟庵の建具。蔀戸の内側に子持ち障子が1本溝で入る
Nested shoji panels set in a single groove inside the latticed shutters at Ryogin'an

桂離宮・新御殿の入側縁
Interior veranda of the Shingoten, Katsura Imperial Villa

慈照寺東求堂・同仁齋。端整な角柱の空間
Square posts neatly delineate the space of the Dojinsai study.

subtemple at Tofukuji temple. The use of half-shoji panels alone (without outside shutters), such as seen at the Ginkaku Pavilion, can be considered a further development of the *mairado*-plus-shoji combination. Rain shutters advanced again with the method of running the wooden panels in a single groove and storing them in a box (*tobukuro*) at the side, a convenience that spread in the early Edo period and survives today. By this method translucent shoji panels could be installed between the posts of the outside row protected from rain and bad weather by rain shutters, and the aisle within them converted to interior space in the form of tatami-mat-floored interior verandas and so forth. Examples are the interior verandas of the Chushoin and Shingoten at Katsura Imperial Villa (as they were renovated in the eighteenth century), and the interior veranda encircling the Choryu-tei pavilion built overlooking the river in 1709 at Enuma Shrine (see p. 335).

Driven by the demands of people's daily lives, improvement and refinements in moveable partition panels figured significantly in the changing forms and spaces of architecture, but it was shoji panels covered with translucent paper, made possible after ways were developed for screening of thin and tear-resistant paper, that made the biggest difference. Shoji screens provided a translucent skin separating inside and outside that permitted light to enter even while closed, brightening interiors considerably over the darkness that had once reigned when doors were closed. Moreover, while the shoji sheltered the inside from the wind and rain outside, all that separated inside from out—the changing weather, the shifting light of day and night, the presence of other people, the hum of insects and the calls of birds in the garden—was a single sheet of paper. The ease with which the panels could be opened and closed bolstered the continuity between inner rooms and the surrounding verandas and enhanced the affinity between the architecture and the garden. The realm under the eaves of buildings—that intermediate territory between inside and out—became increasingly refined in relation to the gardens that were aiming at ever-higher levels of perfection.

The Square Post Aesthetic: The Dojinsai Space

In Japanese architecture, the composition of space and the shape of rooms are determined by the handling of posts (or columns). When the space changes, the posts change, and vice versa. The main theme of volume one of *The Essence of Japanese Architecture* was the architecture of the round columns that marked the spaces of prayer and the features of the round-column culture. The main theme of this second volume is architecture made with square posts, round posts with the bark remaining, and posts with planed sides but natural contours on the corners. These posts defined hybrid architectural spaces that accommodated daily life, social intercourse, education, enjoyment of cultural pursuits, and sometimes religious practice, spaces where people lived, mingled, studied, enjoyed poetry and art, drank tea, and reveled in the beauties of nature—they were, in short, spaces of society.

The era of the square post began with the end of the Kamakura period (1185–1332) and the opening of the Muromachi period (1333–1572). The Kinkaku and Ginkaku pavilions, while both are Buddhist temples, had moved beyond the old pattern of a structural core demarcated by round posts and surrounded by eaves (a pent roof) supported by square posts; both types of space are supported with square posts. Roof structures developed through the establishment and perfection of cantilevers, allowing buildings for both living and entertaining guests to be separated as needed under one roof, shifting toward the subdivision of buildings into small and large spaces. At the same time, the workmanship of *fusuma*, shoji, and other fixtures for the subdivision of space advanced, and sills

の柱まわりを見ると、四方柾のヒノキの角柱で室内を美しく構成するための技法がいかんなく発揮され、すでに完成の域にあったことに気づく。この端整な角柱の空間は、プロポーションの洗練とディテールの集積によってできている。襖や障子が入ると、室内は柱と長押のほかに何本もの縦横材で構成しなければならず、空間に線が多くなる。そのとき、材と材のぶつかるところをどう処理するかは、部屋の完成度に大きく影響する。

同仁齋で柱に対する横材の納まりを見ると、そこにはじつに細やかな配慮がある（p. 115参照）。このような熟練した角柱まわりのディテールは、いつ頃から積み上げられてきたものだろうか。むろん一朝一夕にしてできあがったものではなく、同仁齋だけで使われたものでなかったことはわかる。遺構がないのでその源流をどこまでさかのぼればよいのかわからないが、第4代将軍・足利義持が邸宅兼執務の場として使った三条坊門殿と、第6代将軍・義教の室町殿には、「安仁齋」と名づけられた持仏堂兼書院があったという。代々の足利将軍邸において、角柱空間の美学は一つの筋として連なってきたのであろう。こうして今、私たちは500年以上前にさかのぼる義政の小さな書斎・同仁齋に、その粋を見ることができる。そこは格調高く端整な空間でありながら、どこか和らげな雰囲気を漂わせている。

皮つき柱の空間──都市のなかの囲い

もう一つ、円柱や角柱の建築のほかに、皮つき丸太や面皮柱で形成された茶室や数寄屋の建築空間がある。ここには、価値観の大きな転換があった。その担い手は、それまで文化の主導権を握ってきた公家や武家といった支配者階級や宗教者ではなく、千利休（1522-1591）やその師・武野紹鷗（1502-1555）をはじめとする富裕な堺商人の新興層であった。10年間続いた応仁・文明の乱（1467-1477）、その後、引き起こされた下剋上と呼ばれる政情不安のなかで、武家・公家・僧・富裕町人が社会階層を超えて交流し、知的な刺激を交感し、創造性を高めた時代であった。

利休は4畳半を基準とした茶室を、2畳あるいは1畳台目まで小さくした。それにともない、そういった茶室を構成する建築の素材も、手の掛け方も、プロポーションも、すべてを変えた。柱は角柱から樹皮がついたままの丸太、あるいは、薄皮を角に残したままの面皮柱になった。壁を張付壁（紙）から土壁に変えたのは紹鷗であったといわれるが、利休の土壁は藁を見せた下地用の壁とし、床の間までその壁を塗りまわした。さらに、まるで壁を塗り残したような下地窓を開けて、出入り口は

桂離宮・古書院一の間（手前）と中書院三の間（奥）の床まわりの柱
The tokonoma corner posts of the Koshoin and Chushoin in the Katsura Imperial Villa

2畳台目の草庵茶室・真珠庵庭玉軒
Teigyokuken, the two-and-one-*daime*-mat tea room at Shinjuan Temple

and lintels grooved to carry these partitions and square posts against which they neatly closed became the standard.

When we observe the position of the posts in the Dojinsai study built by shogun Ashikaga Yoshimasa for the Togudo hall at Jishoji temple in 1485, we can see just how important a role the square posts play in refining the composition of a room's interior space, and how well perfected the techniques already were at that time. The trim lines of the square-pillared space are the result of great refinement of proportions and cumulative attention to detail. When *fusuma* and shoji are part of the room, the composition incorporates many more vertical and horizontal members besides the posts, and the crisscrossing lines proliferate in the space. The level of refinement of a room is greatly influenced by the way joints and the intersections of members are handled.

If we look closely at the finishing of the horizontal members vis-à-vis the posts in the Dojinsai room, we observe the great care with which the structure is assembled (see p. 115). We begin to wonder when this handling of the fit of posts and beams reached such a level of detail. Naturally it did not come about overnight, nor are such techniques limited to the Dojinsai alone. It is difficult to trace details for lack of preserved buildings from earlier ages, but we know that there was a buddha hall-cum-study called Anjinsai at both fourth shogun Ashikaga Yoshimochi's palace Sanjo Bomon-dono, which was used as both residence and office, and at sixth shogun Ashikaga Yoshinori's Muromachi-dono palace. The residences of successive Ashikaga shoguns most likely maintained the aesthetic of spaces delineated by square pillars as an unbroken tradition, and it is thus that we can get a glimpse of that chic tradition going back more than 500 years in the small study Yoshimasa included in his villa. It is a style of space that is both dignified and spare but also endowed with a sense of gentleness and ease.

Natural Pillared Space: Rustic Enclosures in the City

In addition to round posts and square posts, there is another category of posts that were developed for tea rooms and *sukiya* architecture spaces—posts left in their natural log shape (*kawa-tsuki maruta*) or planed on four sides with the natural contours left on the corners (*menkawabashira*). The spaces thus formed represent a major shift of values. The people responsible for these buildings were not the courtiers and warriors of the ruling class or leaders of religious institutions who had taken the lead in culture until that time, but wealthy merchants of the city of Sakai like Sen Rikyu (1522–1591) and Takeno Joo (1502–1555), a new stratum of society. The regime of the Ashikaga (also called the Muromachi shogunate after the area in Kyoto where they lived), was weakened by the Onin War, succession disputes beginning in 1467 and lasting until 1477. Turmoil continued, and the ensuing era of political instability turned out also to be one of widespread exchange among warriors, courtiers, the clergy, and wealthy merchants that crisscrossed the social hierarchy, enhancing intellectual stimulation and creativity in society.

Sakai townsman and tea master Sen Rikyu reduced the tea room, which had conventionally been a standard four-and-a-half mats in size, to the smaller two mats and even "one mat and a *daime* (three-quarter sized mat)." He also changed the nature of the materials from which tea rooms were built, the way they were prepared, their proportions—everything. Instead of squared-off posts he used posts partially left as logs, sometimes with the bark or natural contours remaining, or posts planed on four sides with the bark remaining at the corners. It was Takeno Joo who changed from walls covered with

引違い障子からにじり口となった。また、竿縁天井から、ヘギ板や竹などを使った天井に変えた。草庵茶室と呼ばれるものである。それは当時もっとも栄えた文明都市・堺のなかに内包された、きわめて非都市的で虚構的な「囲い」であった。

しかし、そもそもなぜ柱をはじめ、このような素材が選ばれ、意図的にやつす手法が着想されたのか。それは空間を縮める、というところから始まっているように思える。では、なぜ空間の大きさをこれほど小さくしたのか。そこに人と人との新たな関係性を求めたからであろう。

覇権闘争の世に生き、だれもが明日の命も知れぬ日々のなか、極小の草庵茶室は日常を異化する時空であった。亭主と客の息遣いがすぐ間近に感じられ、かすかな仕草や表情でたがいの心の動きが読める。心が裸にされるような、虚勢も思惑も露呈するような空間であった。そこは「市中の山居」と呼ばれ、山里の侘びた庵の体を装うことで成立した。しかし、同時にそれは都市にあってこそ意味のあるものであり、虚構性を帯びた都市的所産であった。華やかなもの、贅を凝らしたもの、磨き抜かれ、洗練をきわめたものの存在なくして、侘びの茶室の対比的な価値を発揮することはできなかったであろう。つきつめれば、それは人間の本性を引き出すことに特化した建築といえるかもしれない。

如庵の侘びた佇まい
Rustic-style design of Jo-an tea room

本書を通して、私はもう一度自分のなかで日本建築と出会い、それをつくった人間、守った人間、なぜその場所に、そのような形で存在するのかを考えた。飛鳥時代の聖徳太子と法隆寺、平安時代の空海と多宝塔、藤原頼通と平等院鳳凰堂、鎌倉時代の重源と東大寺、室町時代の夢窓国師と西芳寺、足利義満と金閣、桃山時代の千利休と待庵、江戸時代初期の八条宮智仁・智忠親王と桂離宮。このような新たな時代をつくった建築は、規模の大小や建物の種類、公私の別を問わず、等価に日本の歴史と文化を形として今に伝えている。また、最大の木造建築である東大寺の大仏殿と、たった2畳の茶室である待庵が、両方とも国宝となり、普遍的価値を有する最高の文化遺産として同等に評価されてきたことにあらためて深い思いを抱いた。伝統とは、私たちがそれに触れることで、何かを表現し、創造する意欲を鼓舞するものである。

paper to uncovered earthen walls, but Rikyu introduced the use of walls left at the *susakabe* or underlayer stage, revealing the rough plaster mixed with straw and even using that technique for the walls of the tokonoma. He was also the one to leave parts of the bamboo wall skeleton unplastered, opening up simple *shitajimado* apertures to let in light, and to convert the entrance from a sliding shoji door to the low wooden *nijiri* (crawl-in) entrance. He also changed ceilings from the more refined board and batten assemblies to simpler forms using thin shingles (*hegi-ita*), bamboo poles, and other simple materials. These tea rooms were in the so-called *soan*, or "grass hut" style. They became extremely "fictive," non-urban enclosures within the city of Sakai, which was the most culturally advanced urban environment of the time.

Why was it that such rough materials, including the crudely prepared posts, were deliberately chosen and methods of intentionally making things crude employed? It is thought that this began as an attempt to shrink down the size of spaces. As for why Rikyu found it necessary to reduce the size of space to this degree, we may surmise that it was because he was attempting to create new relationships between people.

In a world of ever-ending power struggles when no one ever knew whether they would survive to live another day, the extremely small and simple *soan*-style tea room offered a space and occasion removed from the day-to-day. Host and guest were seated close enough to be aware even of each other's breathing, close enough to read the meaning of subtle gestures, expressions and shifts of feeling. It was space where hearts were bared, a place where false courage and scheming would be exposed. These tea rooms were described as "huts in the city," and were built in the rustic fashion of country folk buildings. It was a style meaningful precisely because it was built in the city, however. They were products of a fictive and urban aesthetic. Only when placed alongside the splendid, the luxuriously appointed, and the highly refined and exquisitely polished, did the *soan* tea room show its raison d'etre as the antithesis to it. Ultimately, this was architecture for the sole purpose of bringing forth true human nature.

The compilation of this work has allowed me to return to the roots of Japanese architecture as I see it and contemplate once more the people who built it—Prince Shotoku and Horyuji, the priest Kukai and his Tahoto, Fujiwara Yorimichi and the Phoenix Hall at Byodoin, the priest Chogen and Todaiji temple, Muso Soseki and Saihoji, shogun Ashikaga Yoshimitsu and the Kinkaku Pavilion, Sen Rikyu and Taian, the princes Toshihito and Toshitada and Katsura Imperial Villa. I believe this compilation gives the reader a chance to recall the people who preserved these buildings and the reasons they appeared where they are. Through this architecture, whether it is large or small, and regardless of its style or use for public or private purposes, we can see arrayed with equal value the shapes of Japan's history and culture. What is more, we cannot but be deeply moved to think that the world's largest remaining wooden building, Todaiji's Great Buddha Hall, and one of its most diminutive, the two-mat tea room Taian, are both preserved as National Treasures, protected equally as holding universal value at the highest level of cultural heritage. Tradition is that which has the power to speak to us, stimulating us to artistic expression and energizing our impulse to thinking and creativity.

[凡例]
- 本書の建物名（和文）については、国指定の文化財の場合、おおむね国の指定名称に従った。
- 時代区分は文化庁編集・発行『国宝・重要文化財建造物目録』（2012年）に準じ、以下の通りとした。

    飛鳥時代（593年－709年・和銅2年）
    奈良時代（710年・和銅3年－793年・延暦12年）
    平安時代（794年・延暦13年－1184年・元暦元年）
    鎌倉時代（1185年・文治元年－1332年・元弘2年／正慶元年）
    室町時代（1333年・元弘3年／正慶2年－1572年・元亀3年）
    桃山時代（1573年・天正元年－1614年・慶長19年）
    江戸時代（1615年・元和元年－1867年・慶応3年）
    明治時代（1868・明治元年－1911年・明治44年）
    大正時代（1912年・大正元年－1925・大正14年）
    昭和時代（1926・昭和元年－1988年・昭和63年）

- 建立年代については、おもに文化庁編集・発行『国宝・重要文化財建造物目録』（2012年）に準じた。
- 図面については、おもに文化庁所蔵図面、修理工事報告書を基本とした。古建築の計画尺度は尺寸であるため、図面の寸法は尺（曲尺・約30.3cm）で表わし、適宜メートルを併記した。スケールバーには曲尺とメートルの縮尺を両方示した。
- 巻末にまとめた主要建造物の種別・規模形式については、おおむね文化庁編集・発行『国宝・重要文化財建造物目録』（2012年）に従った。

[Notes]
- Historical periods follow the dates given in *Kokuho juyo bunkazai kenzobutsu mokuroku* (Catalogue of National Treasure- and Important Cultural Property-designated Structures), edited by the Agency for Cultural Affairs and published in 2012:

    Asuka period (593–709)
    Nara period (710–793)
    Heian period (794–1184)
    Kamakura period (1185–1332)
    Muromachi period (1333–1572)
    Momoyama period (1573–1614)
    Edo period (1615–1867)
    Meiji period (1868–1911)
    Taisho period (1912–1925)
    Showa period (1926–1988)

- Construction periods are generally according to the above catalogue (2012).
- The drawings in this volume are mainly from the collection of the Agency for Cultural Affairs and reports of repair projects. The traditional units of length for ancient buildings are *shaku* and *sun* (one-tenth of *shaku*), and so the measurements in the drawings are given in *shaku* (*kanejaku*: approx. 30.3 cm); metric measurements are added where deemed appropriate. The scale bars are shown both in meters and in *kanejaku*.

円覚寺 舎利殿

国宝
建立年代　14世紀―15世紀
所在地　　神奈川県鎌倉市

Engakuji Temple Shariden (Reliquary Hall)

National Treasure
Completed: 14th–15th century
Location: Kamakura, Kanagawa prefecture

時代背景

　禅宗が中国の宋から日本に本格的に伝えられたのは、鎌倉時代初期のことである。13世紀後半に入ると、幕府の拠点がある鎌倉を中心に重要な禅宗寺院が次々と建立され、まずは旧仏教の勢力がおよばない鎌倉で大きな発展を見せた。その擁護者は、既成の秩序や権威の束縛を脱し、新たな思想と信仰を求めた北条氏を中心とする新興の武家階級である。宋代・中国の禅宗寺院を範とし、伽藍配置や諸堂の建築様式についてもその完全な移植を理想に掲げ、本格的な禅宗寺院が誕生した。

　円覚寺は北条時宗（1251-1284）を開基に、宋僧・無学祖元（1226-1286）を開山として、1282（弘安5）年に創立された。大規模な宋風禅寺として整備されたが、度重なる火災で伽藍は焼失と再建を繰り返した。そのなかで、境内のほぼ最奥、開山・無学祖元を祀る塔頭・正続院内に立つ舎利殿は、寺内で最古の建造物となる。

　舎利殿の創立は1285（弘安8）年とされるが、1374（応安4）年、1421（応永28）年、1563（永禄6）年の火災で、正続院とともに焼失したと考えられ、その後、鎌倉尼五山の一つであった太平寺の仏殿を移建したものが現建物である。太平寺仏殿の建立時期は文献を欠くために不明だが、様式・細部手法から室町前期の建物と推定され、円覚寺への移築時期は桃山時代、16世紀末と見られている。

　円覚寺のもともとの舎利殿には、鎌倉幕府第三代将軍・源実朝（1192-1219）が、宋の能仁寺から請来した仏牙舎利（釈尊の歯）を祀るという由来があった。一方、禅院の伽藍構成から現在の舎利殿を位置づけると、無学祖元の頂相（彫像）を安置した開山堂（塔亭）の前面に接続して立つことから、塔亭の礼拝・祭祀のために機能する「昭堂」となる。したがって、この殿堂は、舎利殿であると同時に昭堂の性格もあわせもつことになるが、順序としては、伽藍全体を失った1563年の火災後、太平寺仏殿が昭堂として移建され、江戸時代に入ってからは舎利信仰の隆盛にともない、古くから寺に伝わる仏牙舎利を祀る厨子（宮殿）を内部に設けたことで、以降、舎利殿と呼称されるようになったと考えられている。[*1]

特徴と見どころ

　禅宗の伝来とともに、禅寺の造営にあたり採り入れられた宋の建築様式を禅宗様という。この渡来様式は、奈良時代末から平安時代の400年間、形式美を追求してきた日本建築に新たな活力を吹きこみ、構造・意匠面を前進させた。円覚寺舎利殿は、その代表的な遺構となる。

　山を背に立ち、勾配の強い大きな屋根を載せ、軽快に反り上がる軒先をもつ外観は、引き締まった表情を見せる。扉は桟唐戸、窓は曲線が印象的な火灯窓で、その上部には弓欄間が裳階の四周をめぐる。軒下の見え方は、従来の和様とずいぶん異なる。組物は小ぶりで、柱上のみならず柱間にも同形の斗栱を配した「詰組」である。小さな部材を巧みに組み上げ、端正に配置された組物の整備感と量感は、立体的で細やかな陰影を軒下に刻んでいる。垂木は扇垂木の二軒で、隅のみ扇状に打つ中国式と異なり、全体に放射状に配する。

　禅宗様の内部空間の醍醐味は、部材をそのまま見せるため、力学的要素と装飾的要素が一体化されたかたちで視覚に訴えることである。舎利殿では、方3間の主屋まわりに裳階がまわって下屋の空間をつくるが、両者は海老虹梁と呼ばれる湾曲した繋梁で連結される。虹梁と大瓶束（円形断面の束）による力強い梁組に対し、ひしめき合うように集合した精緻な組物が、立体感をもって上へ上へと積み上げられ、中央・鏡天井の頂点へ向かい、空間の垂直感を高めている。

　禅宗様がもたらした構造手法のうち、もっとも波及力を持ち、従来の日本建築を進展させた要素は、貫の多用による軸組の強化であった。同時に、空間形成への影響という点では、大虹梁に大瓶束を用いた架構法が挙げられる。この手法によって柱の数を減らすことが可能となり、広々とした礼拝空間がつくられるようになった。円覚寺舎利殿においても、須弥壇前面の前側2本の柱が省かれている。

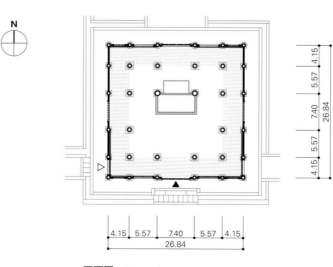

平面図　Floor plan

Historical Background

Zen Buddhism was introduced to Japan from Song China mainly in the late twelfth to early thirteenth centuries. By the latter part of the thirteenth century, important Zen temples were being constructed in Kamakura, then seat of the *bakufu*, the locus of the warrior-led government that exercised actual rule over most of the country at that time. In Kamakura, which is far to the east of the region where the old and established Buddhist temples held sway, the new school of Buddhism rapidly developed its following and the architecture to serve it. The temples were supported by the emergent warrior class coalescing around the Hojo family and their appetite for new ideas and teachings as they challenged the power and control of the old order in Kyoto. Full-fledged Zen temples came into being, and they transplanted not only teachings and practices but emulated the precinct layouts and architectural styles of their Song-dynasty models.

Engakuji was founded in 1282 by Kamakura *bakufu* regent Hojo Tokimune (1251–1284) and headed by the Chinese priest Mugaku Sogen (Ch. Wuxue Zuyuan; 1226–1286). It was laid out as a large-scale Song-style Zen temple, but suffered from repeated fires and was rebuilt over and over. Among its buildings, the Shariden (Reliquary Hall), in a subtemple called Shozokuin dedicated to founder Sogen and located almost at the back of the complex, is the oldest building in the temple.

The Shariden was first built in 1285, but was burned in 1374, in 1421, and again in 1563 along with the whole Shozokuin compound. The current building was a Buddha hall at Taiheiji temple, one of the "five big nunneries" (*amagozan*) of Kamakura. There is no record of when the Taiheiji Buddha hall was first built, but judging from its style and handling of detail, it is believed to be from the early part of the Muromachi period and to have been moved to Engakuji in the late sixteenth century.

The original Shariden at Engakuji was said to have been intended to enshrine a relic of the Buddha (a tooth) that Minamoto no Sanetomo (1192–1219), third shogun of the Kamakura shogunate, had obtained from Song China's Nengrensi monastery. It is presumed to have been located in the Shozokuin compound, but where it was in the compound is not known. As the layout of Zen temple precincts indicates, the Buddha hall moved from Taiheiji was connected to the front of the founder's hall where the portrait statue (*chinzo*) of the priest Sogen was enshrined, and served as a *shodo* (a structure used for worship and ritual). During a phase in the Edo period when reverence for relics of the Buddha enjoyed particular popularity, the *zushi* chest for Buddhist relics that had been passed down at the temple from long before was installed in the *shodo*. The *shodo* came to function also as a relinquary hall (*shariden*). The hall then began to be called Shariden, although it continued to serve as the *shodo* as well.

Characteristics and Highlights

The style of architecture introduced to Japan along with the introduction of Zen Buddhism and used for the construction of its temples is called Zenshuyo. The newly introduced style injected new vigor into traditions that had been focused on an aesthetics of form over the 400 years of the late Nara through the Heian periods and propelled structural as well as design advances. The Engakuji Shariden is a representative example of the new style.

The building rises in compact clean lines against the mountain at back, its roof steeply inclined and eave ends curving upward gracefully. The front has *sankarado* paneled entrance doors and windows in the curvilinear shape distinctive to the Zenshuyo style. Above the doors and windows, "bow"-patterned transom panels (*yumi ranma*) encircle the building under the *mokoshi* pent roof on all four sides. Small identical bracket complexes are closely placed in the *tsumegumi* style not only over the pillars but between them, giving the appearance of the building under the eaves quite a different quality from the Wayo (Japanese style) of previous eras. The skillful assembly of small complexes creates a sense of orderliness and volume, giving depth and shifting shadows to the space under the eaves. The double rafters are set fan-style (*ogidaruki*), radiating all around the roof, as distinct from the Chinese style in which only the corner rafters fan out.

The marvel of Zenshuyo-style interiors is that the structure is in plain sight, with both the dynamic elements and the decorative elements presenting an integrated visual experience. The *mokoshi* surrounding the square 3 x 3 bay core of the Shariden expands the space with an additional bay (*geya*) and the core and *mokoshi* extension are tied together with humpbacked *ebikoryo* tie-beams. Combined with the sturdy beam structure of rainbow beams and large bottle struts (round in cross-section), the dense assembly of intricate bracket-work builds the sense of space upward toward the flat, smooth-board ceiling (*kagami tenjo*) in the center above, heightening the verticality of the space.

Of the structural techniques introduced by the Zenshuyo style, that which had the greatest ripple effect, moving Japanese architecture beyond its previous stage, was the strengthening of the framework through the generous use of penetrating tie beams (*nuki*). Also important, in its impact on the formation of space, was the framing method using large rainbow beams and large bottle struts. This technique made it possible to decrease the number of pillars and realize more spacious settings for worship, as seen in the space before the altar in the Engakuji Shariden.

強く反り上がった軒先、火灯窓、上部に連子を入れた中央の桟唐戸、竪板張の壁など、禅宗様の典型的特徴を備えた外観。二層に見えるが下の屋根は裳階で、内部は天井の高い一層空間となる

With upward sweeping eaves, decoratively shaped windows, wood-paneled doors with lattice-work in their upper parts, and hardwood walls, the Shariden exterior displays the typical features of Zenshuyo architecture. While the building appears to be two-story, the lower roof is a *mokoshi* and the interior is a high-ceilinged single-story space.

裳階・主屋とも二重繁垂木だが、裳階は平行垂木、主屋は中心から放射状に配列した扇垂木である。主屋の組物は三手先斗栱を柱間にも並べた詰組

Both the *mokoshi* and main roofs have double, closely spaced rafters, but for the *mokoshi* the rafters are all parallel along each side while for the main roof the rafters fan out in lines radiating from the center. The bracket complexes are three-stepped with identical brackets both above the pillars and between them.

中央最頂部の鏡天井に向かって垂木を放射状にめぐらせ、上昇感を高める。太い梁組と精緻な小部材との対比が巧みで、力感と装飾性を兼ね備えた表現。須弥壇前方を広く使うため、大虹梁を架け渡し、内陣柱2本を省略して空間を開いている

The radiating arrangement of the rafters directed toward the central smooth-board ceiling heightens the sense of ascent. The stoutness of the beams makes a skillful contrast with the intricacy of the details, expressing both strength and ornamentality. In order to open up the space before the altar, large rainbow beams consolidate the frame of the sanctuary enclosure, allowing the elimination of the front two pillars.

主屋の側柱と裳階の外壁をつなげる海老虹梁。禅宗様では曲線を多用する。繁垂木の直線との対比がたがいを引き立てる

The humpback tie beams (*ebikoryo*) connecting the core pillars to the outer row of pillars supporting the *mokoshi*. Zenshuyo style makes frequent use of curves. The parallel lines of the rafters and the curves of the tie beams set off each other.

裳階外部の隅部ディテール。柱には上部を丸めた粽がつき、頭貫の木鼻には波紋を刻んだ繰形、その上の台輪の木鼻にも繰形がつく

Detail of one corner of the *mokoshi* exterior. The pillars are rounded at the top and the penetrating tie beam nosings are carved with wave patterns. The nosings of the top plates (*daiwa*) also have decorative carving.

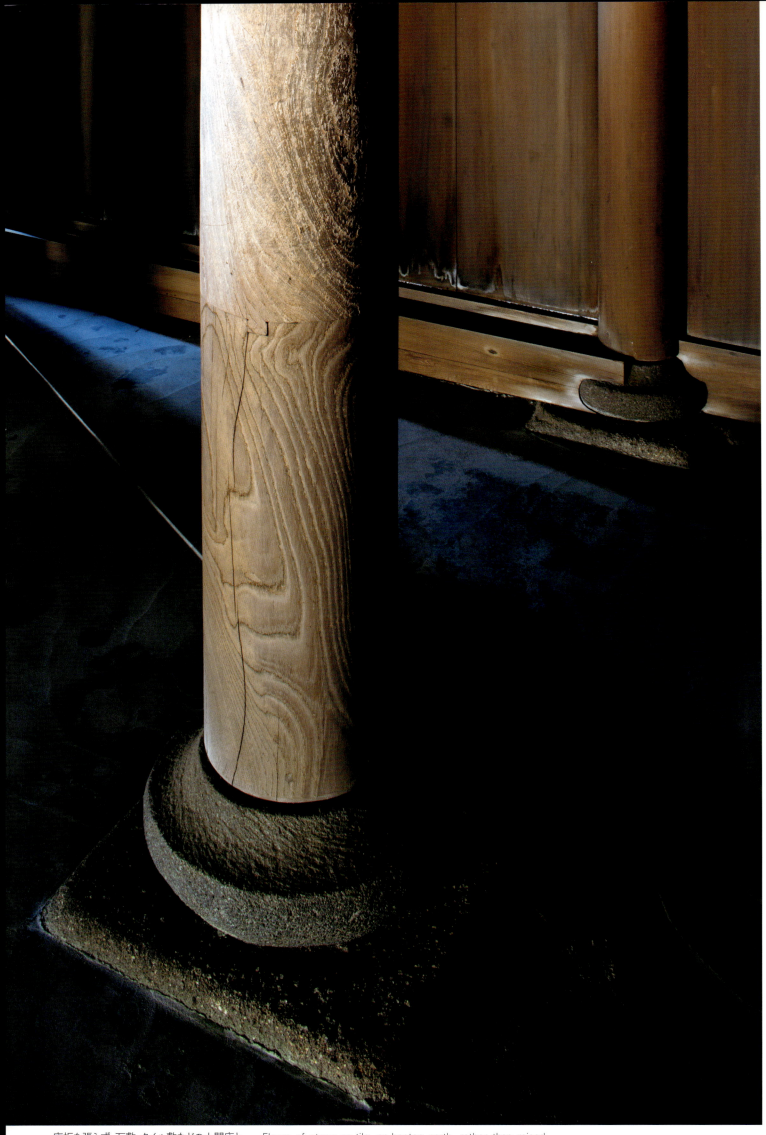

床板を張らず、石敷、タイル敷などの土間床とするのが禅宗様の特徴。柱と礎石の間には礎盤を入れる

Floors of stone or tile, or beaten earth, rather than raised wooden floors are a characteristic of Zenshuyo. Footing stones are inserted between the pillars and the foundation stones.

裳階にまわる弓欄間。障子には火灯窓のシルエットがかすかに映りこむ

The *yumi ranma* transoms around the outer walls of the *mokoshi*. The silhouette of the curvilinear window frame is faintly reflected on the shoji panels.

天井見上げ。外で見えていた組物と扇垂木が内部にも同様に現れる。尾垂木は堂内に入って先端を延長し、その末端尻に平三斗を組んで母屋桁を支える

View looking up at the ceiling. The bracket complexes and fan-style rafters seen on the exterior also appear on the interior. The tail rafters extend inside the hall where their ends pass through the non-projecting three-on-one complexes supporting the purlins (*moyageta*).

東福寺 三門・禅堂

三門	国宝
禅堂	重要文化財
建立年代	15世紀前半
所在地	京都府京都市東山区

Tofukuji Temple Sanmon Gate and Zendo Hall

Sanmon: National Treasure
Zendo: Important Cultural Property
Completed: Early 15th Century
Location: Higashiyama ward, Kyoto, Kyoto prefecture

時代背景

　東福寺は京都市街地の南東、東山連峰の月輪山のふもとに寺地を構える。その歴史は、1236(嘉禎2)年、摂政関白・九條道家(1193-1252)が五丈(約15m)の釈迦像とそれを祀る大仏殿の造立をこころざし、寺院建立を発願したことに始まる。奈良の東大寺と興福寺から一字を取って、東福寺と名づけられた。堂宇の完成には長年の歳月を要し、1255(建長7)年に仏殿の開堂供養、1273(文永10)年には法堂が完成した。その間、1243(寛元元)年には、宋より臨済禅を修めて帰国した円爾(1202-1280)を開山に迎えている。このことで禅宗寺院としての基盤が固められ、三門・仏殿・法堂・方丈・庫裡などを備えた禅宗伽藍に整備された。14世紀前半の鎌倉末から室町初頭に3度の火災に遭って堂宇を焼失し、15世紀前半までに復興されたが、1881(明治14)年の大火で仏殿、法堂、方丈、庫裡などの主要堂舎を失った。これらは明治から昭和にかけて再建されている。

　三門と禅堂は、明治の大火を逃れた室町再建時の遺構である。三門の再建は1384(至徳元)年に始まり、1425(応永32)年までには完成していたと考えられている。二重屋根の2階建て、両脇には上層に通じる階段をつける。禅宗寺院の三門に典型的な形式で、最古の遺例となる。三門とは三解脱門(空門・無相門・無作門)の略で、涅槃に達するために通らねばならない法門とされ、俗界と仏教世界の聖域の境界を暗示する。上層は一室の大きな仏堂になり、天井や柱は極彩色の画で荘厳されている。東大寺南大門に見られるように、従来の二重門(下層は裳階)は仰ぎ見る高さをつくるためのものであったが、禅寺の三門では実際に2階建てとなり、上層は仏堂として法儀に使われる。

　三門の北西に位置する禅堂は、三門より同時期かやや遅れて再建されたと考えられている。現在は座禅の道場であるが、中世においては寺僧が集団で生活(食事・就寝)と座禅を行う場であった。生活も大切な修行とみなす禅宗では、禅堂をはじめ、僧衆が修道生活する建物は南北軸に並ぶ主要堂宇の両脇に配され、廻廊などでたがいが結ばれて、伽藍構成に不可欠な要素となっていた。東福寺では禅堂のほか、その南には僧衆の厠である東司(重文・室町前期)が、三門を挟んで東側には浴室(重文・1459年)が現存し、中世禅宗寺院の日々の営みを今日に伝えている。

特徴と見どころ

　思遠池と名づけられた蓮池を前にして、高くそびえる三門を眺める。その柱間からは、絶妙な遠近感をもって本堂(仏殿兼法堂)が重厚な瓦屋根を見せている。焼失と再建を幾度繰り返そうとも、三門を起点に見るこの南北の軸線は、禅宗伽藍の秩序をなす不変の中心軸である。

　一方、この三門は構造に大仏様を採用しており、東福寺の「東」の字をもらった東大寺とのつながりを想起させる側面をもつ。貫を多用して軸組を固めるのは大仏様・禅宗様ともに共通する手法だが、柱に直接挿しこんだ挿肘木を用いて斗栱を組み上げるのは大仏様の工法である。創建当初、五丈の釈迦像を祀った東福寺の仏殿の建立には、鎌倉再建東大寺の大工と同族の出と推測される物部為国が建立を担当していることから、仏殿の前に立つ門についても、その規模や仏殿との調和を鑑みて、大仏様で建設されたと推測されている。14世紀末の再建工事に際し、大建築に有利な大仏様の構造技術を踏襲しつつ、禅寺の三門にふさわしい禅宗様意匠が組み合わされたと考えられている。

　三門の北西に立つ禅堂は、大きな切妻の瓦屋根が印象的な建物である。桁行7間、梁間4間の主屋、その周囲に1間の裳階をまわし、主屋内部は梁間を二分して高い柱列6本が吹放ちで立つ大きな気積の一室空間である。主屋と裳階との境は竪繁格子で仕切られており、裳階の火灯窓や弓欄間から入射した光は、この格子を通して主屋内部に拡散する。さらに、主屋の頭貫と飛貫の間には格子欄間がめぐらされており、二重の欄間は内部では光の帯となって、刻一刻と変化する美しい光で堂内を充たす。

禅堂
Zendo

Historical Background

Tofukuji is located at the foot of Mt. Tsukinowa in the Higashiyama range, southeast of Kyoto's main business district. Its history begins in 1236 when then regent Kujo Michiie (1193–1252) made a vow to build a great temple to enshrine a 15-meter tall statue of the Shakyamuni Buddha. Taking one character each from the great temples of Nara (Todaiji and Kofukuji), the temple was named Tofukuji. The buildings took a long time to complete, with the Buddha hall opened and dedicated in 1255 and the lecture hall (*hatto*) in 1273. In 1243 the priest Enni (1202–1280), who had returned after studying Rinzai Zen in Song China, was put in charge of founding the temple. Under his leadership, the temple became firmly established as a Zen temple and was equipped with the requisite monastery structures—gate (*sanmon*), Buddha hall (*butsuden*), lecture hall (*hatto*), abbot's residence (*hojo*), kitchen (*kuri*), and so on. In the first half of the fourteenth century, the temple suffered fires three times, destroying all the original buildings. During the Muromachi period (1333-1572), the complex had been completely reconstructed by the first half of the fifteenth century, but in 1881 a great fire destroyed most of the main structures once more. What we see today are primarily reconstructions completed in the period between 1890 and 1934.

The Sanmon gate and Zendo meditation hall shown here are the structures that escaped the flames in 1881 as they had been rebuilt in the Muromachi period. Reconstruction of the gate began in 1384 and is thought to have been completed by 1425. It is a two-story structure with stairways from both sides leading to the upper story. It represents the classic style of Zen temple gate and is the oldest example preserved.

"Sanmon" (lit., three gates) is the abbreviation of *san-gedatsu-mon*, referring to the three spiritual "gates" to be passed through before enlightenment, marking the boundary line between the secular world and the realm of the Buddha. The upper floor is one large Buddha hall and the ceiling, pillars, and beams are elaborately decorated with colored paintings. As seen in the Nandaimon gate at Todaiji temple, earlier two-layered gates (the lower roof is a *mokoshi* skirting) had been built to achieve a height that would tower over the visitor, but the *sanmon* gates of the Zen temples were built as two separate stories, and the upper floor used as a Buddha hall for ceremonies.

The Zendo meditation hall located northwest of the Sanmon is thought to have been reconstructed either about the same time or somewhat after the gate. Today it is used as a zazen meditation hall, but in medieval times it was the collective residence of the priests (eating and sleeping) as well as being used for zazen training. In Zen Buddhism, in which daily life is considered an important part of training, the Zendo and other buildings used for the training of the priests were an indispensable part of the temple compound. They were laid out along both sides of the north-south axis of the temple consisting of the main buildings, and they were linked together by corridors. At Tofukuji, three structures—the Zendo meditation hall, the monastery toilets called the Tosu (Important Cultural Property; early Muromachi period) to the south of the Zendo, and the bathhouse (Important Cultural Property, 1459) to the east of the gate—survive to recall what daily life was like at a medieval age Zen temple.

Characteristics and Highlights

The Sanmon rises up over a lotus pond called Shionchi, its massive pillars framing in exquisite perspective the staunch tile roof of the main hall (which serves as both Buddha hall and lecture hall) beyond the gate. While the temple burned down over and over, the north-south axis originating on the Sanmon forms the unchanging central core of the order of a Zen temple.

Another feature of the Sanmon is that it employs the Daibutsuyo style, reminding us of its connection with Todaiji, from which it took one character of its name. Both the Daibutsuyo and Zenshuyo styles share the technique of lavish use of penetrating beams to achieve structural strength, but it was Daibutsuyo that built bracket complexes with the bracket arms inserted directly into the pillars. When Tofukuji was first built, the master carpenter put in charge of the construction of the Buddha hall to enshrine the 15-meter high Buddha statue was Mononobe no Tamekuni, who is thought to have been of the same family that had been in charge of the Kamakura-period rebuilding of Todaiji temple. So it may be surmised that when the Sanmon was built in front of the Buddha hall, it was decided to adopt the Daibutsuyo style in order to achieve harmony of style and scale. At the time of the reconstruction toward the end of the fourteenth century, the architects must have decided to follow the structural techniques of Daibutsuyo that were advantageous for large-scale structures and combine them with the decorative aspects of Zenshuyo as suited to the gate of a Zen temple.

The Zendo, standing northwest of the Sanmon gate, is striking for the immense gable of its tile roof. Its core is seven bays wide and four bays deep, and an extra bay covered with a *mokoshi* roof surrounds the core. The interior is one vast room, open floor to the ceiling, divided by a row of six tall central posts. The core and *mokoshi* are divided by latticed partitions with closely spaced muntins. Light filters into the interior via the cusped *katomado* windows and "bow"-patterned transom panels. Above as well, the opening between the head-penetrating tie beams (*kashiranuki*) and the neck-penetrating tie beams (*hinuki*) is latticed, so the interior is filled with a beautiful play of light filtering through the transoms on two layers.

中世における禅寺三門の威風を伝える唯一の遺構。前面に蓮池を湛え、中央柱間から見える本堂（仏殿兼法堂）とは南北軸線上に並ぶ。両脇には階段をつけ、その出入り口となる山廊を付設する

The sole monument of a medieval Zen *sanmon* gate surviving today, the Tofukuji Sanmon rises over the lotus pond. The main hall (Buddha hall and lecture hall), visible through the central bay of the gate, is aligned with the gate on the north-south axis. Stairs at both ends lead to the upper floor, each equipped with a detached *sanro* entrance hall.

正面5間は等間隔の柱間。上下層の二軒・平行繁垂木が刻む細やかなリズム、
禅宗様の高欄と各柱間に入る桟唐戸、挿肘木の三手先組物、簡潔な平三斗の
中備──和様・禅宗様・大仏様が渾然一体となっている

Note the finely articulated rhythm of the parallel rafters along the eaves of both the upper and lower roofs. In the balustrade (*koran*) along the upper story, the *sankarado* panels between the pillars, the simple intercolumnar brackets, and the three-stepped bracket complexes that incorporate *sashihijiki* bracket arms, we see a splendid merging of the three styles——Wayo, Zenshuyo, and Daibutsuyo.

整然と幾重にも並んだ組物が華やかなリズムを刻む。肘木の繰り上げ曲線が丸く、木口に塗った割れ止めの胡粉がその形を強調する。大仏様の三手先挿肘木を用い、中備は平三斗。組物間に壁はなく、透けているのが特徴

Under sweeping eaves a dense and orderly succession of bracket complexes sets up a splendid rhythm. The *gofun* pigment painted on the bracket arms to inhibit cracking accentuates their upward-curving shapes. The bracket complexes are of the three-stepped type of Daibutsuyo style with intercolumnar brackets. In a feature distinctive to the gate, the spaces between the bracket complexes are left open, not walled in.

柱は東大寺南大門のように通し柱ではなく、上層の床で止まる。そのため、地震時の水平の揺れに対処が必要で、貫を何重にも交差・貫通させた構造とし、数多くの組物がそれを支える

The pillars are not *toshibashira* that rise through the second story, but stop at the second-story floor level. To counteract horizontal seismic movement, then, a multi-layered interlocking structure of penetrating tie beams is used and supported by numerous bracket complexes.

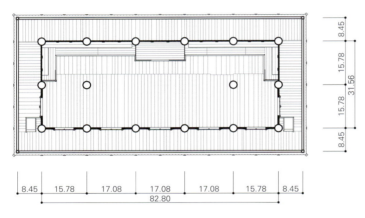

2階平面図　Second floor plan

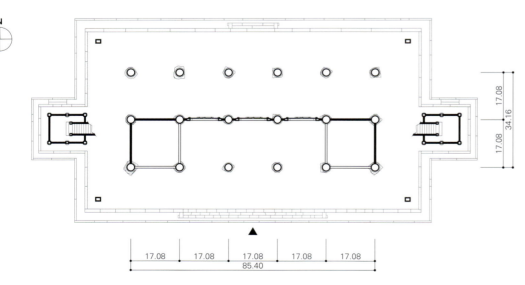

1階平面図　First floor plan

上層の縁と軒裏。伽藍を遠望するとともに、内部を仏堂として使う。上層を人が利用できる空間としたのは禅宗建築が先駆けである

Veranda of the upper story and underside of the eaves. The upper story not only affords a bird's-eye view of the precincts but can be used as a Buddha hall. This is one of the first two-story Zen buildings whose upper story can be used for temple affairs.

上層内部。力感あふれる禅宗様の構造に極彩色の空間。大虹梁をかけ、中間に大瓶束を立て、さらに二重目虹梁にも2カ所に大瓶束を配置し、挿肘木を組んで鏡天井を受けている。宝冠釈迦如来坐像を中尊に祀る

The interior of the upper story displays the powerful structures and extravagant coloring of the Zenshuyo style, with massive rainbow beams, thick bottle struts in the center, and bottle struts in two places inserted with brackets to hold the beam supporting the smooth board ceiling. The main statue enshrined is of the seated Shakyamuni Buddha with Jeweled Crown.

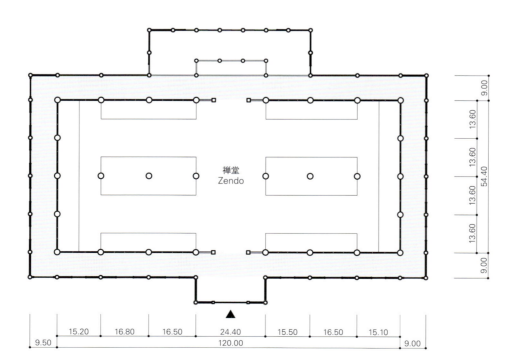

平面図　Floor plan

(左上)禅堂・妻側。大きな切妻屋根を載せ、直線と曲線を対比した明快な壁の分割。裳階には火灯窓を取り、その上に弓欄間をまわす。裳階屋根の上、主屋との取りつき部分にも格子欄間をめぐらせる

(Upper left) Gable end of the Zendo. The walls are subdivided with distinct straight and curvaceous lines. The *mokoshi* extension is punctuated with *katomado* windows and "bow"-patterned transoms surrounding the entire building. Above the *mokoshi* roof as well, latticed transoms surround the core of the building.

(上)深い軒は雨から建物を守るとともに、彫りの深い陰影をつくる。妻飾りは二重虹梁に大瓶束、装飾性の強い蕪懸魚がつき、肘木は禅宗様の渦紋入り木鼻を持つ

(Above) The deep eaves protect the walls of the building from rain and cast deep shadows. The gable ends are topped with double rainbow beams and large bottle struts and are decorated with the elaborate *kaburagegyo* (turnip-style) bargeboard pendants and swirl-carved bracket arms characteristic of the Zenshuyo style.

禅堂。欄間から射しこむ一条の朝日。座禅のための単布団が整然と並び、凛とした空気に包まれている

A band of morning light enters the Zendo interior through the upper transom. The alignment of the cushions transmits an atmosphere of discipline and simplicity.

内部より裳階空間を見る。裳階と主屋との境を上げ下げの竪繁格子で区切り、外側の火灯窓、弓欄間を通して主屋内部に採光、通風する。線の重なりと透けが繊細な光の空間をつくる

View of the *mokoshi* space from the interior. The *mokoshi* and core of the building are divided by lattice partitions with closely spaced muntins that can be raised and lowered vertically, bringing in light and ventilation through the *katomado* windows and "bow"-patterned transoms in the outside walls. The lattice lines and openings create delicate patterns of light and shadow

主屋の内部は大きな一室空間である。弓欄間と格子欄間から入る二重の光の帯。切妻の深い庇に覆われて、落ち着いた光で包まれる

The interior of the building core is one large open room. Bands of light from the upper and lower transoms shine into the space. With the deep eaves under the gables, the light is muted throughout the day.

鹿苑寺 金閣

建立年代　1955年（再建）
庭園　　　特別史跡・特別名勝
作庭年代　14世紀末
所在地　　京都府京都市北区

Rokuonji Temple Kinkaku Pavilion

Completed: 1955 / reconstruction
Garden: Special Historic Site; Special Place of Scenic Beauty
Garden Design: Late 14th century
Location: Kita ward, Kyoto, Kyoto prefecture

時代背景

　鹿苑寺の金閣は、室町幕府第三代将軍・足利義満（1358－1408）が営んだ山荘・北山殿のなか、舎利殿として建てられた楼閣である。慈照寺・銀閣と並び、室町時代を代表する庭園建築として知られる。

　京都の北山に位置し、北を左大文字山、南西を衣笠山に限られた風光明媚な寺域は、鎌倉時代前半、権勢をふるった公卿・西園寺公経（1171－1244）が菩提寺と山荘を築いた土地であった。1397（応永4）年、義満は西園寺家のこの所領を入手し、寝殿をはじめとする公務の建物、仏堂、会所や泉殿といった庭園建築、住居からなる堂舎群を建て、政治・外交・文化の中心的な舞台とした。西方浄土とも換えがたい、と形容されたほどの壮麗な北山殿のなか、池（鏡湖池）のほとりに建てられた金の舎利殿は、義満が思い描いた理想郷の象徴的な存在であったことは想像に難くない。

　金閣の構想の源泉となったのは、禅僧・夢窓疎石（1275－1351）が築いた西芳寺であった。禅に深く傾倒し、夢窓を崇敬した義満は、西芳寺にたびたび参禅した。そこには池（黄金池）を中心に仏堂や亭などが土地の起伏を利用して巧みに配置され、山水の景色のなか、別天地のような環境が創出されていたという。池の北側には、金閣造営の範とされた楼閣「瑠璃殿」が立っており、それは上層に仏舎利を祀った舎利殿であった。

　金閣には当初、その北側に隣接して、西園寺家時代から引き継いだ2階建ての会所（文芸・芸能のための専用建物）があったという。天鏡閣と呼ばれ、金閣とは中空に渡した廊でつながれていたと伝えられる。その建築的な痕跡は残ってはいないものの、かつて西園寺公経が築いた建物のいくつかは、池や滝などの遺構とともに北山殿に引き継がれ、造営計画に活かされたと考えられている。

　北山殿は義満の没後、舎利殿などごく一部を残し、諸堂の大部分は解体されてゆかりの寺へ下賜された。その後は禅宗寺院に改められ、義満の法号にちなみ、鹿苑寺と称せられた。北山殿の唯一の遺構として伝えられてきた金閣であったが、1950（昭和25）年に焼失。1955（昭和30）年には明治の解体修理（1904－1906年）の記録や部材調査をもとに復元再建され、さらに昭和の大修理（1986－1987年）、のちの金箔の張りかえを経て、燦然と輝く姿をよみがえらせた。

特徴と見どころ

　日本では、上階に人を収容する重層の建物は、禅宗建築の影響を受けて初めて出現したと考えられている。金閣が画期的なのは、それが先例のない三層の楼閣建築という点である。この光り輝く舎利殿は、庭園の景観形成の中心的な構成要素となるだけでなく、上層内部に人が入り、そこから見下ろす眺めが主題となっている。視点の高さと俯瞰、階ごとに様相を異にする庭の景と展望——このような垂直方向の空間体験は、水平の広がりを特徴とした従来の日本建築に新たな空間の領域をもたらした。

　火灯窓など禅宗様の意匠を持つ3階の「究竟頂」という名称は、最上、という意味と伝えられるが、これ以上の高いところはない、という身体的な感覚とともに、これ以上の観念的な世界の高みはない、という二重の意味がかけられているのだろう。だからこそ、この層は外だけでなく内部も金で覆われている。金は永遠を象徴する色であり、その建築は現世を超えた光を放つかのように佇んでいる。

　そして、何よりも金閣の美しさを至上のものにしているのは、それを取り巻く庭園であり、山々を借景にした環境である。池の水を海に、水中に浮かぶ石を山や島に見立て、蓬莱仙境の世界を喚起する。海景や山水を庭のテーマとする象徴的表現の文脈のなかで、金をまとった金閣もまた、抽象性を帯びた光の建築となっている。

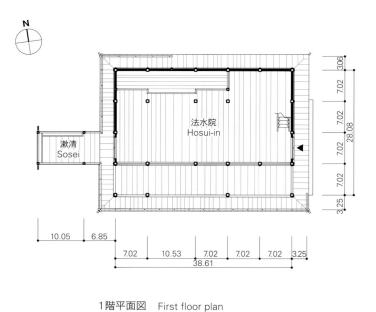

1階平面図　First floor plan

2階平面図　Second floor plan

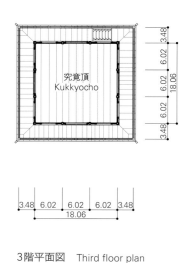

3階平面図　Third floor plan

Historical Background

The Kinkaku (Golden Pavilion) at Rokuonji temple was built as a *shariden* (reliquary hall) by third Muromachi shogun Ashikaga Yoshimitsu (1358–1408), for his villa in the Kitayama area of northern Kyoto. Along with the Ginkaku (Silver Pavilion) at Jishoji temple, it stands among the leading examples of Muromachi period (1333–1572) garden architecture.

Framed on the north by the Hidari-Daimonji peak and on the southwest by Mt. Kinugasa, this now scenic temple area was during the thirteenth century the place where the powerful court noble Saionji Kintsune (1171–1244) built his family temple (*bodaiji*) and villa. In 1397 Yoshimitsu procured these grounds from the Saionji family and erected *shinden*-style buildings for performing his official duties, Buddhist halls, the *kaisho* (meeting place), the *izumidono* (spring pavilion) and other garden structures, and buildings for his living quarters. The estate, which came to be known as the Kitayama villa, became a central stage upon which the politics, diplomacy, and culture of the time unfolded. It may not be so farfetched to imagine that Yoshimitsu sought to make the golden *shariden* pavilion on the edge of the "mirror" pond (Kyokochi) within the Kitayama villa—the magnificence of this villa was praised as "irreplaceable even by the Pure Land of the West"—the symbolic representation of the Shangri-la he envisioned.

The idea for the Kinkaku pavilion was inspired by Saihoji, a temple erected by the Zen priest Muso Soseki (1275–1351). Yoshimitsu was a devout Zen Buddhist who revered Soseki and had visited Saihoji many times. There at Saihoji, it is said, *butsudo* (halls enshrining Buddhist statues) and huts were built surrounding the Ogonchi (Golden Pond), ingeniously taking into account the undulations of the terrain to create an otherworldly atmosphere within the scenic landscape. On the north side of Saihoji's pond stood the Ruriden (Lapis lazuli) pavilion, a *shariden* enshrining relics of the Buddha in the upper floor.

Initially, just north of and next to the Kinkaku stood a two-story *kaisho* (a meeting hall specifically for literary and performing arts) in existence from the time when the land belonged to the Saionji family. Known as the Tenkyokaku (Sky Mirror Pavilion), it was said to have been connected to the Kinkaku via a roofed corridor connecting their upper stories. No architectural traces remain, but a number of the buildings built by Saionji Kintsune, along with structural parts of its ponds and waterfalls, are thought to have been preserved and incorporated into the design of the Kitayama villa.

After the death of Yoshimitsu, the majority of the halls on the villa grounds, except for a select few such as the Kinkaku pavilion, were dismantled and given to temples associated with the Ashikaga family. Later, the site was turned into a Zen monastery, and was given the name Rokuonji based on Yoshimitsu's posthumous Buddhist name. The Kinkaku pavilion enjoyed the distinction of being the only original structure from the Kitayama villa complex, but was burned down in an act of arson in 1950. In 1955 it was rebuilt based on records made during extensive Meiji-era renovations (1904–1906). In the Showa-era restoration and repair project of 1986–1987, the pavilion was re-covered with gold leaf, and the building returned to its original splendor.

Characteristics and Highlights

In Japan, multistoried buildings with upper stories that can withstand practical use first appeared due to the influence of Zen architecture. As a three-storied structure, the Kinkaku pavilion was without precedent. Not only was this sparkling *shariden* the central feature of the garden's composition; a major theme of its conception was that it would provide a high vantage point from which the garden scenery could be viewed. High vantage points, bird-eye views, each floor offering an entirely different vista of the garden and its surroundings—the experience of the vertical dimension of space—created a totally new realm in the world of Japanese architecture, which until then had been characterized by its horizontality.

The third floor, which displays many Zenshuyo style features such as the *katomado* (cusped windows), is called the Kukkyocho, or "pinnacle of the ultimate." This is said to mean "the highest," but is probably imbued with the dual meaning of both the physical experience of being above everything in the world while aware that there is nothing conceptually higher in the world. No wonder that not only the exterior, but also the interior of the top story is covered in gold. Gold represents eternity, and this building emits an aura that transcends our present world.

Further exalting the Kinkaku, setting off its beauty above everything else, is the garden that surrounds it, and the assimilation of the natural surrounding mountainous scenery into its landscape. Seeing the pond as the ocean and the rocks in the water as substitutes (*mitate*) for mountains and islands, we can envision the image of the realm of the immortals (*horai*) of myth and legend. In the context of symbolic expression of ocean views and mountain scenery as the themes of the garden, the gold-covered pavilion also becomes an abstract symbol of the architecture of light.

紅葉の頃、葦原島を前景に金閣を見る。園池や山々と切り離せないかたちで融合した比類なき庭園建築である

Kinkaku amid autumn foliage, the Ashiharajima island in the foreground. The inseparable merging of garden pond and landscape beyond makes for an unparalleled work of garden design.

金は松の深い緑とよく調和する。奥の葦原島の石組、手前中央の浮石、そのほかにもいくつもの岩島や石を配し、金閣へ向けた絶妙な遠近感をつくる

Gold strikes a fine harmony with the deep green of the pines. The rock arrangements on Ashiharajima (center of the photo), the partially submerged rocks in the foreground, and the other rock islets and stones set up a superb perspective focused on the Kinkaku.

西に張り出し、池中に建てられた小亭・漱清。金閣の西縁とつながる。寝殿造における釣殿や涼殿を思わせ、風雅な趣を持つ

Jutting out from the west side over the lake is the small deck named "Sosei" ("cleansing fresh"). It is connected to the western veranda of the Kinkaku, and has an aura of elegance similar to the fishing decks and cooling pavilions of *shinden*-style dwellings.

3階の屋根の軒先には、下層の柿葺屋根に雨水を落とさない配慮から
金箔張の雨樋を四周にまわす

To prevent rain from falling upon the cypress-shingled roof of the lower story, rain troughs covered in gold leaf surround the eaves of the third story roof.

2階の広縁。柱は5寸角（151mm）に面取りおよそ1／10。床は黒漆塗。二軒の大疎垂木で、垂木間を板軒天井に仕上げた簡潔なデザイン。禅宗様の木鼻がつく

The deep, second-floor veranda. The pillar is 151-mm square in cross section and 1/10 chamfered; the floor is finished in black lacquer. The eaves have double rows of rafters, wide spaced, with plain-designed ceiling boards showing between them. The ends of the rafters have carved nosings in the Zenshuyo style.

2階・潮音洞は観音堂である。岩屋観音像は四天王像に護衛され、天井には迦陵頻伽や草花、楽器の画。すべてが黒漆塗の床に映りこむ。西面壁(左)に腰掛けがつく

The Choondo ("sound of the sea grotto") located in the second floor is a worship hall for the Kannon Bodhisattva. The statue of Iwaya Kannon is protected by the Four Heavenly Devas (Shitenno). The ceiling is painted with pictures of celestials (*kalavinka*), flowers, and musical instruments, which are all reflected on the black lacquered floor. There is also a bench along the western wall (left).

2階の縁を二手先の挿肘木による持ち送りで支え、下層の庇も兼ねる簡潔で巧みな構成。下層と同様に柱を1本抜き、広縁の開放感を高めている。ここからは庭が一望できる

The structure, with the second-floor veranda supported by two-step bracket complexes with bracket arms inserted in the posts that simultaneously support the eaves of the first floor, is both simple and ingenious. As on the lower floor, one post has been eliminated, heightening the sense of open space in the deep veranda. This is the vantage point from which the entire garden can be seen.

3階の屋根は宝形造、2階の屋根は3階の縁の腰組から四方へ葺き下ろす。
矩形平面の下層の上に方形平面の3階を載せるため、屋根は大きな振隅と
なる。このずれがあることで、庭から見る角度により、建物の姿は変化に富む

The third-floor roof is a *hogyo* style square pyramidal roof, and the second-floor roof slopes downwards from the brackets at the base of the third-floor veranda. Due to the fact that a square third-floor sits upon a rectangular lower story, the hip rafters in the corners bisect at an angle larger than 45°. Because of this distortion the building appears different depending on the position from which it is viewed in the garden.

3階・究竟頂の南縁から奥の出島方向を眺める。火灯窓、勾欄、木鼻、柱の粽など禅宗様式でつくられている

View from the southern veranda of the third-floor Kukkyocho towards the peninsula extending into the pond. The latticed *katomado* windows, the decorative railings (*koran*), the carvings of the beam nosings (*kibana*), and the rounding of the tops of the pillars (*chimaki*) are all features of Zenshuyo architecture.

究竟頂の内部。ここの根本的なあり方は舎利殿である。金の輝きに包まれ、現世を超越した光の空間。床は漆の最高級仕上げである黒蠟色漆塗。艶やかな光沢が金を引き立てる

Inside the Kukkyocho, which serves as a *shariden* (reliquary hall). Filled with the sheen of gold, the room is a space of pure light transcending anything in this world. The floors are finished with top quality high-gloss black lacquer, its sheen heightening the brilliance of the gold.

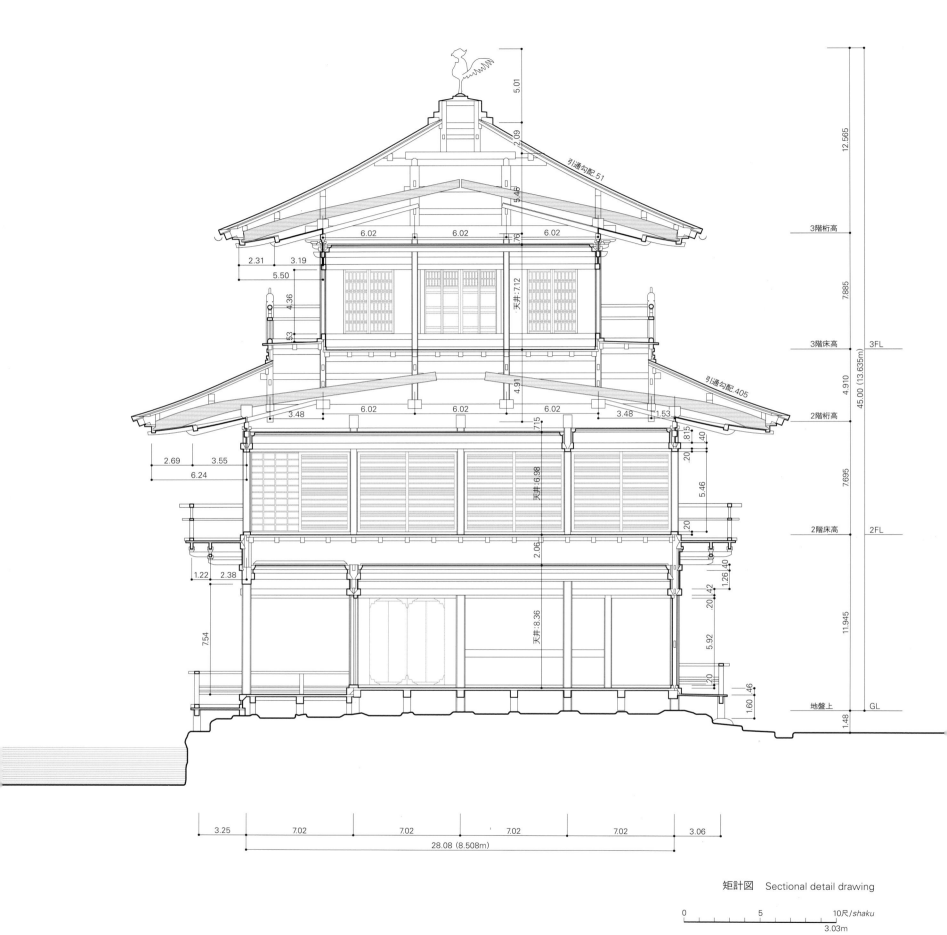

矩計図　Sectional detail drawing

金閣は計画時に全体のプロポーションを決めてから各部の寸法を割り出したと考えられる。1階と2階の柱間は約7尺、3階の柱間は約6尺。右ページの立面図にある赤の右下がり線は1:1、青の右上がり線は1:2の近似値となり、もっとも単純な素数の組み合わせによって、設計の基礎としていることがわかる

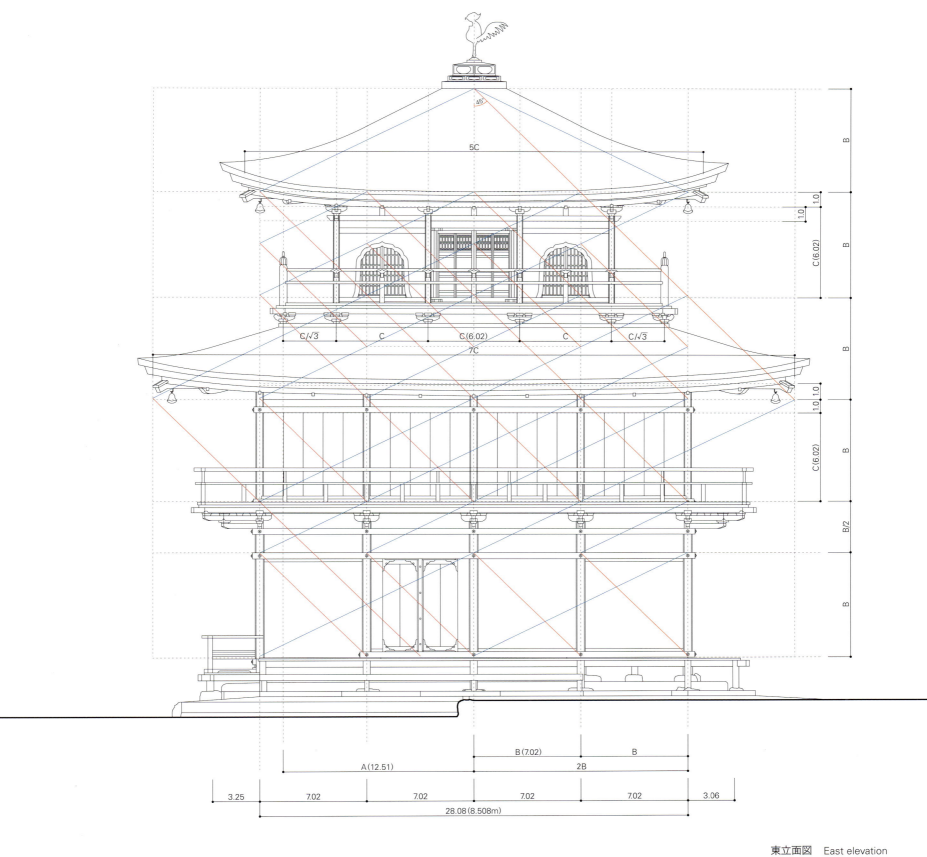

東立面図　East elevation

In the planning of the Kinkaku pavilion, the measurements of each part seem to have been determined after establishing the proportions of the whole. The first- and second-floor bays are about 7 *shaku* (2.1 meters) wide and those on the third floor about 6 *shaku* (1.8 meters). The design is based on the simplest combination of figures: the red lines descending to the right at the proportion of approximately 1:1, and the blue lines descending to the left at approximately 1:2.

金閣には縦樋がついていないので、雨水は3階の横樋（右ページ）から池中に直接落ちる。夜泊石（手前2石）とその奥の石との間に水滴が落ち、波紋が石の間に広がる

Since the Kinkaku does not have vertical rain troughs, rainwater drops directly into the pond from the lateral gutters (right page). Water drops between the *yodomari* rocks (the two rocks in front) and a rock towards the back, sending out ripples.

3階、金箔張の雨樋。軒先をいかに軽快に見せるか、そのとき雨樋をつけるかつけないか。つけるのであれば、全体とどのように調和を図るか。庇のある建築には永遠のテーマである

Third-floor roof rain trough covered in gold leaf. To keep the eave-ends simple yet elegant, should rain troughs be added or not? If they are to be attached, how can they be incorporated harmoniously with the whole? The handling of rain runoff is the eternal theme of architecture with extended eaves.

池に張り出して立つ金閣は、毛細管現象で上がってくる水を切る処理が必要となる。外周は自然石の上に支柱を立て、なかでは亀腹の上に柱を立てている

Since the Kinkaku projects into the pond, there has to be a way to cut off the water that rises due to capillary action. For the outer rim posts are erected upon natural stones, and in the middle pillars stand upon white plaster-covered mounds (kamebara).

広縁の外側にさらに落縁をつけ、縁を延ばす。一段落とすことで、水や庭との結びつきをさらに高めている。手前の石敷が船着き場となる

The veranda is extended with an *ochien*—an outer veranda one step lower. Lowering it a step increases the sense of unity with the garden and water. The stone paving in the forefront is the pier.

日が昇る頃、美しい姿を池に映じる　　At dawn, Kinkaku's beautiful silhouette shimmers upon surface of the pond.

慈照寺 銀閣・東求堂

国宝
建立時期　銀閣1489年(上棟)／東求堂1485年
庭園　　　特別史跡・特別名勝
所在地　　京都府京都市左京区

Jishoji Temple Ginkaku Pavilion and Togudo Hall

National Treasures
Completed: Ginkaku, 1489 (framework); Togudo, 1485
Garden: Special Historic Site; Special Place of Scenic Beauty
Location: Sakyo ward, Kyoto, Kyoto prefecture

時代背景

　室町幕府第八代将軍・足利義政（1436-1490）は将軍職を退き、隠遁生活を送るため、京都の東を区切る大文字山のふもとに山荘・東山殿を造営した。工事は1482（文明14）年から始まり、義政がこの地で没する1490（延徳2）年まで、常御所（つねのごしょ）、会所、仏堂、山上の亭など10余りの建物が築かれた。義政没後にはその菩提（ぼだい）を弔い、臨済宗の禅寺に改められて慈照寺と号し、諸建物はそのまま維持されたが、1558（永禄元）年の戦乱で罹災し、ほとんどの堂舎を焼失した。そのなかで観音殿（1489年上棟）と東求堂（1485年）は火難を免れ、東山殿の貴重な遺構として今日に伝えられる。銀閣の通称で知られる観音殿は、観音仏を安置する2階建ての楼閣、東求堂は阿弥陀如来像を祀る持仏堂兼書斎である。両者ともに仏教建築でありつつ、住宅的要素をあわせもつ。

　義政の東山殿は、祖父・義満の北山殿と比較対照されてきたが、それぞれが建てられた社会的背景や目的は異なる。義満が北山殿を建てたのは、南北朝を合一し終えた権力の絶頂期であり、一方、義政が東山殿の造営を開始したのは、10年以上にわたって都を戦乱に巻きこんだ応仁・文明の乱（1467-1477）が鎮まった5年後の、幕府が弱体化の一途をたどった時期であった。両者とも山荘を営むにあたり出家したが、義満は為政者として引き続き君臨し、北山殿には公務の建物群があって、晴れの場を兼ね備えていた。他方、義政は政治の舞台から身を引き、東山殿を占めたのは、花鳥風月を愛でる風流のための施設や私的な仏堂であった。

　銀閣も東求堂も池（錦鏡池）のほとりに立ち、園地と不可分の関係で結ばれた庭園建築である。やはり義政も、夢窓礎石（むそうそせき）の作庭の系譜を引き継いだ。敷地にこの山麓を選定したのも、山上・中腹・山麓の土地の起伏を利用して築かれた西芳寺の庭園形式を踏襲するためであった。義政は堂舎の多くを西芳寺の諸建物に倣って造営し、命名についても、西来堂（西芳寺）——東求堂（慈照寺）のように発想の拠りどころにした。東求堂とは、東方の人が西方極楽浄土に往生することを求める意味という。禅的な仙境への憧憬の一方で、平安以来の浄土教信仰が義政の構想の背景に重ねられていることが指摘されている。*2

　銀閣の工事は東山殿の造営の最終時期にかかり、義政は完成を見届けずにこの世を去った。観音殿が「銀閣」と呼ばれるようになったのは、江戸時代のことである。

特徴と見どころ

　朝、大文字山の向こうから昇る太陽に照らされ、慈照寺は生気と清らかさに満ちたひとときを迎える。銀閣は真正面から朝日を浴び、池に向かって開かれた広縁には、水面に反射した光が戯れる。心空殿（しんくうでん）と名づけられた1階は軽やかな住宅風の構えで、東正面の広縁の前に落縁をつけ、その柱間には腰高の明り障子を入れる。広縁はまた、平面で見ると建物内部の一部分でもあり、建具の入らない吹放ちの部屋である。そこは外と内とが融け合うような、魅力的な中間領域がつくられている。ここから望む巧みな遠近感をもって築かれた林泉の景趣は、日本の庭園芸術における一つの頂であろう。

　金閣が3階建てであるのに対し、銀閣は2階建てであるが、いずれも上層（金閣は最上層）は方3間の仏堂で、禅宗様とする。銀閣の東西面は火灯窓（かとうまど）が各柱間に出窓の形で入り、出張り部分は内部では浅い腰掛となる。三連の火灯窓と宝形屋根の組み合わせは、庭や山から閣を眺めたとき、鮮やかな印象を残す庭園の中心的な構成要素となっている。

　錦鏡池の東北部に位置する東求堂は方3間半の建物で、平面を南北に分け、南半分は平安時代以来の私的な阿弥陀堂の流れを汲んだ仏間を中心とし、北半分は書院造の原形的な構えを備える4畳半の書斎・同仁斎（どうじんさい）と6畳間からなる。

　四畳半の同仁斎は、付書院と違棚を造りつけにした最古の遺例で、初期の書院造のあり方を今に提示する。この部屋は、隠棲した将軍の私的な書斎であるとともに、うちとけた雰囲気のなかで人と語らう場であった。その意味で、のちに形式化・格式化し、晴向きの対面の場となる書院造とはずいぶん雰囲気が異なる。義政の時代、書院は部屋の目的に合わせて飾りつけをする奥向きの交流の場であった。同時代に書かれた『蔭涼軒日録』（いんりょうけんにちろく）には、義政が永眠するまでの1年の間に、宴、歌、詩、茶、雑話などの用途でこの部屋が使われた記録が約50回残るという。*3

　同仁斎の格調高い空気感は、部材の寸法構成や研ぎ澄まされた比例感覚によってもたらされている。北向きの付書院から射しこむ静謐な光が、さらにその美しさを際立たせている。

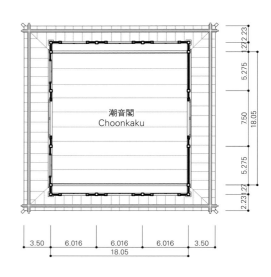

2階平面図　Second floor plan

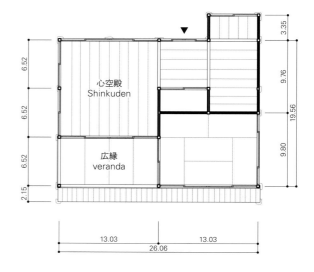

1階平面図　First floor plan

Historical Background

To live in seclusion after his retirement, eighth Muromachi shogun Ashikaga Yoshimasa (1436–1490) built his Higashiyama villa in the hills on the eastern edge of Kyoto. Between the start of construction in 1482 and Yoshimasa's death in 1490, more than ten buildings had been completed. After his death, the villa was made a Rinzai school Zen Buddhist temple and named Jishoji. Although the buildings were preserved as they were, a number were lost to fire during fighting in 1558. Fortunately, the Kannonden hall (framework completed in 1489) and Togudo hall (1485) managed to evade the fires, and stand today as precious testimony to the time of the Higashiyama villa. The Kannonden, known popularly as the Ginkaku (Silver Pavilion), is a two-story building enshrining a statue of the Kannon Bodhisattva, and the Togudo hall is part study and part worship hall enshrining a statue of Amida Buddha. Both Buddhist halls incorporate numerous features of residential architecture.

Numerous comparisons have been drawn between Yoshimasa's Higashiyama villa and his grandfather Yoshimitsu's Kitayama villa, but the social background and purposes for which they were constructed were vastly different. Yoshimitsu built his villa during the period after the union of the Southern and Northern courts, when the political power of the Ashikaga shoguns was at its height. In contrast, Yoshimasa started his Higashiyama villa five years after the Onin War (1467–1477) had ravished the capital, in a period in which the shogunate was in decline. When they built their villas, both men became priests; however, Yoshimitsu continued to rule the country, requiring that his villa have many buildings for performing official duties and as sites for rites and rituals. On the other hand, Yoshimasa had retired entirely from politics, so his villa consisted of facilities for marveling at the beauties of nature and worshipping the Buddha.

The designs for the architecture of the Kannonden and Togudo halls, both standing on the edge of Kinkyochi ("brocade mirror") pond, make them integral parts of the garden setting. Like his grandfather, Yoshimasa also followed in the footsteps of Zen master Muso Soseki in constructing his garden. He chose the villa's grounds in order to emulate Soseki's Saihoji temple, which was built incorporating the natural contours of the top, middle, and foot of a mountain. Yoshimasa took inspiration for many of his pavilions and halls from the buildings of Saihoji temple, and even drew on them for names: Jishoji's Togudo is said to mean "a man of the East wishing for peace in the afterlife in the Pure Land of the West," and Saihoji's Sairaido implies "the Amida Buddha coming from the Pure Land of the West." It has been noted that in addition to his aspiration for a Zen-like retreat, beliefs in Pure Land teachings prevalent since the Heian period lie behind Yoshimasa's conception for the villa. The Kannonden was one of the last buildings to be constructed, and Yoshimasa passed away without having seen its completion. It was named "Ginkaku" much later, during the Edo period.

Characteristics and Highlights

When the morning sun rising over Mt. Daimonji casts its rays upon Jishoji, for a moment the temple is filled with freshness and purity. The morning light shines directly onto the front of the Ginkaku, and beams reflected by the water dance upon the deep veranda opening on the pond. The first floor, named the Shinkuden ("Heart Emptiness" hall), has an airy residential-style structure; the deep veranda on the eastern facade has an outer veranda one step lower (*ochien*) and between the pillars are half-shoji panels. Furthermore, looking at the Ginkaku floor plan, we can see that the deep veranda is part of the building interior that has been left open to the outside, without any partitioning panels, creating an attractive middle zone where outside and inside merge. The view from here, with its tasteful scene of woods and water built through masterful manipulation of perspective, is one of the highpoints of Japanese garden art.

In contrast to the three-story structure of the Kinkaku (Golden Pavilion), the Ginkaku is two storied. In both cases, however, the top story is built in the Zenshuyo style consisting of a square room with three bays on each side. The combination of the three bell-shaped windows and *hogyo* style pyramidal roof is striking when seen from the garden or hillside, making it the centerpiece of the garden's composition.

The Togudo hall, located on the northeastern side of Kinkyochi pond, is a three-bay square building. Its southern half centers around a room with a Buddhist altar (*butsuma*), which follows the style of private worship halls for Amida Buddha seen since the Heian period. The northern half consists of the four-and-a-half-tatami study Dojinsai structured in a prototypical *shoin* style, and a six-tatami room.

The Dojinsai is the oldest example of a *shoin* room with built-in recessed desk (*tsukeshoin*) and built-in staggered shelves (*chigaidana*), showing us the early structures of *shoin-zukuri* buildings. This room, while functioning as the personal study of the retired shogun, was also a place where he could socialize in an informal environment. In that sense, it is quite different from the later *shoin-zukuri* study, which through conventionalization and formality, became a place for public meetings. In Yoshimasa's time, a study was a place for private interaction, with the decorations and furnishings changed according to the occasion. The *Inryoken nichiroku*, the official diary of the chief monks of the Inryoken, a cloister within the Rokuon'in, a subtemple of the Shokokuji, written in the same era, records about fifty gatherings in this room in the last year of Yoshimasa's life, for parties, poetry, tea ceremonies, and general conversation.

The elegant atmosphere of Dojinsai is the result of the carefully calculated dimensions of its components and an extremely refined sense of proportion. Light shines serenely through the windows of the recessed desk on the north side, further heightening its beauty.

新緑のなか、朝日を浴びる銀閣こと観音殿。向月台（左端・盛砂）あたりから見る。
東面のみ縁側があるので縋破風つきの庇で軒を延ばしている

Surrounded by the spring greenery, morning sunlight bathes the Kannonden hall, also known as Ginkaku (Silver Pavilion). The view is as seen from near the "Moon Viewing Platform" (Kogetsudai, sand cone in the left corner). On the eastern side only, the eaves are extended with different-sized bargeboards (*sugaruhafu*).

錦鏡池の畔に立つ。1階は書院造の住宅風、2階は禅宗様の仏堂。1階の腰高明り障子が軽やかな印象をつくる。護岸石組や浮石、石橋（分界橋）の配置が巧みな遠近感をつくる

Ginkaku stands at the edge of the pond. The first floor is in residential *shoin-zukuri* style and the second floor is a Buddhist worship hall in Zenshuyo style. The half shoji panels introduce an impression of lightness. The arrangement of rocks along the water's edge (*gogan ishigumi*), the half-submerged rocks (*ukiishi*), and the stone bridge (*ishibashi*) skillfully set up a dynamic perspective.

朝、錦鏡池に反射した光が広縁の奥まで明るく照らす。腰高明り障子は14世紀末建立の金閣には使われていない建具で、15世紀後半の文明年間から遺構例がある。以降、広縁や落縁に明り障子を組み合わせた縁の空間が発展する

Morning light reflecting off the "brocade mirror" pond shines on and well into the back of the deep veranda. Half shoji panels were not used in the Kinkaku (Golden Pavilion) built in the fourteenth century; extant examples date back only as far as the latter half of the fifteenth century. Veranda spaces developed from this time onward, with deep verandas and lower *ochien* verandas combined with shoji panels.

南東から見る銀閣は庭に融けこむようにしてある。小川のせせらぎを聴きながら、
園路を進むにつれて変化に富む景観が展開する

Viewed from the southeast, the Ginkaku blends into the garden. The garden path leads to scenes of rich and changeful variety, the sound of the gurgling brook never far away.

錦鏡池が凍る2月。薄氷の張る水面に東求堂の屋根が映りこむ。
このあたりの石組みは作庭当初の意匠と考えられている

In February, ice forms on the "brocade mirror" pond. The corner of the Togudo reflects in spots between thin ice. The rock arrangements in this area are thought to date back to the very first building of the garden in the fifteenth century.

東求堂。方形の建物だが屋根の棟を後方(北側)にずらして通し、
前面はゆるやかな勾配で葺き下ろして、優雅な屋根の流れをつくる。
手前には一石づくりの緊張感みなぎる仙桂橋がかかる

Togudo hall. Though the building is square, the roof ridge has been moved to the back (north), and the front side slopes downwards at a gentle angle, creating a large, elegantly flowing slope. Adding a terse line in the foreground is the rustic Senkeikyo bridge, a single stone laid across the water.

阿弥陀如来像を安置する仏間・東求堂南面。中央間には桟唐戸、両脇間には腰壁の上に竪繁桟の障子が入る。内部は折上小組格天井で、壁上のジャボコ（竪の湾曲材）が繊細で美しい

The Togudo's southern side houses an altar enshrining a statue of Amida Buddha. Between the center columns is a pair of paneled doors (*sankarado*), and next to it on both sides are latticed windows with closely spaced vertical muntins and wainscoting. Inside the ceiling is coved, coffered and finely latticed. The curved muntins (*jaboko*) atop the walls are especially delicate.

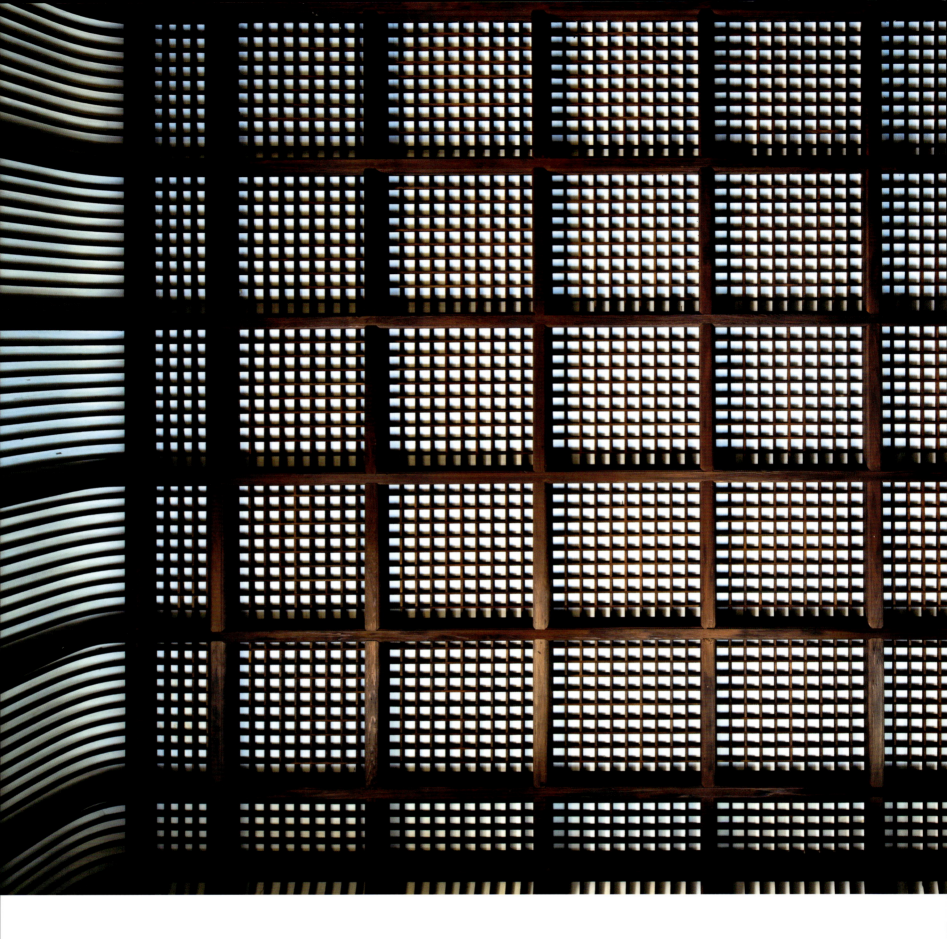

仏間・折上小組格天井を見上げる。正方形のみで割り切らずに格子を割りつけたところが、むしろ瀟洒な印象を生む

Looking up at the coved, coffered, and finely latticed ceiling over the altar. The fact that it is not all divided into squares, with the lattices halved on the edges, serves to enhance its elegance.

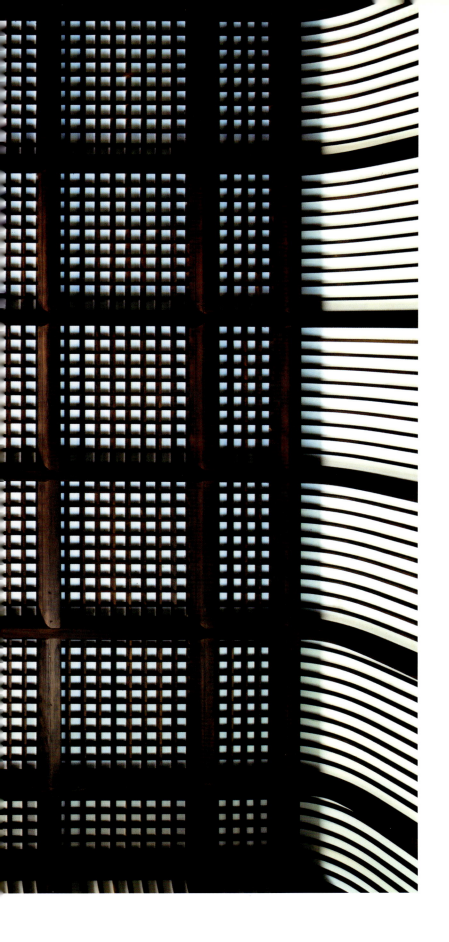

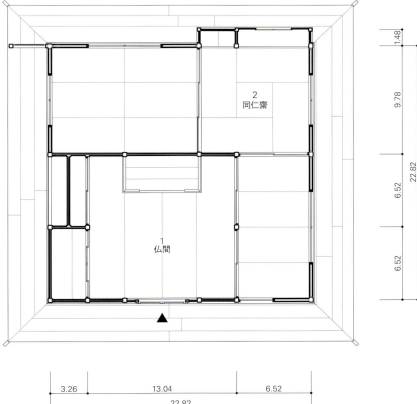

1 worship hall
2 Dojinsai study

(右)東求堂・平面図。方形平面を南北に分け、仏間のある南半分を2間、書院のある北半分を1間半とし、屋根の棟もこの東西線に通す。仏間以外の部屋には畳を敷きつめる

(Right) The plan of the Togudo hall shows how the square structure is divided between north and south, the southern half for the worship hall being two bays wide, and the northern half with the study one-and-a-half bays wide. The ridge of the roof follows this divide. All the rooms are floored with tatami mats, except for the worship hall.

東庭の建具を開いた書斎・同仁齋。縁には二軒疎垂木の軽快な軒がかかる。夕方、太陽が北西にまわる頃、庭木に当たる西日が反射し、書院窓を明るくする

The Dojinsai study has sliding doors opening onto the eastern garden. The simple yet elegant eaves with widely spaced double rafters extend over the veranda. In the evening, when the sun comes around to the northwest, sunlight reflects off the garden trees, illuminating the interior of the study.

4畳半の同仁齋は、500年以上の歳月をさかのぼる和室の源流である。鴨居の高さは畳より5尺8寸(約176cm)で、部屋をまわるこの線の高さが、今も和室のプロポーションの要となる

This four-and-a-half tatami study Dojinsai is the source of a five-hundred-year-old tradition of Japanese-style rooms (*washitsu*). The head jambs (*kamoi*) are positioned five *shaku* and eight *sun* (approximately 176 centimeters) above the tatami mats. The height of the *kamoi* line that circles the room is key to good proportions in traditional Japanese rooms to this day.

同仁齋・付書院の外側。舞良戸4枚に引き分け明り障子を立てた3本溝の建具使いは、室町時代、書院造の発展とともに工夫された。上方の欄間には蔀を吊る

Dojinsai study from outside. The three-grooved panel moldings, holding four wood-panel doors with parallel crosspieces (*mairado*) and shoji panels, was devised along with the development of the *shoin-zukuri* style during the Muromachi period. Note the *shitomi*-style shutter (here raised) over the transom panels.

付書院の押板上には文具や本が飾りつけられた。明り障子を開けると、手入れのよい北庭の景が縁取られ、爽やかな風が通り抜ける。押板は厚み73mm（2寸4分）、畳面より233mm（7寸7分）の高さ

Writing implements and books were displayed on the baseboard (*oshiita*) of the recessed desk. The shoji panels open to frame the well-groomed scenery of the northern garden and a refreshing breeze blows through the room. The baseboard is 73 millimeters thick and rises 233 millimeters above the tatami mats.

違棚は21mm（7分）厚のケヤキ板である。木口には端喰、飾り金物をつけ、上下の棚板をつなげる海老束は銀杏面取りで繊細に見せている

The staggered shelves are made of zelkova boards 21 millimeters thick. The crosscut end (*koguchi*) is covered with strips of wood (*hashibami*) and adorned with metal fittings (*kazari kanamono*), and the small pillar connecting the shelves (*ebizuka*) has rounded chamfering, giving it a delicate look.

柱と長押の原寸。四方柾・木曾ヒノキの柱は115mm（3寸8分）、面取り1／10。柱の面取り部分の1／2に内法を納めたディテール。同仁齋の端整な空間は、このような細部の集積で成り立っている

A pillar and a non-penetrating tie beam (*nageshi*) at full size. The Kiso cypress pillar showing straight grain on all four sides is 115 millimeters square in cross section and 1/10 chamfered. The frame for the sliding panels is set within 1/2 of the chamfered section of the pillar. The atmosphere of refined taste in the Dojinsai is the result of the accumulation of such minute details.

相國寺 鐘楼

京都府指定有形文化財
建立年代　1843年
所在地　　京都府京都市上京区

Shokokuji Temple Bell Tower

Kyoto Prefectural Tangible Cultural Property
Completed: 1843
Location: Kamigyo ward, Kyoto, Kyoto prefecture

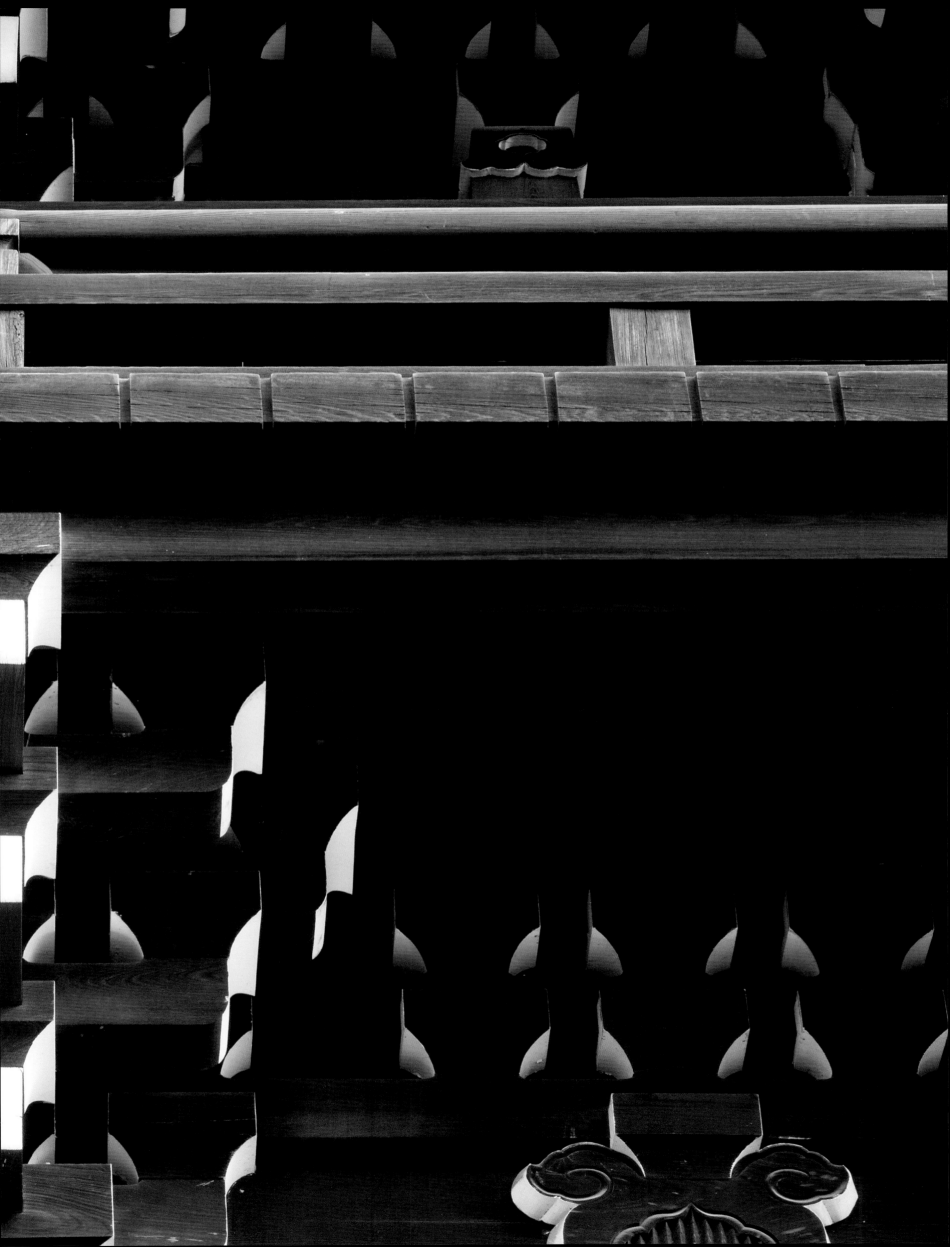

時代背景

　室町は禅宗の時代である。足利尊氏（1305－1358）の夢窓礎石への帰依に始まり、歴代の足利将軍家はとくに臨済禅を厚く保護した。なかでも三代将軍義満は、夢窓の直弟子で甥に当たる春屋妙葩（1312－1388）を幼い頃から禅師とし、熱心に参禅修道に勤め、1382（永徳2）年には相國寺の建立を発願した。寺地は御所の北、義満が居を構えた室町殿の東隣である。30数年前に示寂した夢窓を追請開山に、春屋を実質開山に迎え、法堂・仏殿・三門・禅堂などを持つ禅宗式伽藍が1392（明徳3）年に完工。五山官寺の制度のなか、天龍寺に次ぎ、京都五山の第二位に列せられた。その後は4回の大火に見舞われ、焼失と再興を繰り返す歴史を歩んだ。そのなかで禅宗寺院の中心的建物となる法堂は、1605（慶長10）年、豊臣秀頼（1593－1615）の寄進により建立されたものが災禍を免れて現存し、全国でも最古の法堂となる。今日の伽藍は天明の大火（1788年）を経て、おもに江戸時代後期の1807（文化4）年に整えられた建物で構成されている。臨済宗相國寺派大本山で、足利義満が開基の鹿苑寺、足利義政が開基の慈照寺を山外塔頭に持つ。

特徴と見どころ

　天明の大火で鐘楼も焼失し、現鐘楼は1843（天保14）年に再建された。洪音楼と号する。梵鐘は1629（寛永6）年造立のものを吊るす。下層には袴腰がつき、内部階段で上層に昇って鐘を撞く。小部材を精緻に組み上げた斗栱とその圧倒的な量感に加え、木口に塗られた白い胡粉の鮮やかなリズムと立体感が見どころである。胡粉は腐り止めではあるが、こうなると美的処理の域に達している。大きな入母屋の屋根を載せるが、全体のプロポーション、スケール感に狂いがないため重苦しさがなく、大寺院の鐘楼にふさわしい品格がある。大きな要素と小さな要素との形の対比がよく、冴えたデザインの感性でまとめられた建築である。

Historical Background

The Muromachi period was the heyday of Zen Buddhism. The Ashikaga shoguns, beginning with Takauji (1305–1358), who became a devout follower of the priest Muso Soseki, were strong protectors of its Rinzai school. Among them, third shogun Yoshimitsu devoted himself from boyhood to Zen training under Muso Soseki's nephew and direct disciple Shun'oku Myoha (1312–1388), and in 1382 made a vow to build Shokokuji temple. The temple was situated north of the imperial palace and east of and adjacent to Yoshimitsu's residence in the Muromachi quarter of the city. The temple was built with Muso Soseki, who had died 30 years earlier, as its "posthumous founder" and Shun'oku as its founder. In 1392 the temple's Zen-style compound was completed with lecture hall (*hatto*), Buddha hall (*butsuden*), gate (*sanmon*), and meditation hall (*zendo*). Among the Gozan or five leading Rinzai Zen temples in Kyoto, Shokokuji was second only to Tenryuji. After that, it was burned down four times, so the temple's history is one of repeated renewal out of the ashes of fire. Among its buildings, the *hatto* lecture hall built in 1605 with the support of Toyotomi Hideyori (1593–1615) has escaped the flames and been preserved to this day, making it the oldest *hatto* hall in the country. The compound suffered a major fire in 1788 and now consists mainly of buildings completed as of 1807 (late Edo period). Shokokuji is the main or head temple of the Shokokuji branch of the Rinzai school of Zen, the parent temple of Rokuonji (known as Temple of the Golden Pavilion), founded by Ashikaga Yoshimitsu, and Jishoji (Temple of the Silver Pavilion), founded by eighth shogun Ashikaga Yoshimasa.

Characteristics and Highlights

Shokokuji's bell tower burned down in the great Tenmei fire of 1788, and the current structure was rebuilt in 1843. The tower was named the Ko'onro ("flood-of-sound tower") and its bell was cast in 1629. The lower floor has flaring skirt-like walls that house the stairway leading to the platform from which the bell is rung. The structure projects a tremendous sense of volume and stands out for the density and complexity of the bracket arms and bearing blocks under the veranda and eaves. The painting of selected faces of the bearing members with white *gofun* pigment brings out the striking rhythm of the architecture. The *gofun* serves to inhibit decay but also enhances the building as far as aesthetic appreciation is concerned. The structure is topped with a massive hip-and-gable roof, but thanks to the finely calculated sense of proportion and scale, it provides just the right amount of weight and dignity requisite to the bell tower of a major temple. The fine matching of massive features with elements of detail gives it an overall sense of refined design.

斗栱を組み、屋根を跳ね出す技術を大陸から移入して1,000年以上を経た江戸末期の組物。盛期は過ぎても、時代の生彩が吹きこまれて新鮮味のある意匠となっている。斗栱の圧倒的な量感がつくる禅宗様独特の集合美が強調され、軒や縁に華を添える

These bracket complexes were built more than a thousand years after the technology for extending roofs and eaves supported by bracket arms and bearing blocks was introduced from the continent. While honoring the classical style long after its heyday has past, the freshness of the workmanship reflects the time the tower was rebuilt. The bearing block and bracket arm complexes evoke an overwhelming sense of volume, projecting the dense intricacy characteristic of the Zenshuyo style and imbuing the eaves and veranda with a touch of splendor.

小建築ながら強いシンメトリーの形に、すみずみまで統制された規矩感。中備の間の透けが軽やかである。腰組の下段には蟇股を入れている

For such a small building, the tower exudes a strong sense of symmetry in which every piece is governed by precision and regularity. The openings in the intermediate supports (*nakazonae*) open the complexes to light and air. The lower row of bracket complexes under the veranda have frog-legged struts.

縁を支える三手先斗栱。15世紀建立の東福寺三門とくらべると、白い胡粉を塗った肘木の曲線は丸みがなく角張り、かっちりとした端整な印象である。肘木には割れ防止に背割を入れている

The three-stepped bracket complexes supporting the veranda. Compared to the *sanmon* gate at Tofukuji constructed in the fifteenth century, the projecting arms (their ends painted white with *gofun* pigment) are no longer rounded, but squared, giving an impression of spare, clean lines. The bracket arms have wedge-cuts (*sewari*) to prevent cracks from forming.

梵鐘の音が格子の壁を通してあたりに鳴り響く。松林の間から浮かび上がるようにして張り出す深い庇と入母屋造の大きな屋根。その下には広々とした縁がまわる

The sound of the bell resounds through the latticed wall of the belfry. The tower's hip-and-gable roof and deep eaves flare out broadly, as if floating up among the great pines. Encircling the building beneath the eaves is the spacious veranda.

龍安寺 方丈庭園

史跡・特別名勝
作庭年代　15世紀末–16世紀
所在地　　京都府京都市右京区

Ryoanji Temple *Hojo* Garden

Historic Site and Special Place of Scenic Beauty
Garden completion: Late 15th–16th century
Location: Ukyo ward, Kyoto, Kyoto prefecture

時代背景

　日本における枯山水の歴史は古い。平安時代に書かれた最古の庭園書『作庭記』では、枯山水という語がすでに使われており、池もなく遣水(やりみず)もなきところに石を立つることあり、と定義される。中世に入ると、「石立僧」と呼ばれ、半専門的に作庭を手掛ける僧が皇族の別業（別荘）などの作庭に関わった記録が残り、庭園における庭石の占める重要性を物語る。さらに室町初期には、夢窓疎石(むそうそせき)が禅の境致を作庭で表現し、これを範にして禅の庭園文化が盛んとなった。禅宗寺院の枯山水は、禅の哲学や神仙的な自然観を、水を用いずに、石組を主として象徴的に表わしたものである。とくに室町後期以降、禅宗寺院の塔頭化(たっちゅう)が進み、限られた空間のなかで単純化と象徴化を深めた枯山水の表現が発展した。

　龍安寺は臨済宗妙心寺派大本山妙心寺の末寺で、1450（宝徳2）年、室町幕府管領・細川勝元（1430-1473）が妙心寺五祖・義天玄承(ぎてんげんしょう)（1393-1462）を開山に招いて創建した。1467年、応仁・文明の乱で堂塔・塔頭を全焼したが、勝元の子・政元（1466-1507）が4世住持・特芳禅傑(とくほうぜんけつ)（1419-1506）とともに再興に着手し、1499（明応8）年には方丈が上棟した。以来、塔頭20余を数える伽藍が整備されたと記録されたが、1797（寛政9）年の火災により方丈・開山堂・仏殿を焼失した。現在の方丈（重文）は、1606（慶長11）年に建てられた塔頭・西源院の方丈を移築したものである。

　龍安寺石庭として広く知られる枯山水の方丈前庭は、いつ、だれによって創意・作庭されたかは明らかではない。創意者として幾人もの名が挙がり、作庭時代の推定についても寺の創建当初、あるいは15世紀末の再興時とする説から、作庭技法や様式からの推定により17世紀初頭とする説まで、かなりの隔たりがある。

　この庭園は方丈と対の関係でつくられたものだが、上述のように、方丈は1797年の火災後に移築されたものなので、その際、庭まわりにいくつかの改修が施されたと考えられている。そのため石庭の地割と建物とは多少ずれており、方丈の東西長さより石庭は西（向かって右）にやや長く、したがって火災前の方丈の東西長さは現在の方丈よりも長かったことがわかる。また、勅使門（重文・1606年）の位置は、かつては南側の油土塀と同じ線上にあり、現在の東側の高塀はなく、さらに石庭との境は明け放ちとなっていた可能性も指摘されている。*4　時とともに変化を経た箇所はあるものの、庭石の形態の対照の妙、配石の張りつめた均衡は不変であり、卓越した象徴性をもって眺める者の黙想を誘う。

特徴と見どころ

　築山も池もなく、平坦な地面に石が配置されているだけの平庭形式の石庭である。油土塀で区切られた矩形の枠内に白砂が敷かれ、方丈から見て、左から右へ5・2・3・2・3石の5群15石で構成されている。枠内には一草一木も植えられておらず、庭として変化する最大の要素を欠くこととなり、結果、その表現を著しく抽象度の高いものにしている。他方、自然石でなければこの景観が成立しないのはいうまでもない。風霜(ふうそう)にさらされて滲み出た石の寂びた色合い、質感、天然の形態の妙が、さらにこの空間に時間の魔法をかける。油土塀は石の古色にふさわしい額縁となり、外界からこの小宇宙を区切っている。

　石組と配石の均衡感がこの庭の醍醐味ではあるが、見方を変えれば、むしろ石ではなく、白砂の余白——海であり水の象徴か——をいかに生かすかがこの庭の主題であるように思える。石組のつくりだす巧みな間合いが、白砂の無の空間を活性化し、空間全体の象徴性を高めている。これは描かれた部分が、何も描かない空白を生きたものとする水墨画の手法と似ている。その間合いをつくる基点は、やはり方丈の室中(しっちゅう)（中心に位置する主室）前の広縁からのぞむ眺めとなろう。現状は方丈が東に寄っているので、室中の西寄りとなるが、そこからはこの庭が象徴する大海原の眺めが大きな広がりを見せ、同時に、海に浮かぶ島々（石組）を視界に収めることができる。広縁に立つ柱の垂直性、縁の深い庇と油土塀の伸びやかな水平線は、さらに遠近感を強調している。

　石庭はまた、方丈の縁の美しさと一体となっている。広縁の長さは約22m、落縁を含めて縁の幅は約4.3mもある。正面・南からの光は石庭の白砂にきらきらと反射し、深い庇がそれを受けとめて、和らいだ光で縁の空間を照らす。光はさらに鎮められて奥へと導かれ、室内を淡い光で充たしている。縁に座って庭を眺めると、舟で海へと漕ぎ出していくようにも感じられ、外と内の中間にたゆたう魅力的な空間がつくりだされている。

Historical Background

The history of dry landscape gardens (*karesansui*) goes back quite far. The term already appears in the famous Heian-period manual on gardens, the *Sakuteiki*, defining it as the arrangement of rocks without a pond or stream. Records from the medieval period, which tell of semi-specialists known as *ishidateso* (rock-arranging priests) involved in the planning of gardens for royal family villas, give us a sense of the importance of this aspect of garden building. It was in the fourteenth century that Muso Soseki described garden building as an integral part of Zen training and his examples inspired the garden culture of Zen temples for centuries after. The dry landscape gardens of Zen temples use rock arrangements as symbolic expressions of Zen philosophy and the Daoist view of nature with its legends of the islands of the immortals. Particularly from the late fifteenth century onward, the subtemples of larger temples proliferated, and in the process dry landscape gardens of increasing simplicity and refined symbolism flourished, crafted to fit into very limited spaces.

Ryoanji is a subtemple of Myoshinji, which is the headquarters of the Myoshinji branch of Rinzai Zen; it was built in 1450 by shogunal deputy Hosokawa Katsumoto (1430–1473), who invited a Zen priest Giten Gensho (1393–1462) to be its founder. In 1467, during the Onin War (1467–1477), the temple's main buildings and subtemples were all burned to the ground, but its reconstruction was launched by Katsumoto's son Masamoto (1466–1507) together with Tokuho Zenketsu (1419–1506), its fourth-generation head priest. The *hojo* abbot's quarters ridge-raising ceremony was celebrated in 1499 and from that time, it is recorded, more than 20 subtemples were built. But in 1797 again the abbot's quarters, the founder's hall (*kaizando*), and Buddha hall (*butsuden*) burned down. The current abbot's quarters was originally built in the subtemple Seigen'in in 1606 and moved to Ryoanji after the 1797 fire.

Who designed the *hojo* rock garden is not known, though several possible creators have been named. Opinion is quite divided over when it was built as well, with some saying that it was made when the temple was founded, others asserting that it goes back to the time of the restoration in the late fifteenth century, and still others, judging from the techniques and style of garden building, placing its origins in the early seventeenth century.

The rock garden was designed as part of the original abbot's quarters, and with replacement of the building following the various fires, it is thought that a number of repairs and changes were made. Because of the different dimensions of the replacement building, there is some disjunct with the garden layout. The rock garden is somewhat longer east-to-west than the building on the west end, indicating that the original *hojo* was longer east-to-west than the current building. In addition, it is said that the location of the Chokushimon (gate for use by an imperial envoy; Important Cultural Property) was previously aligned with the earthen wall on the south side of the garden, and that the current high east-side wall was not in existence, suggesting the possibility that the boundary to the garden was open on that side. While it is likely that a number of changes took place in the surroundings, the uncanny contrasts among the shapes of the garden rocks and the fine tension set up by their arrangement remain unchanged. Their superb symbolism draws the visitor instinctively into meditation.

Characteristics and Highlights

The rock garden is in the flat style, without any hill (*tsukiyama*) or pond, but composed entirely of rock arrangements. Within a rectangular frame surrounded on two sides by earthen walls (*aburadobei*, made with oil-permeated clay) are 15 rocks, clustered in groups of five, two, three, two, and three (left to right when viewed from the veranda) across an expanse of white pebbles. The absence of elements that bring about change in the appearance of a garden heightens the quality of its abstraction. At the same time, what we find is needless to say a scene that could not have been composed except with natural rocks. It is precisely the subdued hues of rock weathered by wind and frost, the qualities and textures, and the beauty of the natural shapes that cast the magic of time over this space. The earthen wall serves as the perfect backdrop for the patinas of the rocks and shields the resulting microcosm from the world outside.

The fascination of this garden lies in the sense of balance in the rock arrangements and their interrelationships, but if we shift our perspective slightly, we can also imagine that the theme of this garden was not so much the rocks as how to bring out the best in the expanse of white pebbles—whether it is symbolic of the ocean or of water. The adroitly created spaces marked out by the rock arrangements enliven the "blank," pebbled-covered expanse, enhancing the symbolism of the whole. The pivot of the Ryoanji rock garden from which its spaces are created is the view from the veranda in front of the main room of the *hojo*. The building today is shifted to the east, so the center of the garden is aligned with a point in the western part of the building, and it is from there that one can hold within one's field of vision the entire expanse of the "vast seas" and encompassing all the "island groups" (rock arrangements) rising from them.

The rock garden is also integrated with the beauty of the *hojo* veranda, which measures 22 meters in length and 4.3 meters in width, including the outer, slightly lower level *ochien*. Light coming in over the garden from the south reflects brightly on the white pebbles. The long eaves embrace the reflected light and soften it, illuminating the veranda space. Further dimmed, the light penetrates far back into the rooms, its faint glow filling the interior. Sitting on the veranda gazing out, one finds oneself in a fascinating middle place, as if floating between outside and inside or sitting in a boat that is rowing out into the sea.

春の朝、薄明の静寂のなか、白砂が徐々に輝きを増すひととき。正面の油土塀の高さは
南(左)へ向かうにつれて低くなり、方丈から眺めたときの遠近感を強めている

The glow of light gradually builds over the white pebbles of the garden on a spring morning. The height of the earthen wall at the west end (back of the photo) slants slightly downward to the south (left), augmenting the sense of the depth when the garden is viewed from the veranda.

方丈と庭。深い軒と広々とした縁。軒の出は5.8m、広縁3.2mに落縁1.1m。
清々しくも引き締まった空気感が漂う

Forming an atmosphere both fresh and bracing, the *hojo* eaves sweep for 5.8 meters, the inner veranda reaches out 3.2 meters and the lower *ochien* veranda another 1.1 meters.

広縁からの眺め。柱、落縁、深い軒と低い油土塀の水平線が奥行きを深める。
庭のほぼ中央にあたり、すべてを見晴らす

View from the interior over the veranda. The verticality of the post and the horizontal lines of the outer veranda, deep eaves, and the horizon provided by the low earthen wall add depth to the perspective. From this position aligned with the center of the garden, the entire garden may be seen.

1　Chokushimon gate
2　*hojo*
3　inner veranda
4　outer veranda
5　garden

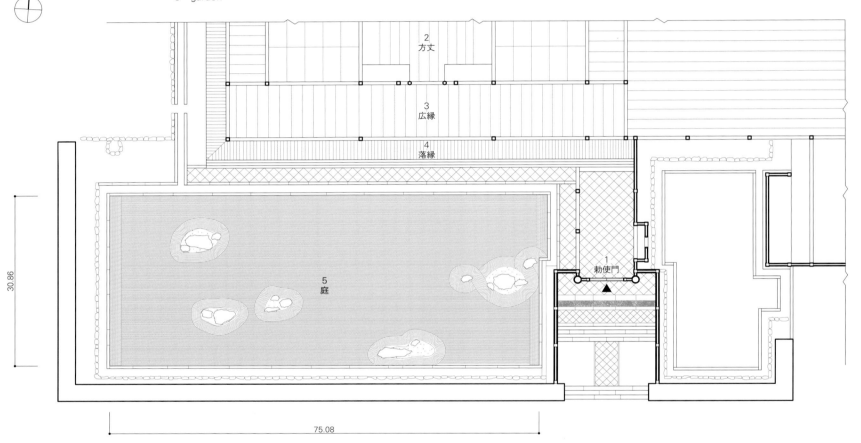

平面図　Plan

（右）唐破風のついた勅使門。1797年の火災後、方丈とともに塔頭・西源院より移築。四半敷のアプローチ、方丈の廊、さらに奥の北庭まで視線が通り抜ける

(Right) Chokushimon gate with a *karahafu* undulating gable. After the loss of the original building in 1797, this gate along with the *hojo* building was moved from the Seigen'in subtemple. A square of the garden on the north side can be seen through the approach with a *shihanjiki* pattern of square paving stones, the gate and the hallway and passage of the *hojo*.

園城寺光浄院 客殿

国宝
建立年代　1601年
所在地　　滋賀県大津市

Onjoji Temple Kojoin Guest Hall

National Treasure
Completed: 1601
Location: Otsu, Shiga prefecture

時代背景

　琵琶湖の南西、長等山の中腹に位置し、三井寺の通称で知られる園城寺は、天台寺門宗の総本山である。創建は7世紀末にさかのぼり、9世紀中盤には入唐僧・円珍（814-891）が中興し、発展の礎を築いた。以来、朝廷や貴族、為政者の信仰を集めてきたが、1595（文禄4）年、豊臣秀吉（1537-1598）の勘気を蒙り、堂舎の大半が破却された。3年後には赦され、現在の伽藍は慶長年間に整えられた。

　光浄院は、室町中期（15世紀前半）、瀬田城を築いた山岡資広（-1442年）が開いた園城寺の子院である。以来、山岡家が代々住持を勤めてきた。なかでも光浄院の院主で、のちに還俗した山岡景友（のちに道阿弥：1540-1604）は動乱の世にあって、織田信長（1534-1582）、豊臣秀吉、徳川家康（1542-1616）に仕え、秀吉による一山破却ののちには寺の復興に多大な貢献をした。関ケ原の戦い（1600年）では徳川方の東軍につき、戦功を立てている。1601（慶長6）年の建立とされる光浄院客殿は、その名の通り接客用の殿舎であるが、武将であり高僧でもあった道阿弥の存在があっての普請であろう。なお、寺内には光浄院客殿と類似する形式の勧学院客殿（国宝・1600年）が残り、両者ともに初期書院造の遺構として名高い。

特徴と見どころ

　中世と近世のはざまに位置し、古代の伝統的形式を引く寝殿造の要素と、近世的特徴を表わす書院造の要素をあわせもつ建築である。屋内には畳を敷きつめ、間仕切りには襖を入れる。賓客をもてなす最奥の広間は座敷飾りの装置を備えた書院造で、2間の床、違棚、帳台構え、上段の付書院を備える。一方で、床は奥行きの浅い押板の形式で、付書院は上段構えの小室となって広縁に突き出し、古式な書院の形式を見せる。外まわりでは軒唐破風をつけて車寄せとし、平安以来の建具である蔀戸を吊り、簡略化された形ながら寝殿造に由来する中門廊を備えている。

　書院造のなかに融けこんだ寝殿造の手法が見どころで、それは中門廊と縁の空間に凝縮されている。妻戸を開くと広がる中門廊は、本屋根と直交する切妻屋根で覆われ、庭へと吹放たれたみやびやかな中間領域をつくっている。そこからは広縁が奥の付書院へ向かって延び、一段下がって落縁がめぐる。屋根構造の発達により、1間ごとに柱を立てる必要はなくなり、広縁の外まわりの中間柱は抜かれて、庭と縁との連続感が高められている。縁と部屋との境には、もはや蔀戸はなく、舞良戸2枚に明り障子1枚を立てこみ、端整な佇まいを見せる。

　いわゆる主殿造の典型とされ、室町末期の「洛中洛外図」に描写された細川管領代の主殿正面と立面を同じくし、また、江戸幕府の大棟梁・平内家の秘伝書『匠明』（1608年成立）に「昔の主殿」（「昔六間七間ノ主殿之図」）として載る間取りと近似するのは、これまで指摘されてきたところである。

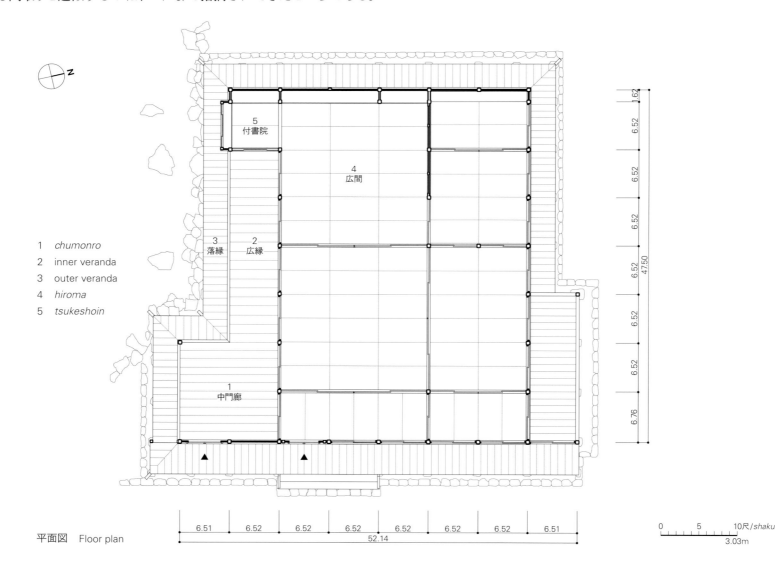

1　chumonro
2　inner veranda
3　outer veranda
4　hiroma
5　tsukeshoin

平面図　Floor plan

Historical Background

Onjoji temple, popularly known as Miidera, sits halfway up a hill called Nagarayama at the southwest corner of Lake Biwa; it is the head temple of the Jimon branch of the Tendai school of Buddhism. Originally founded sometime in the late seventh century, the temple was restored in the middle of the ninth century by Enchin (814–891), who had studied in China. He laid the foundation of its further development. For centuries the temple counted courtiers, aristocrats, and statesmen among its followers, but in 1595, it incurred the wrath of hegemon Toyotomi Hideyoshi (1537–1598) and suffered the destruction of most of its buildings. It was pardoned three years later and rebuilt itself to the state we see today by the early seventeenth century.

Kojoin is a subtemple of Onjoji founded in the first half of the fifteenth century by Yamaoka Sukehiro (d. 1442), a warlord who had built the Seta castle overlooking the lake. His descendants served as abbots of the temple for generations thereafter. Among the abbots of Kojoin was Yamaoka Kagetomo (he later left the priesthood and took the name Doami; 1540–1604). Kagetomo's relatively long life coincided with times of continual turmoil and strife, and he served under all three of the country's unifying leaders—Oda Nobunaga (1534–1582), Toyotomi Hideyoshi, and Tokugawa Ieyasu (1542–1616)—and contributed in major ways to the restoration of the Onjoji temple after the abovementioned destruction wreaked on it by Hideyoshi. In the decisive battle of Sekigahara in 1600, Kagetomo sided with the Tokugawa forces that emerged victorious and distinguished himself in battle. The Kojoin's Kyakuden (Guest Hall), believed to have been built in 1601, was used for entertaining guests, and its construction reflects the presence of Doami, a leading warrior and high-ranking priest as mentioned. Also within the precincts of Onjoji is the Kangakuin guest hall (1600, National Treasure), and the two buildings are famous extant examples of early *shoin-zukuri* architecture.

Characteristics and Highlights

Built at a time of transition between medieval and early modern times, the Kojoin incorporates elements of both the traditional *shinden-zukuri* style passed down from the ancient period and of early *shoin-zukuri*, which was to become the standard in residential architecture in the early modern period. The interior floors are covered with tatami mats and the partitions are *fusuma* panels. The *hiroma*, or innermost chamber for entertaining guests, is a *shoin-zukuri* structure equipped with various ornamental features: the alcove of two-mat width (*niken no toko*), staggered shelves (*chigaidana*), decorative partitions (*chodaigamae*) leading to rooms that were originally the sleeping quarters, elevated chamber with built-in desk (*tsukeshoin*), and the like. The *toko* alcove, meanwhile, is of the shallow *oshiita* style and the *tsukeshoin* is a small chamber one step up from the main room built out into the inner veranda (*hiro-en*), displaying the old style of *shoin*, or study alcove. Outside, the building has the *karahafu* gable at eave ends (*nokikarahafu*) over a carriage approach (*kurumayose*) porch. It also has the *shitomido* (reticulated shutters), a type used since the Heian period, and has a shortened *chumonro* corridor, a vestige of *shinden-zukuri* style.

The Kojoin is known for its use of *shinden-zukuri* techniques merged into the *shoin-zukuri* style, features of which are condensed in the *chumonro* corridor and veranda space. The hinged doors (*tsumado*) at the front lead into an elegant intermediate realm—sheltered under the overhang of the gabled roof that runs perpendicular to the main roof—wide open to the garden. From there the long and broad inner veranda continues all the way back to where the *tsukeshoin* projects from the interior. Alongside the veranda is the narrow, one-step-lower veranda that surrounds the hall. With advances in roof structure, it was no longer necessary to insert posts for every bay, so intermediate posts on the outside of the inner veranda have been eliminated, enhancing the continuity between the garden and veranda. The boundary between the rooms and the veranda is no longer partitioned with *shitomido* but with a tidy design made up of pairs of *mairado* panels that can be opened to reveal single shoji panels.

軒唐破風をつけた非相称形の東側正面。唐破風下の両開き板扉
(妻戸)が賓客を迎える正式な出入り口となる。建具は4間に蔀戸、
北端1間に舞良戸を入れる

Asymmetric east facade with *karahafu* gable at eave ends (*nokikarahafu*). Beneath the gable is a set of hinged doors for welcoming and sending off guests in formal style. Four of the front bays are filled with *shitomido* reticulated panels (raised here) with the far north-side bay fitted with *mairado* panels.

戸口の構成は見どころの一つ。位階に応じ出入り口を三段階に区別する。左へ向かうにつれ、格を下げる。右端に正式な妻戸の入口、次に客の様子をうかがう横連子を開け、その隣にもう一つの妻戸、さらに左端に片開きの脇戸がつく

One noteworthy feature is the handling of the doors, with separate entrances for persons of different ranks. The further to the left the lower the rank of the user. The most formal entrance for persons of highest rank lies directly under the *karahafu* gable. Next to that is the wall fitted with horizontal lattice from which persons inside can observe who is visiting. Further to the left is another set of hinged doors, and at far left the single hinged door on the outside of the building.

古建築のなかでも随一の美しさを誇る縁空間。妻戸を開けると中門廊（広縁風の廊）に出る。一方、脇戸は落縁と通じている。寝殿造における中門廊の流れを引き、閑雅な雰囲気が漂う

This is one of the most beautiful examples of veranda space in traditional architecture. The hinged doors open out upon the foreshortened *chumonro*, which is a veranda-style vestibule, while a side-door opens upon the outer veranda (*ochien*), one step lower than the inner veranda. It is a space that inherits the *chumonro* corridor tradition of *shinden-zukuri* with gracious elegance.

奥の広縁前は柱を4間飛ばしており、庭と縁の間を遮るものは何もない。
内部との境には舞良戸と明り障子、奥の付書院には腰高障子を入れる。
広縁を覆う長い疎垂木が簡潔で美しい

Four posts that would ordinarily stand at the edge of the inner veranda are eliminated, leaving nothing to obstruct the view of the garden from inside. The boundary between interior and out is composed of *mairado* and shoji, and the *tsukeshoin* at the back has shoji from waist height up. The long wide-spaced *mabaradaruki* rafters that support the eaves over the veranda form beautifully clean lines.

雨が生んだ建築の形。主屋の本屋根に直交して中門廊には切妻屋根がかかり、落縁には矩折の先端まで軒が深々と覆う。ここから眺める雨の景はひときわ美しい

These forms of architecture are the product of rain. Running perpendicular to the main roof over the main building, a gabled roof covers the *chumonro* vestibule and provides a deep awning over the outer veranda. The rain is especially beautiful when viewed from within this space.

背後の山の杉木立を縫い、秋の光が付書院のあたりを照らす。この柱の存在感は格別。柱はまた、眺めの奥行きをつくる。屈折して延びていく縁の流れを付書院が受けとめる

In autumn, the sunlight filters through the cedars on the mountain behind, casting its rays over the area around the *tsukeshoin* panels. The presence of this pillar is formidable; it creates depth of perspective. The veranda extends, with its outer edge turning this way and that, the *tsukeshoin* beckoning.

付書院。2畳敷きの上段の間となり、広間のなかにあって、さらに特別な一室とする。広縁に突き出した形で、腰高障子を開けると南庭が目前に広がる

The *tsukeshoin*. A two-mat room one level higher than the *hiroma*, it is yet a more special space within the guest-reception space. The room projects into the veranda, and the waist-high shoji open out directly on the garden on the south side.

広間は接客の場である。畳を敷きつめ、竿縁天井を張り、正面に2間床（押板）と違棚、南側（左）には付書院、北側（右）には帳台構えを設け、初期書院造の形式を示す

The *hiroma* is a room for entertaining guests. It is floored with tatami mats and has a board and batten (*saobuchi*) ceiling, with a two-mat wide but shallow *oshiita* (left) and staggered shelves (*chigaidana*). On the south side (left) is the *tsukeshoin* and on the north side (right), the decorated doors leading to the sleeping quarters (*chodaigamae*). These are typical features of early *shoin-zukuri* style.

高台寺 霊屋

重要文化財
建立年代　16世紀末―17世紀初頭
所在地　　京都府京都市東山区

Kodaiji Temple Otamaya Sanctuary

Important Cultural Property
Completed: Late 16th– early 17th century
Location: Higashiyama ward, Kyoto, Kyoto prefecture

勾欄、柱、長押には楽器散らしの蒔絵、木階には花筏の蒔絵が施され、流麗な表現が漆黒のなかに浮かび上がる。厨子内には随求菩薩を祀る

The graceful designs stand out brilliantly against the black lacquer background. The *makie* motifs featured on the balustrades, posts, and lintel are scattered musical instruments and those on the risers of the steps rafts and cherry blossoms in swirling streams.

時代背景

　高台寺は豊臣秀吉夫人の北政所(1548−1624)が建立した臨済宗建仁寺派の寺院である。豊臣から徳川の世へと時代が移り変わるなか、北政所は逝去するまでの17年間、この地で亡夫の冥福を祈りつつ、自らの菩提所とした。諸堂が完成したのは1606(慶長11)年のことで、伽藍は仏殿と方丈を備え、持仏堂(現開山堂・重文・1605年)、化粧殿(北政所の住まい)、茶室の傘亭(桃山時代・重文)・時雨亭(江戸初期・重文)などで構成されたが、これらは秀吉の伏見城の遺構や、北政所の生母の菩提所であった康徳寺の建物を移建したものと伝えられる。その後、江戸後期から明治の間に3度の火災に遭い、創建時の方丈や仏殿を失ったが、霊屋をはじめ傘亭・時雨亭などは被災を免れ、桃山から江戸初期にかけての建造物を今に伝える。

　霊屋は北政所の廟堂で、高台寺蒔絵として名高い華麗な蒔絵や、狩野光信(1561−1608)の障壁画を室内装飾に施す。1955(昭和30)年の解体修理の際、秀吉の木造を安置する厨子の扉裏に針刻の銘文が見つかり、この部分の蒔絵は1596(文禄5)年、室町時代以来の蒔絵師の主流派・幸阿弥(長晏)の手になると推定されている。この年は秀吉の伏見城の造営時期と重なっており、銘文は霊屋が伏見城から移建されたとする伝えを傍証する。一方で、ほかの部分の蒔絵や内陣・外陣の障壁画の様式・技法上などの比較検討から、それぞれの制作時期は一時期ではなく、ある程度の振幅を持つとの指摘もあり、建物自体の由来を確定するまでにはいたっていない。*5　いずれにしろ、この堂は伏見城や大坂城、聚楽第など、一連の「失われた秀吉の建築」の流れを引き、絢爛豪華をきわめたと伝えられるその室内装飾の様相を鮮やかに想起させる遺構である。

特徴と見どころ

　工芸の密度を建築の大きさにまで押し広げ、目くるめく美しい異次元のごとき空間をつくりあげる。平等院鳳凰堂や中尊寺金色堂の螺鈿の空間しかり、鹿苑寺金閣の金箔の空間しかり、そして、霊屋の蒔絵の空間がある。いずれも各時代における最高峰の工芸の表現と技術を用いて、為政者が現実の世界の、さらにその先に思い描いた理想郷を具現してきた。工芸と建築の合体。そのとき選択された方法は、彼らの時代精神を表わすのにもっとも適した工芸であったが、秀吉の時代、蒔絵が大きな役割を担ったのである。

　蒔絵はことさら細密な技巧を要する工芸である。霊屋に施された蒔絵は、漆塗りの面に図柄を描き、そこに金粉を蒔いた平蒔絵と呼ばれる比較的シンプルな技法がふんだんに使われており、描かれた線は伸びやかで、生き生きとした表現力を備えている。城郭や殿館といった大規模な建築を装飾する場を得て、そのスケールにふさわしい蒔絵の表現法が追求されたことがその背景にはあるのだろう。この廟堂はまた、近世に成熟を遂げた霊廟建築の流れに連なり、装飾が主役となる建築の時代の到来を象徴するものである。

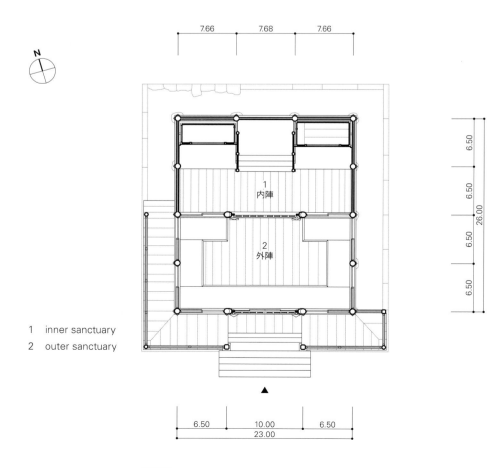

1　inner sanctuary
2　outer sanctuary

平面図　Floor plan

Historical Background

Kodaiji is a temple of the Kenninji branch of the Rinzai school of Zen Buddhism, built by Kita no Mandokoro (1548–1624), principal wife of the late sixteenth-century hegemon Toyotomi Hideyoshi, in memory of her husband. In the era when power shifted from the Toyotomi family to the Tokugawa in the early seventeenth century, Kita no Mandokoro lived in the temple compound for 17 years until her death, praying for the repose of her husband's soul and maintaining it as her family temple. The buildings were completed in 1606, consisting of the Buddha hall, the abbot's quarters (*hojo*), *jibutsudo* (1605; currently founder's hall Kaizando; Important Cultural Property), *kewaiden* (Kita no Mandokoro's residence), the tea houses Karakasatei (Momoyama period, Important Cultural Property) and Shiguretei (early Edo period; Important Cultural Property), and other buildings, and it is said that they are mainly relics moved from Hideyoshi's Fushimi castle as well as from Kotokuji temple, which was the family temple of Kita no Mandokoro's birth mother. The Kodaiji compound later suffered fires three times between the end of the eighteenth and the second half of the nineteenth century, and the original abbot's quarters and Buddha hall were lost, but the Otamaya (which houses the statues of Hideyoshi and Kita no Mandokoro) and the tea houses survived the fires as testimony to the architecture of the Momoyama to early Edo periods.

The Otamaya is the official mausoleum of Kita no Mandokoro and is famous for the interior decorations—the gold-inlay lacquerwork known as *Kodaiji makie* and screen and wall paintings by Kano Mitsunobu (1561–1608). In the dismantling and repair project conducted in 1955, a needle-engraved inscription was found on the inside of the doors of the *zushi* chest housing the wooden statue of Hideyoshi, and according to the inscription this part of the *makie* was done in 1596 by Koami (Choan) in the mainstream of *makie* masters that continued from the Muromachi period. That year coincides with the time when Hideyoshi's Fushimi castle was being built, and the inscription corroborates the story that the Otamaya was moved from the site of Fushimi castle. On the other hand, the style and techniques of the *makie* of this and other parts of the building and paintings on the screens and walls of the inner and outer sanctuaries indicate that they were not all the product of a single era but were completed over a certain span of time. So it is difficult to confirm the provenance of the building itself. In any case, the hall embodies, along with Fushimi castle, Osaka castle, and the Jurakutei palace, part of the legacy of Hideyoshi's "lost architecture," a vivid reminder of the unsurpassed splendor of interior decoration that must have filled such edifices.

Characteristics and Highlights

The density of craftsmanship is amplified by the very size of a building, creating a dazzlingly beautiful other worldly space. This is true of the mother-of-pearl inlay of the Phoenix Hall of Byodo-in temple and of the Konjikido hall at Chusonji temple; it is true of the gold-leaf-covered Kinkaku pavilion at Rokuonji temple; and it is true of the *makie* in the Otamaya. In all these examples, the rulers of the time mobilized the most sophisticated arts and the most advanced technologies of their times to embellish and embody not just the real world but paradise as they imagined it. Craft and architecture became one. The methods selected were the crafts that were most suited to expressing the spirit of their times, and in Hideyoshi's day, it was *makie* that played that role.

Makie demands the ultimate in detailed workmanship. The *makie* that was created for the Otamaya used the comparatively simple technique of flat *makie*, by which the patterns were engraved on the lacquered surface and the engraved lines filled with gold powder, but the execution of the lines is superb, achieving a marvelous flow and vigor. That must have been possible because of the opportunity to use *makie* to decorate large-scale buildings such as castles and pavilions, and because of the efforts made in the process to develop methods of expression suitable on that scale. This hall, moreover, is linked to the lineage of mausoleum architecture that reached its height in the early modern period, and it is a symbol of the period when decoration played a leading role in Japanese architecture.

内陣。蒔絵と障壁画で荘厳された空間。多様な意匠、繊細な質感が重なり合う。
右の厨子内には秀吉公の座像を、左の厨子内には北政所の座像を安置する

The inner sanctuary (*naijin*) is gorgeously decorated with *makie* lacquer decoration and screen and wall paintings. Diverse motifs are depicted with an extremely refined sensibility. The *zushi* cabinet on the right houses the statue of Hideyoshi; the cabinet on the left that of his wife Kita no Mandokoro.

北政所像の厨子・表扉。松竹の文様。地黒の少ない空間充溢的な構図の蒔絵で、梨地や赤漆を使い、秀吉像の厨子扉とは意匠と技法をやや異にする

The front doors of the *zushi* cabinet holding the statue of Kita no Mandokoro. Pictures of pine and bamboo crowd into the space, leaving little of the plain black ground. The *makie* techniques used include *nashiji* ("pear-skin") and red lacquer, forming an interesting contrast with the sparer, more magnanimous style of the Hideyoshi cabinet.

秀吉像の厨子・表扉。風にそよぐススキに、今にもこぼれ落ちそうな露玉。円弧を描く伸びやかな線のリズミカルな反復の間に、柔らかなススキの穂が揺れる。背景の黒漆（地黒）を活かし、簡潔な平蒔絵と針描の技法で描出され、細密さに拘泥しないおおらかな表現が特長

The front doors of the *zushi* cabinet holding the statue of Hideyoshi. Dewdrops, looking as if they may fall at any time, sparkle on graceful blades of swaying *susuki* grass. Among the rhythmical arcs of the grasses, curvaceous seed tassles ripple in the wind. Making use of the background expanse of black lacquer, simple flat *makie* and needle engraving techniques are applied to decoration on a large scale and in flowing lines that contrast with the usual tendency of *makie* for the small and minute.

小高い地に南を正面に立つ。おもむきに富んだ野石の乱層積み。
外側より平唐門、唐破風の向拝、宝形屋根と高まっていき、三つの
屋根の重なりが優美で格調高い佇まいをつくる

The building stands on a rise, facing south. Tastefully chosen field stones of various shapes are piled up for the retaining wall. The combination of the *hirakaramon* gate (featuring undulating bargeboards on each gable end) on the outside wall, *karahafu* undulating gable on the step canopy (*kohai*), and pyramidal roof (*hogyo yane*) give this mausoleum its imposing and elegant appearance.

姫路城

特別史跡
国宝・重要文化財
建立年代　17世紀初頭
所在地　　兵庫県姫路市

Himeji Castle

Special Historic Site
National Treasure, Important Cultural Property
Completed: Beginning of 17th century
Location: Himeji, Hyogo prefecture

時代背景

　天守閣を備えた近世の城は、織田信長の安土城（1579年完成）に始まるといわれる。以降、およそ半世紀の間に、武将たちの軍事・統治拠点として各地で盛んに城が築かれた。とくに関ケ原の戦い（1600年）前後の政情不穏を背景として、また、頻繁に命じられた大名の国替により、慶長期（1596－1615）の後半は築城の最盛期を迎えた。姫路城もこの時期、1601（慶長6）年から1609（慶長14）年にかけて築かれたものである。

　近畿と西国の境に位置する姫路が、軍事上の要所と見なされたのは徳川政権以前からのことであった。最初に城塞が築かれたのは室町時代初め、14世紀前半のことで、16世紀半ばには黒田孝高（官兵衛・1546－1604）が居城とし、1581（天正9）年には信長の命を受けた豊臣秀吉が、中国地方で勢力を持つ毛利への前衛としてここに本格的な城を築いた。1600年には関ケ原の戦功により、徳川家康の娘婿である池田輝政（1564－1613）が播磨の国主として姫路城に入り、この要衝の地を治めることとなった。輝政は秀吉の建てた城を全面的に改め、縄張りを構成し直した。大天守と小天守3基が渡り櫓で連結される防備力の高い本丸を標高45mの丘陵（姫山）に建て、次第に低くなる地形を利用して巧みに建築群を配置した。それとともに石垣と塀を築いて螺旋状に通路をめぐらせ、堅牢な要塞とした。そもそもここは東西に川が流れ、北に山を背負った天然要害の地であった。姫路城は地の利を活かしつつ、防備と技術面、様式と意匠面において完成された城郭建築の白眉である。

　1617（元和3）年には、徳川の重臣・本多忠政（1575－1631）が入城し、西の丸を新たに造営し、三の丸を整備した。その後、めまぐるしく城主は変わったが、1749（寛延2）年からは酒井家が10代世襲し、明治維新を迎えた。姫路城は最高度の軍備を持ちながら、一度も攻撃を受けることのなかった不戦城であった。

特徴と見どころ

　城づくりは町づくりであり、今日でいう都市計画であった。姫路城下は、城のある内堀、藩士が居住した中堀、町人や足軽が暮らした外堀からできており、今の姫路駅前あたりが外堀の周縁となる。駅からは真っ直ぐに延びる軸線上・約1km先に威風堂々と城がそびえ立つ景観が今も眺められ、ここが城をランドマークとする城下町であったことをあらためて思い起こさせる。城は軍事拠点でありつつも、領民の生活と安全を保障する秩序のシンボルでもあった。また、人心の統一を図り、内外に権力を誇示する役割を担っていた。そのため、難攻不落の築城術とともに、実用のなかに造形美が追求された。

　姫路城の面白さは、まず平面計画にある。渦郭式と呼ばれ、本丸を中心にして二の丸、三の丸以下を渦巻き状に配置したものである。城の計画は、どこかを閉じて、どこかを開けなければならない。敵は入れないが、味方は出入りしなければならないからである。姫路城の場合は左渦郭式と呼ばれ、南から攻めてくる敵を西へと迂回させながら、要所で討つ戦略となっている。そのとき要となるのが、城の表玄関となる菱の門を入ってすぐにある三国堀である。ここで右に向かうと追いつめられて討たれるため、敵は左方向に流れていく。石垣と塀が動線をつくり、迂回させたり、坂を上ったと思ったら下ったり、道幅を狭めたり広めたりして巧みに迷路化し、敵の方向感覚を失わせ、かく乱する。塀には、鉄砲や弓矢で敵を狙い撃ちするための狭間が開けられている。16世紀中盤の鉄砲の導入により戦術が変化し、築城には重厚な総石垣を要した。姫路城は天守や櫓などの建物群と、石垣や土塀とが有機的に結びついている。

　大天守は外観五重だが、石垣上に6階、石垣内に地下1階を設けた計7階建ての高層木造建築である。構造は地階から6階床下まで、中心の東西に24.6mの通し柱を立てて全体の構造を固めている。さらに地階―2階・4階―5階・5階―6階の一部にも通し柱を使っている。このような構造の強化は、慶長伏見大地震（1596年）で天守上層が倒壊した秀吉の伏見城を一つの契機としたのかもしれない。

　城は軍備のために築くものであるから、工期の短縮が求められた。池田輝政はこの城を8年で完成させている。礎石や石垣をはじめ、瓦などの素材も、黒田・豊臣時代のものを一部再利用したことがわかっているが、それにしても驚異的な速さであり、当時の大工棟梁の手腕に感心する。

Historical Background

The first castle with a donjon (*tenshu*) in Japan is said to be Oda Nobunaga's Azuchi castle (completed 1579). From that time until around 1615, countless castles were built as the headquarters of local warlords across the country. Castle building was at its height in the period of turmoil before and after the decisive Battle of Sekigahara (1600) when the forces led by Tokugawa Ieyasu settled the struggle for warlord supremacy, and under the early Tokugawa shogunate with the frequent transfer of daimyo from one fiefdom to another during its efforts to bring independent-minded warlords under control. The Himeji castle we see today was built between 1601 and 1609, in the midst of that era.

Located at the border between the Kinki area centering on the capital and the "western regions" (western end of Honshu), Himeji was regarded as a place of strategic importance long before the establishment of the Tokugawa shogunate. Fortifications were first built there in the early fourteenth century and, in the middle of the sixteenth century, were placed in the hands of Kuroda Yoshitaka (better known as Kuroda Kanbee; 1546–1604). In 1581, Oda Nobunaga ordered Toyotomi Hideyoshi to build a full-fledged castle in Himeji for their advance guard against the forces of the Mori family to the west. After the Battle of Sekigahara, Tokugawa Ieyasu assigned his son-in-law, Ikeda Terumasa (1564–1613), to govern this area of vital importance. Ikeda entirely remodeled the fortifications built by Hideyoshi, reorganizing the castle's layout and component structures. The main series of keeps stands on a 45-meter-high hill, consisting of the donjon (*daitenshu*), connected by *watariyagura* parapets to three subsidiary keeps (*kotenshu*). The structures are arranged with skillful use of the sloping topography. The whole is also surrounded with a maze of passageways lined by stone ramparts and plaster-covered walls, making the castle highly defensible. The area was a natural stronghold with mountains on the north and rivers running along its eastern and western sides. Making the most of its geographical setting, Himeji castle is a masterpiece of castle architecture in terms of defense and technology, style, and design.

In 1617 Honda Tadamasa, a key retainer of the Tokugawa shogun family, became the lord of Himeji castle. He newly built the west compound (*nishi-no-maru*) and rebuilt the third compound (*san-no-maru*). Subsequently the master of the castle changed hands many times until 1749, when it was assigned to the Sakai family, which continued to be the lords of the castle for ten generations up to the Meiji Restoration of 1868, when the Tokugawa shogunate ended. Despite being equipped with the best of defenses, Himeji castle was never attacked—it is a castle with no experience of battle.

Characteristics and Highlights

Castle building was also town building in its time—what we would call city planning today. The Himeji castle town is made up of the *uchibori* (inner moat) area where the castle itself is located, the *nakabori* (middle moat) area where the retainers of the lord of the castle lived, and the *sotobori* (outer moat) area where the townspeople and foot soldiers lived and where Himeji station stands today. Looking out from the station even today, to where the great castle looms up about one kilometer in the distance, we are reminded that this is a castle town, where everything revolved around this imposing stronghold. The castle was not only the headquarters of warrior power, but a symbol of the order that stood by the lives and safety of the people of the domain. It also played the external and internal role of a display of power aimed at inspiring people's loyalty to their domain. To that end, its builders sought not only the features of an impregnable fortress but beauty in practicality.

Part of the fascination of Himeji is in the plan of its layout. It adopts the so-called *kakaku-shiki* or spiral configuration, with the *ni-no-maru*, *san-no-maru*, and other compounds wrapped around the *honmaru* at the center. The plan for a castle has to be closed off, but it also has to be open. The enemy cannot be allowed to enter, but friendly forces have to gain access. Himeji castle's layout is of the "left swirl" type, designed for the strategy of deflecting an enemy assault from the south toward the west and then attacking. The stone ramparts and plastered walls create maze-like lines of movement, turning left and right, taking one uphill and then down, widening and narrowing, confusing and upsetting the enemy's sense of direction. The walls are punctuated with embrasures for shooting at the enemy with guns or bow and arrow. With the introduction of guns to Japan in the mid-sixteenth century, fighting strategies changed and castles needed to be fortified with thick stone walls. The donjon and keep architectural parts of Himeji castle are organically linked to the stone ramparts and plastered walls.

The donjon appears to rise in five stories on the exterior, but in fact it is a high-rise building seven stories high, with one more story above the ramparts and one story sunk into the stone foundation. The structure is consolidated around two 24.6-meter main pillars, set on the east and west sides, that rise continuously from the underground podium to the floor of the sixth level. It is further strengthened by continuous pillars running from the podium to the second floor, from the fourth floor through the fifth floor, and so on.

Because the castle was built as a military stronghold, it had to be put up as quickly as possible, and Ikeda Terumasa completed this strategically sound and aesthetically grand complex in a matter of eight years. It is known that the foundations and stone walls as well as tile and some other materials were partially recycled from the older castles built by Kuroda Kanbee and Toyotomi Hideyoshi, but when we think of the speed with which it was built, we cannot but admire the skill and competence of the master carpenters of that day.

西の丸、約63m長さの石垣の上にカの櫓（右）とワの櫓（左）が立つ。櫓の壁や塀には石落としがつき
石垣の監視や射撃に用いる。当初西の丸は、本多家の居館が連なる曲輪であった

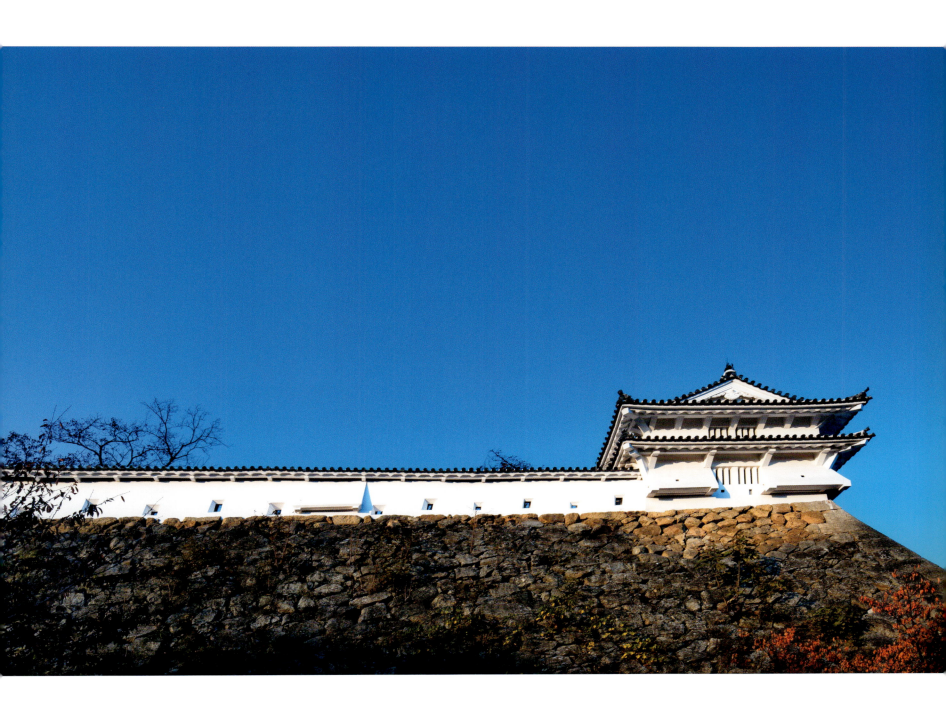

The Ka-no-yagura (Ka Turret), right, and Wa-no-yagura (Wa Turret) sit atop the 63-meter parapet along the front of the *nishi-no-maru* compound. Apertures (*ishi-otoshi*) through which stones were dropped to turn back enemy warriors attempting to scale the walls are built into the bases of the towers and along the wall; they were also used for shooting and defense of the walls. Initially, *nishi-no-maru* was the compound where the Honda family lived.

右より、大天守、西小天守、乾小天守を見る。千鳥破風や比翼入母屋造、軒唐破風などを組み合わせ、複雑で華麗な屋根の構成。その姿から白鷺城と呼ばれてきた。外壁は壁から軒裏まで、漆喰の総塗籠とし、耐火構造とする。大天守は瓦の目地も白漆喰で塗り、瓦止めとしている。外観5層、地下1階、地上6階

From right, the donjon (*daitenshu*), west keep (*nishi-kotenshu*), and northwest keep (*inui-kotenshu*). Arrangements of triangular gables (*chidori hafu*), paired wing hip-and-gable roofs (*hiyoku irimoya-zukuri*), and undulating eaves (*noki karahafu*) make for the complex and splendid roof composition reminiscent of a great winged bird that gives the castle one of its nicknames: the Great Heron Castle. The entire castle is finished with plaster, from the exterior walls to the surfaces under the eaves to make the structure fire-resistant. The seams between the tiles on the donjon are also white plaster, fixing the tiles in place. The donjon is six floors above ground and one basement floor.

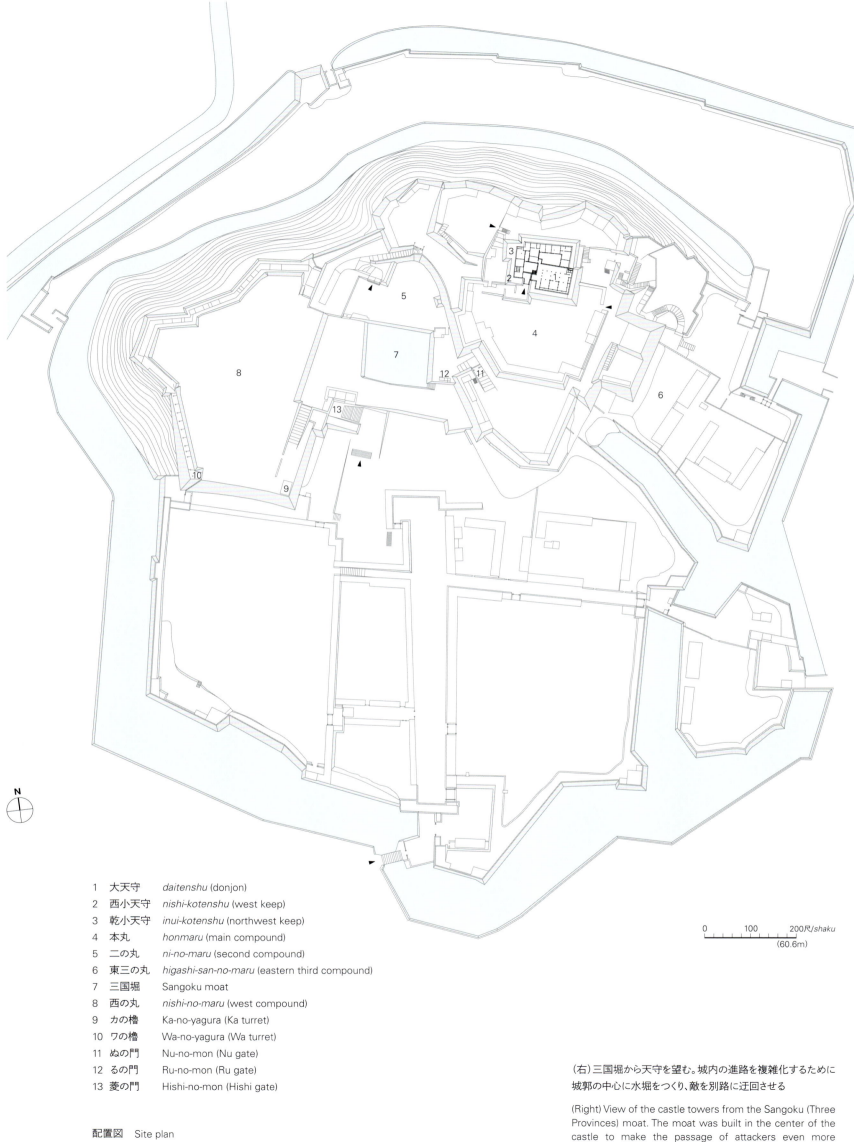

1	大天守	daitenshu (donjon)
2	西小天守	nishi-kotenshu (west keep)
3	乾小天守	inui-kotenshu (northwest keep)
4	本丸	honmaru (main compound)
5	二の丸	ni-no-maru (second compound)
6	東三の丸	higashi-san-no-maru (eastern third compound)
7	三国堀	Sangoku moat
8	西の丸	nishi-no-maru (west compound)
9	カの櫓	Ka-no-yagura (Ka turret)
10	ワの櫓	Wa-no-yagura (Wa turret)
11	ぬの門	Nu-no-mon (Nu gate)
12	るの門	Ru-no-mon (Ru gate)
13	菱の門	Hishi-no-mon (Hishi gate)

配置図　Site plan

(右)三国堀から天守を望む。城内の進路を複雑化するために城郭の中心に水堀をつくり、敵を別路に迂回させる

(Right) View of the castle towers from the Sangoku (Three Provinces) moat. The moat was built in the center of the castle to make the passage of attackers even more complex and divert enemy attack away around the castle.

本丸の南正面に出入口はなく、敵は西側にまわって侵入することとなるが、何度も門を潜り、細い進路が渦巻状に配され、迷路のようになっている。丸や三角の鉄砲狭間、長矩形の矢狭間を空け、白塀に意匠効果を与えている

There is no entrance to the *honmaru* on the south side, so any attacker would have to circle around to the west side to invade the castle, but to get there would be forced to pass through many gates and navigate a maze of narrow, spiraling passageways. The lineup of round, triangular, or rectangular embrasures add a decorative touch to the white walls.

(左)るの門。三国堀の東にあり、門の前は袋小路になっている。穴門とし、味方の連絡通路となる

(Left) The Ru-no-mon gate (Ru gate) stands east of the Sangoku moat, and the area in front of the gate is a cul-de-sac. This *anamon* ("hole gate"), cut through the stone rampart, provided a passageway for the defenders.

(上)ぬの門は厳重な三層の櫓門となる。左は扇勾配と呼ばれる上部が垂直に切り立つ石垣。敵が上ってくるのを防ぐ

(Above) The Nu-no-mon gate (Nu gate) has a forbidding three-story structure. At left, note the distinctive *ogi kobai* curvature of the stone wall with the upper part vertical designed to prevent the enemy from scaling the wall.

本丸の北西。内部は台所で、格子窓は採光と通気のためのもの。城は象徴的な表の形だけではなく、籠城時のための倉や室が必要となり、それぞれに見合った形の開口を取っている。各窓下には鉄管の雨水抜きがつく

Northeast side of the *honmaru* compound. Inside this part is the kitchen, so the lattices were intended to provide light and ventilation. The castle needed to have not only an imposing symbolic outward form but house storehouses and rooms for various purposes, and the openings in its walls are shaped differently in accordance with the use of the inside. Beneath each window are pipes for drainage of rainwater.

2階・東側内部。大きな瓦葺の庇を支えるには、跳ね出しの梁が必要となる。木は剪断力に弱いため、支点を補強するために大きく長い肘木をつけている。隅柱の脇には筋交いを入れて補強する

Interior on the east side of the second floor. Large and sturdy overhang beams are needed to support the projecting eaves with their tile roofs. Wood is vulnerable to shearing force, so the beams are buttressed with long and thick bracket arms. The corner post is reinforced with a diagonal brace.

姫路の町を見下ろすようにして立つ。大天守、小天守、櫓で構成された群のつくりだす美

Himeji castle looks down on the city around it, displaying the beauty of the clustered donjon, keeps, and turrets.

妙喜庵 待庵

国宝
建立年代　16世紀末
所在地　　京都府乙訓郡

Myokian Temple Taian Tea Room

National Treasure
Completed: Late 16th century
Location: Otokuni disrict, Kyoto prefecture

時代背景

　妙喜庵のある山崎は、1582（天正10）年、本能寺の変で織田信長を討った明智光秀（-1582）の軍と豊臣秀吉の軍が交戦した地であった。妙喜庵は室町時代の明応年間（1492-1501）に建立された臨済宗東福寺派の古刹で、千利休（1522-1591）の遺構とされる2畳の茶室待庵を今に伝える。

　待庵は書院（15世紀後半・重文）の南端に接続して構えられ、両建物の部材の納まりから、ある時期に移し建てられたことはほぼ確実と見られている。[*6] 妙喜庵の住持・功叔士紡（-1594）は茶人として知られ、利休と親交のあったことが知られるが、一方でこの茶室を利休作と裏付ける確かな拠りどころはいまだ見つかっておらず、建てられた年代や移建された経緯についても精確にはわかっていない。

　1606（慶長11）年に描かれた「宝積寺絵図」のなか、妙喜庵のところに「かこひ」（囲い）と書き入れられていることから、その「かこひ」を待庵とすると、この時点までには移建を終えていたと見ることは可能となる。なお、この絵図内には妙喜庵の近くに利休の屋敷も記されていることから、一時利休が山崎に居を構えていたことが知られ、それは秀吉が山崎の合戦から大坂城へ移る1583（天正11）年までの間、宝積寺も含めた山崎城を居とした時期と重なるのではないかと推察されている。

　また、江戸中期の史料には、「妙喜庵利休滅亡後スキヤくずしをく　立ル」とあり、一時期解体されていたことが示唆されている。これらを考え合わせて、待庵は利休の山崎の屋敷にあった茶室であり、利休没後に崩し置かれていたものを、のちに妙喜庵に移し建てられたとする説が立てられた。[*7] あるいは、利休の屋敷ではなく山崎城内につくられたもので、秀吉の大坂転居にともない山崎城が廃城となった際、待庵も崩し置かれ、それがのちに妙喜庵に移築されたとする説もある。[*8] いずれにしろ、間取りや空間構成の手法、素材の選び、空間の質から鑑みて利休が直接関与した茶室とされ、利休と山崎との縁から、1582年から翌年にかけてを成立年と考えるのが定説である。待庵はまた、草庵による侘茶の発生を象徴する茶室でもあり、その最古の遺例となる。

特徴と見どころ

　同一人物の息がかかったものであれば、それが茶室であれ、道具であれ、ものとものとの間には必ず脈略がある。待庵ほど、このことを強く感じさせる茶室はない。その核心に触れた覚えを持ったのが、400年以上をさかのぼり、利休が直接に関わった道具をこの茶室に置き合わせる機会に恵まれたときだった。本書の写真はそのときに撮ったものである。

　これらの道具を置き合わせた途端、待庵の空間が一変した。それまで利休の「遺構」として目に映っていた空間が、まるですぐそこに利休の息遣いが感じられるような、生き生きと呼吸する空間に変容したのである。縁という言葉が頭に浮かんだ。室床の花釘にかけられた利休作・竹の一重切「小田原」は、ここにこそがゆかりの場所であり、ようやくその懐にもどれたといわんばかりに強い存在感を漂わせながら、これ以上にはないというほどしっくりとスサ壁の床の間に収まっている。利休は塗框に張付壁であった従来の床の間を土壁の塗床とした。しかも、待庵は隅柱を塗りまわした室床である。室床は2畳という極小空間を広く見せる効果を発揮するが、それにも増して利休が意識したのは、茶室から余分な線を消し去り、自らの美意識を反映した道具の存在感を最大限に引き立てる演出を可能とする空間づくりであっただろう。このざっくりとした野趣ある床の間には、無論従来の名物ではなく、竹の花入に活けた折々の花がじつによく似合う。

　利休ゆかりの道具を待庵に置き合わせてみて、初めて道具の力と空間の本領が十二分に発揮される。竹の一重切とともにこのことを実感したのは、真塗手桶の水指である。これは利休が、足の広さは畳の目二つの内に入るほどの寸法がよい、と細かく指示してつくらせたものと同形のものであるが、高さが26cm強、蓋径が25cm強あり、単独で見るかぎりは小さな待庵の、しかも隅炉の脇に置き合わせるには少し大きすぎるのではないかという印象であった。だが実際に置いてみると、たっぷりとした姿が待庵の空間にあって悠然と佇むかのようである。とろけるような漆黒の質感はあたりの光を映しこんでいる。これに利休形の黒棗と黒樂の茶碗「不是」（常慶作）を合わせると、利休が求めた黒の世界が現前とする。

　究極の簡潔さを持つとともに、すべてを包み含むような複雑さをあわせもち、洗練と素朴が同居する。無駄を削ぎ落とした形、研ぎ澄まされた寸法と比例感覚、光を吸収する素材と反射する素材の巧みな選択——道具と茶室はまさに一体であり、その美意識は両者に徹頭徹尾、浸透している。

東側の壁。左は掛け障子でありながら下枠をつけ、右の片引き障子は戸当たりとなる
釣竹を天井まで延ばし、絶妙な壁の分割となる。角柄が極端に短く、ぎりぎりの寸法を
求めており、形に緊張感が宿る。利休のつくった竹花入の節切りと共通する手法である

Bringing together the bamboo flower vase and tea utensils associated with Rikyu, the all-black world he sought in the tea room unfolds in dappled shafts of tranquil afternoon light.

午後の木漏れ日が射し入る静謐な時間。利休の求めた黒の世界が広がる。利休作の竹一重切花入「小田原」、与次郎作の阿弥陀堂釜、余三作の真塗手桶水指、常慶作の黒樂茶碗「不是」、宗長作の黒棗、淀屋个庵作の茶杓「おち葉船」

Historical Background

Myokian temple is located at Yamazaki, known for the 1582 battle between Toyotomi Hideyoshi and Akechi Mitsuhide (d. 1582), two generals of the powerful warlord Oda Nobunaga, just after the Mitsuhide had assassinated Nobunaga. Hideyoshi's victory at Yamazaki paved the way for his succession to the hegemony established over most of Japan by Nobunaga. Myokian is a venerable temple of the Tofukuji branch of the Rinzai school of Zen Buddhism established in the late fifteenth century. The temple has preserved the two-mat Taian tea room, which is said to have been created by Sen Rikyu (1522–1591), although so far there is no reliable evidence to corroborate such accounts and no details about when it was built or moved to its present location. The tea room is attached to the south edge of a *shoin* building (late fifteenth century: Important Cultural Property) and, judging from the fit of the structural members, it is more or less certain that the tea room was moved to this location at some point in time.

A picture of "Hoshakuji" painted in 1606 contains the letters for "kakoi" (enclosure) within the area where Myokian lies in the sketch, and if that "kakoi" is the Taian tea room, it may be possible that it was built by at least that time. The Hoshakuji sketch shows, moreover, that Rikyu's residence was close to Myokian, indicating that he was then residing in Yamazaki. From that, we may surmise that his time in Yamazaki overlapped with the period when Hideyoshi, following the battle of Yamazaki, was briefly at Yamazaki castle before moving to Osaka castle in 1583. An Edo period historical source contains the passage suggesting that the tea room was dismantled at one point. Based on these accounts, some hypothesize that the Taian tea room was part of Rikyu's residence in Yamazaki and that, after Rikyu was forced to commit suicide (1591), it may have been dismantled and stored, after which it was later rebuilt at Myokian. Others hold that it had been built, not in Rikyu's residence, but within the compound of Yamazaki castle, and after Hideyoshi left the castle to make his headquarters at Osaka castle, Taian was dismantled and stored, and then later reconstructed at Myokian. Whichever the case, in terms of the layout, design of the space, choice of materials, and the quality of the space, it is generally accepted that Rikyu was directly involved in its creation and that, judging from Rikyu's connection with Yamazaki, it was built between 1582 and the following year.

Characteristics and Highlights

When it comes to things created under the influence of a certain person—whether it is a tea room or tea ceremony utensils, or whatever—there always appears to be a context, a kind of dialogue, among the things themselves. I have never felt that as strongly as I did in the Taian tea room. And my conviction was confirmed when I was fortunate enough to see utensils directly associated with Rikyu going back 400 years placed together within Taian.

The moment these utensils were brought in, the room was transformed. One could virtually feel the presence of the living, breathing Rikyu there on the tatami. The space—which until then had seemed like nothing more than a "relic"—came alive, rekindling the atmosphere of the time when it was originally in use. I found myself thinking of the word "karma." The "Odawara" bamboo flower container (*ichijugiri*), cut from a trunk of bamboo by Rikyu himself, was hanging on the darkened wall of the tokonoma, vigorously projecting its presence. One could almost hear it tell us that it finally had returned to its real home, to the place where it firmly belonged. The completely plastered tokonoma (*murodoko*) serves to give a sense of enlarged space in the confined two-mat space of the room, but what Rikyu seems to have been trying even more to accomplish was to eliminate lines as much as possible from the room, crafting the space so as to focus attention as much as possible on the presence of the utensils reflecting his personal aesthetic.

Placing the tea implements associated with Rikyu within Taian fully demonstrates the power of such implements and the real appeal of space. Like the bamboo vase, the plain black lacquered fresh water container (*shinnuri teoke*) seemed to have a similar resonance with the space. Made in Rikyu's time by a craftsman in the same form as another piece that had been made according to Rikyu's detailed instructions, it stands 26 centimeters high, with the lid 25 centimeters in diameter. It might seem, when seen separately, to be somewhat too large to fit next to Taian's sunken hearth, but when actually in place, its generous form exudes calm and composure. The almost liquid quality of the black lacquer sparkles in the gathering light. And when the Rikyu-style black lacquer tea container and black Raku tea bowl (named "Fuze") are added, we see before us the all-black world that Rikyu was seeking to create. There he has placed the ultimate in simplicity together with an all-encompassing complexity where refinement and simplicity coincide. Forms that eliminate all excess, minutely refined dimensions and proportions, selection of materials that absorb light and those that reflect light—by these means he practiced an aesthetic that completely penetrates the implements and the room, making them one.

East side wall. The sill added below the hanging shoji (*kakeshoji*) on the left side and the vertical extension to the ceiling of the frame of the right-side shoji draw striking lines on the wall. The left lower corner of the frame injects an element of tension with its closely joined angle.

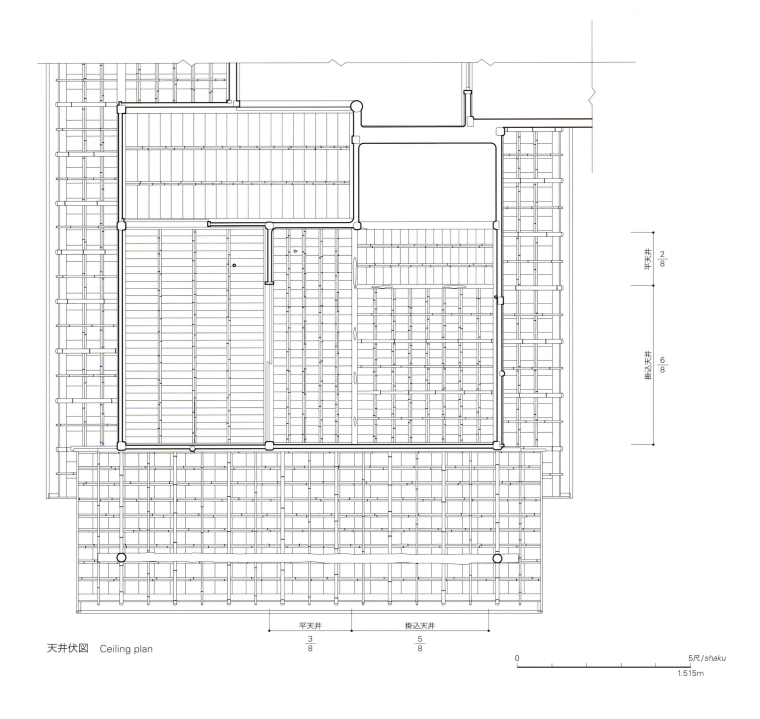

天井伏図　Ceiling plan

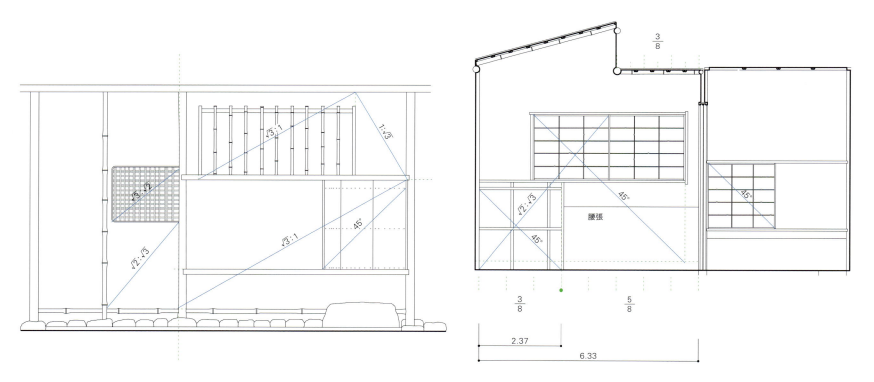

待庵には幾何学がある。日本には古くから規矩術があり、すなわち「規」はコンパス、「矩」は曲尺で、これらの道具を使い比例を分割したり、合成したりして建物の形が整えられてきた。たとえば、一つの壁はその面だけの比例で完結するのではなく、壁面・床の間・天井・床面における全体の立体的な関連づけが行われ、それらが密接に絡み合ってプロポーションができている。待庵では、畳の短手を4、長手を8の枡目に分割し、平面を構成している

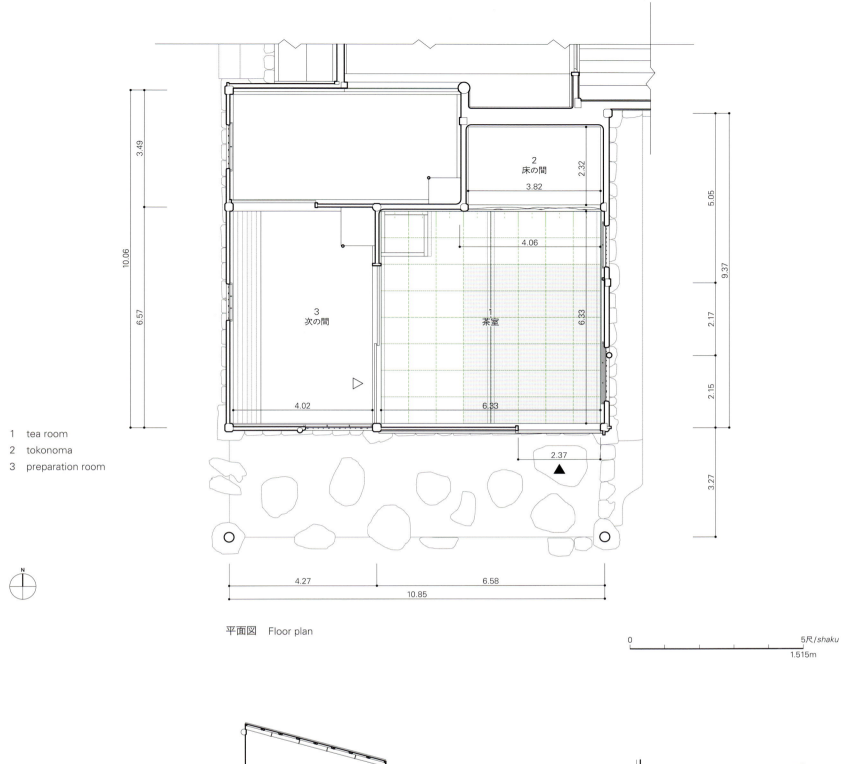

1 tea room
2 tokonoma
3 preparation room

平面図　Floor plan

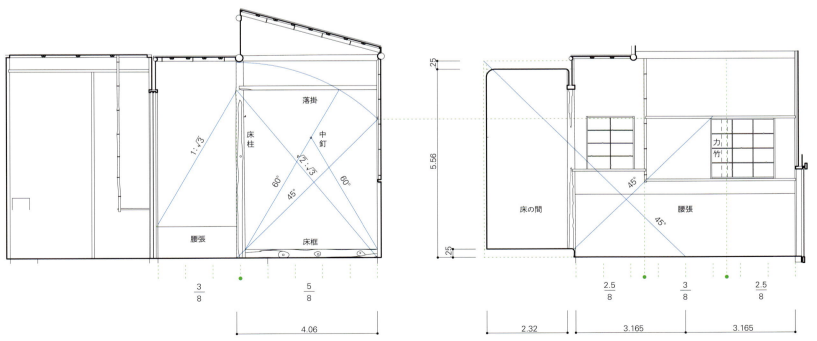

Taian has a geometry all its own. From olden times, carpenters utilized mathematical rules of geometry called *kikujutsu*, through which the members of a building were arranged according to measurements (*ki*) and angles (*ku*). The proportions of the design of a wall are worked out, for example, not in isolation but through the intricately intertwined proportions and three-dimensional relationships with the whole, including the tokonoma, ceiling, and floor. The layout of Taian is based on the division of the tatami into four (short side) x eight (long side) squares.

天井の構成と落し掛け。亭主が座る点前座と正客が座る床前には
天井を張り、残りは掛込み天井とする。落し掛けは柱つきに面皮を
残し、丸太の床柱と繊細な納まりを見せる

Note the varied ceiling composition. Flat ceilings cover the seat for the host and the seat of the main guest, while the rest of the room comes under the sloped *kakekomi* ceiling formed by the underside of the roof. The end of the tokonoma lintel where it clasps the alcove post (*tokobashira*; left front corner post of the tokonoma) is left in the rounded-log form to better harmonize with the rough-hewn style of the post.

有楽苑 如庵

国宝
建立　　1618年頃
所在地　愛知県犬山市

Urakuen Jo-an Tea Room

National Treasure
Completed: c. 1618
Location: Inuyama, Aichi prefecture

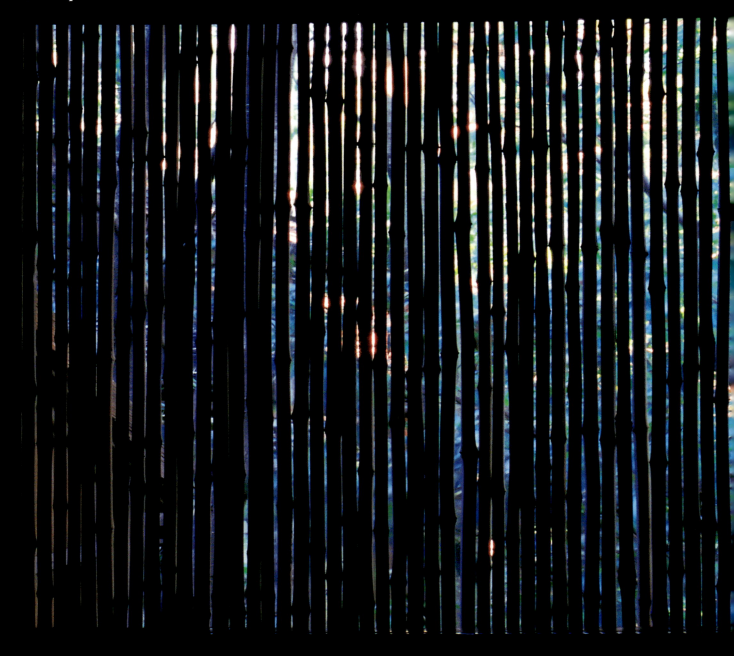

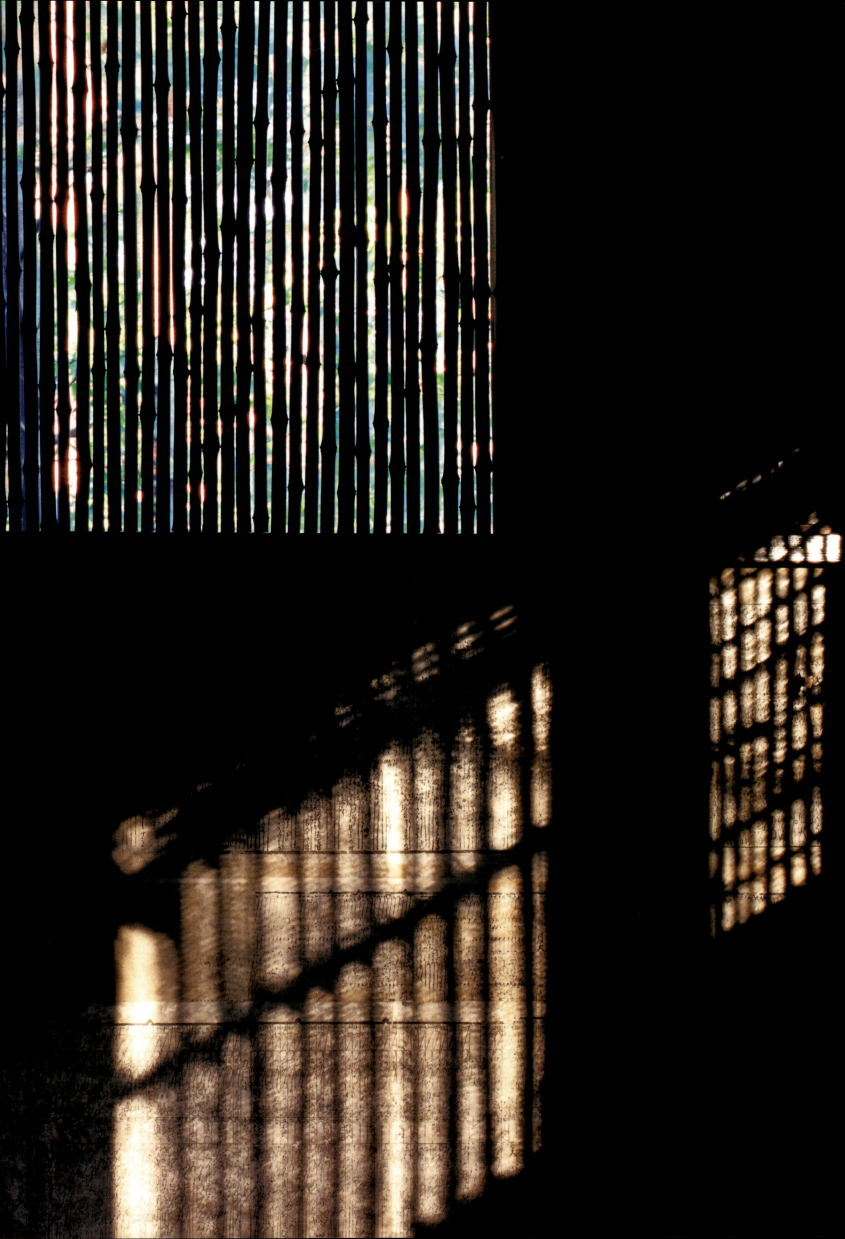

時代背景

　如庵は1618（元和4）年、織田有楽（1547−1621）が京都の建仁寺塔頭・正伝院に隠棲した際、その屋敷内に建てた茶室である。有楽は織田信長の弟で、信長亡きあとは豊臣秀吉に重用され、さらに徳川家康とも交流し、関ケ原の戦いでは徳川方について勲功を立てた。豊臣秀頼の母・淀君（−1615）の叔父という立場から、淀君の相談役として大坂城に居を構え、徳川と豊臣が戦った大阪冬の陣（1614年）では和議調停に活躍したが、豊臣が滅びることになる大坂夏の陣（1615年）では戦いの前に大坂城を出て京都に隠居し、余生を送った。有楽は桃山から江戸へと移行する激動の時代、政治情勢の中枢部、いわば台風の目のなかに身を置きながら生き抜いた武将であり、茶人であった。千利休を師とし、侘茶を根本としながらも利休の追随にとどまらず、新たな茶の境地を開くことに熱心であったという。そのような茶風は、有楽が最晩年に建て、すみずみにまで創意工夫の冴えわたったこの茶室が、400年を経た今も物語っている。

　1908（明治41）年、如庵は東京の三井家に移建され、1938（昭和13）年には神奈川県大磯の三井家別邸へ、さらに1972（昭和47）年には名古屋鉄道の所有となって愛知県犬山市の名鉄ホテル・有楽苑に移され、正伝院の書院と露地とともに再興されて現在にいたる。移建には細心の注意が払われ、よく古材を残し、当初の姿を今に伝える。

特徴と見どころ

　品格、完成度、構成美——如庵はまさしく珠玉の空間と呼ぶにふさわしい草庵の最高峰であり、利休の待庵と双璧をなす茶室である。この茶室を通して伝わってくるのは、有楽の研ぎ澄まされた感性であり、人生の最終章にあっても、茶の湯の固定化に安住しない茶人としての気概、新たな空間体験への飽くなき探求心である。

　にじり口を開けて入席するとき、まず目に入ってくるのが、火灯形に割り抜いた薄い袖板とその奥の有楽窓である。この点前座の景は、人の心を一瞬にしてとらえる傑出した意匠である。有楽窓は障子の外側に直径6mmほどの竹を詰め打ちしたもので、1本1本の細い隙間から光がこぼれ入る。

　2畳半台目（2畳＋半畳＋台目畳1畳）の変則的な間取りではあるが、平面の基本はほぼ正方形の4畳半で、そのなかに床の間も納めている。点前畳の炉先に立てた袖板は、その先の半畳と亭主の点前座とを仕切るが、それを薄い板とした発想が秀逸で、軽やかで瀟洒な結界となっている。割り抜かれた曲線は、五角形の内角を丸く滑らかにつなげたような形である。この曲線と響き合うのが、床の間の脇に敷いた三角形の板で、鱗板と呼ばれる。袖壁の曲線と三角形の対比は、この空間を幾何学的な刺激で充たしている。如庵では茶道口（亭主口）と給仕口が兼用となっているので、この板をつけることで、亭主の背後を出入りする半東（補佐）の動きに余裕をつくっているのである。鱗板に沿って壁を立て、その角は塗りまわして茶道口へと滑らかにつなげている。人の動きを視覚化して、空間のデザインとして取りこむところは、有楽だからこそできる離れ業であろう。

　鱗板の角に立つ床柱は、如庵の魅力の中核である。柱のなぐり方に勢いがあり、技巧的な作意がない。荒々しいほどの強さをもちながら、粗野に堕ちず風格がある。しかもこの野性味を秘めた床柱に、真塗の床框を組み合わせて、空間全体の品格を高めている。この床柱の材種は、以前からイチイ（アララギ）といわれている。

　如庵といえば、別名「暦張りの席」と呼ばれたように、壁の腰張りに古い暦を使っていることが一つの特徴となっている。一方で、洞庫（押入れ式の棚）や茶道口には紅色を帯びた襖紙が張られていることはあまり注目されない。当初からの紙ではないだろうが、茶室ではほとんど使われてこなかった赤系の色が今も踏襲されているというのは、何か古くからのいわれがあるのではなかろうか。そこで思い浮かぶのが、イチイの木肌である。伐採したばかりのイチイに鋸を入れると、そのなかは赤い。この赤みは時間が経つと褪色するが、床柱がイチイだとしたら、如庵ができあがった当初はまだその材に生命感のある赤みが残っていたかもしれない。それに合わせて、襖紙も赤系にするというのはありうるだろう。織部流の茶書『数寄一流之巻』に、如庵について「腰張りしゆせんしのこよみ」とあり、これは修善寺の紅色の紙に刷られた暦のことではないかとの指摘がある。[*9] そうなると、空間は紅めく色に囲まれて、今よりも華やいだものであったのかもしれない。しかも朝、有楽窓は外の葉の色をひろって緑に染まる。そこには紅と緑の鮮やかな対比がある。侘びの茶室に紅色は似合わないと眉をひそめる人がいたかもしれないが、それをできるのが、円熟した茶人有楽の融通無碍な数寄の精神ではなかったか。

Historical Background

The Jo-an tea room, which is preserved today in the city of Inuyama, Aichi prefecture, was built around 1618 by Oda Uraku (1547–1621) for his retirement residence in the compound of Shoden'in, a subtemple of Kenninji in Kyoto. A younger brother of hegemon Oda Nobunaga, Uraku became a trusted retainer of Oda's successor Toyotomi Hideyoshi and was also on good terms with Hideyoshi's later rival and successor to power, Tokugawa Ieyasu. At the 1600 battle at Sekigahara where Ieyasu-led forces vied with those of the Toyotomi family for supremacy, Uraku sided with the Tokugawa and distinguished himself in battle. As the uncle of Yodo-dono, mother to Hideyoshi's heir Hideyori, Uraku lived in Osaka castle as an advisor. At the time of the winter siege of the castle (1614) by the Tokugawa forces, he played an active role in peacemaking, but prior to the summer siege (1615) that led to the annihilation of the Toyotomi family, Uraku had left the castle for Kyoto, where he went into seclusion.

Uraku was a warrior general who survived the tumultuous transitional era between the end of the Momoyama period and the beginning of the Edo period, even while being active within the very vortex of political events. And he was also a man of tea. A disciple of Sen Rikyu, he basically followed Rikyu's *wabi*-style tea, but is said to have been an eager explorer of new dimensions in the way of tea. We can see the traces of his approach to tea in the creative details crafted into every corner of this tea room, which Uraku built in the final years of his life.

In 1908, the Jo-an tea room was purchased by the wealthy Mitsui family of Tokyo and in 1938 it was moved to the Mitsui villa in Oiso, a seaside resort town on the coast of Kanagawa prefecture. In 1972, its ownership passed into the hands of Nagoya Railroad (Meitetsu) and it was moved to the Japanese-style garden Uraku-en on the grounds of the Meitetsu Inuyama Hotel in the city of Inuyama. Along with the Shoden'in temple's *shoin* reception building and the *roji* tea garden, Jo-an has been preserved there in its original form. Great care has been devoted to the reconstruction, utilizing old structural materials and endeavoring to transmit the original appearance of the buildings.

Characteristics and Highlights

Jo-an is like a polished gem of refinement, perfection, and compositional beauty, one of the finest *soan* tea rooms extant on a par with Rikyu's Taian. What comes across to us from this tea room is Uraku's highly refined sensibility, and, though he was in the last phase of his life, his firm commitment as a teaman never to lapse into rigidity but to continue the tireless search for new experiences of space.

When you enter through the *nijiriguchi*, what first meets your gaze is the projecting wing wall with the arch-shaped cut-out and the *urakumado* windows. This scene of the *temae-za* where the host sits is an outstanding design of instantaneous appeal. An *urakumado* is a shoji-covered window on the inside with a vertical lattice of bamboo strips each about 6 millimeters in cross section on the outside. The pattern of light cast by this lattice is beautiful.

The tatami flooring is irregular, consisting of two regular mats, a half mat, and one *daimetatami* (which is about 3/4 the size of a regular mat), but basically the room is a four-and-a-half mat square including the tokonoma. The wing wall adjacent to the hearth forms a partition between the host's tatami and the half tatami beyond, but the notion of using a thin board makes it a brilliantly conceived boundary line, both lightweight and tasteful. The shape of the arch has its echo in the triangular board—the *uroko-ita* ("fish-scale" motif board)—at the side of the tokonoma. It is the contrast of the wing-wall curvature with the triangle that gives the space its bracingly geometrical quality. At Jo-an the host's entrance (*sadoguchi*) serves also as the service doorway (*kyujiguchi*), and the addition of this board opens up space behind the host for the coming and going of the assistant (*hanto*). Uraku's feat was in visualizing human movement and incorporating that into the design of space.

The *tokobashira* post, which stands at the corner of the triangular board, is really the central attraction of Jo-an. Its surface reveals the energy of rough adze-work rather than technical precision. It has both an almost wild strength and character, yet without being coarse. Indeed, the refinement of the space as a whole is elevated by the combination of this wild-looking post with the fine lacquer-covered crosspiece (*tokogamachi*) at the bottom front of the tokonoma. The wood of the post is yew.

Another name for Jo-an is "Koyomibari no seki" (The Calendar-walled Tea Room), because the walls are covered to waist height with old calendars. Not much attention is usually given to the *doko* wall cupboard and *sadoguchi* entrance, which are papered with thick *fusuma* paper with a rouge tinge. The paper itself is of course different from the original, but the fact that the paper is infused with a reddish color, which had hardly ever been used in tea rooms, suggests that there was some reason behind the use of this type of color. Perhaps it is related to the color of yew wood. When you put a saw to a newly cut yew log, the inside is red. As time passes, the red fades, but given that the *tokobashira* is yew, it is possible that when Jo-an was newly constructed, the wood still glowed with its vibrant red color. So the *fusuma* paper might have been given a red tint to go with the wood. The color of this space might have been much brighter than it is today.

床柱（手前）と中柱との絶妙な間合い。そして、茶室のなかに火灯形の曲線を挿入した面白さ。イチイの床柱は、伐採したばかりの丸太をまず六角形に削ってから、杣鉈でなぐったのではないか

Note the fine-tuned distance between the tokonoma corner post (*tokobashira*) and the *nakabashira* in the center of the room. The arched opening in the wing wall injects interest into the tea room. The tokonoma corner post appears to have been made by first hewing a newly cut yew log into a hexagonal shape and then trimming it with an adze.

竹を詰め打ちした二つの有楽窓。南側の下地窓(右端)は点前座を明るく照らす。中柱で仕切られて、左は点前座となり、右の半畳は客座というよりは「余白」となり、空間にゆとりをつくる

The two *urakumado* with bamboo slats on the outside. The *shitajimado* made as an aperture showing the internal wall grid on the south side shines light on the host's seat. With the *nakabashira* as the demarcation line, the left side is the host's seat and the right side is not so much for seating of a guest as a kind of open area that gives leeway to the space.

中柱の通りを境に天井を二分し、北側の床前から点前座にかけては平天井を張り、
南側は化粧屋根裏とする。東側に二つの有楽窓、南側に下地窓と連子窓（右端）、
天井に突上げ窓を開け、光を得て、内部から膨らむような広さを感じさせる

With the *nakabashira* at its border, the ceiling is divided into two. The north side, from the front of tokonoma and over the host's seat is a flat ceiling, while the south side shows the underside of the roof. The east side has the two *urakumado*, and the south side the *shitajimado* (left) and a *renjimado* (right). When propped open, the skylight on the south side brings in more light and swells the feeling of the space inside.

たった9㎡のなかに図られた緊密な構成は、天井を見ても明らかである。平天井の下は正客と亭主の座、化粧屋根裏の下は相伴の客座。平天井は竿縁・廻り縁ともに竹、化粧屋根裏は竹垂木に竹木舞。侘びた風情をつくる

The tightly knit composition achieved in this 9-square-meter space is reflected even in the ceiling. Beneath the flat ceiling are the seats of the host and the main guest, and the other guests are seated beneath the slanted open-beam ceiling. The flat ceiling has bamboo battens and the open-beam ceiling bamboo rafters and laths, giving the whole a rustic look.

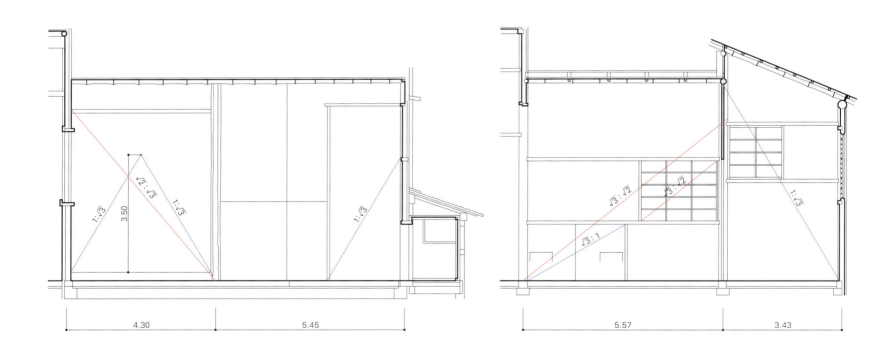

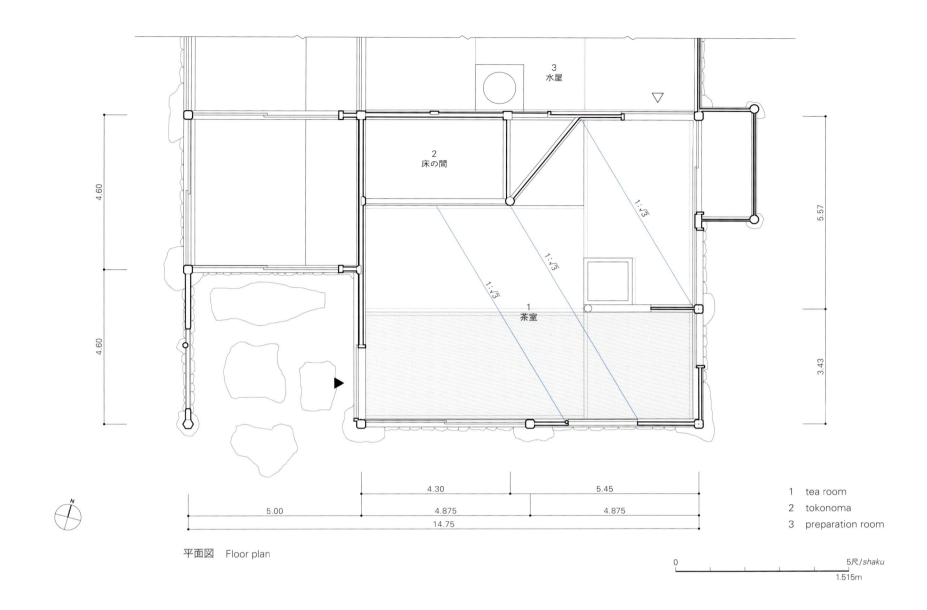

平面図　Floor plan

1　tea room
2　tokonoma
3　preparation room

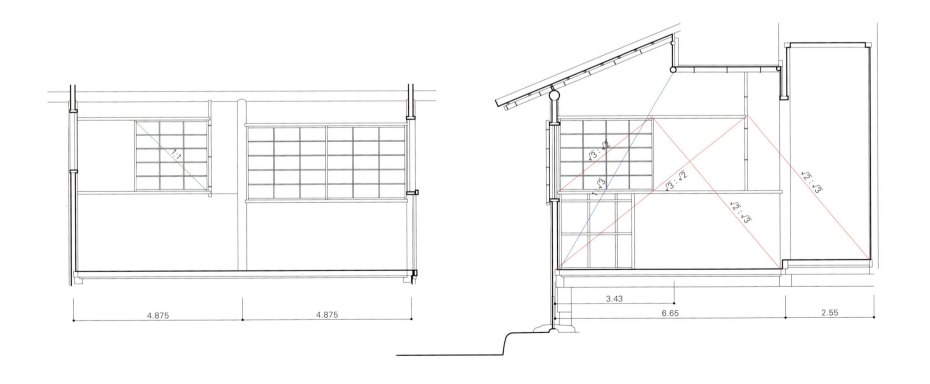

如庵の壁面の比例は、待庵のように8×4分割の畳割を基礎としたものではなく(186–187ページ参照)、$1:\sqrt{3}$と$\sqrt{2}:\sqrt{3}$の2種類の比例の組み合わせだけでシンプルに構成されている

The Jo-an walls are not, as in the case of Taian, based on the division of the tatami into 8 x 4 squares (pp. 186–187), but on a very simple combination of proportions of two kinds $1:\sqrt{3}$ or $\sqrt{2}:\sqrt{3}$.

なぐりの床柱に真塗の床框を組み合わせて格調を高め、床柱を引き立てる。三角形の鱗板を挿入し、茶道口からの斜めの動きを意匠化している。これで半東のサービス動線を確保した秀逸な空間処理

Combining the roughly hewn lines of the tokonoma corner post with a lacquer-covered crosspiece at the front of the alcove both refines the design and brings out the qualities of the post. The incorporation of the triangular board into the flooring transforms the diagonal movement of serving from the *sadoguchi* entrance into an element of design, a superb treatment of space taking into account the movement of the serving assistants.

年輪の詰んだ杉板は樹齢600年ほど、直径1.3mほどはある大木から取った中杢板である。鋭利な刀で迷いなく刳り抜いたような歯切れのよい曲線と、板の薄さが空間を洗練へと導く

The wing wall board is cut for the flat grain (*nakamoku*) from a huge old cedar tree about 1.3 meters in diameter that had probably stood for 600 years. The graceful arch, cut with a razor-sharp blade in an unerring sweep, and the thinness of the board are elements that refine the quality of the space.

方形のなかに床の間も組みこんで全体をまとめた間取り。床の間が前面に出たようなかたちとなり、床脇の余った空間に壁を斜めに立てて塗りまわしている

The layout is a square, incorporating the tokonoma into the whole. It looks as if the tokonoma projects into the room, with the extra space (the remainder of the one-mat space) divided diagonally with a wall. The corner intersection of the walls is plastered over.

床柱に杉の落し掛けが取りつく部分。落し掛けの下端にわずかな面皮を残して納まりを馴染ませている。床柱に挿した竹の廻り縁(左半分)と竿縁(右半分)。すみずみまで神経を行き届かせ、技が冴えている

Detail of the joint of the cedar-wood tokonoma lintel and the *tokobashira* corner post. Note how a scant area of the bark surface is left on the underside edge to harmonize with the rough-hewn post it joins. The bamboo pole serves as the binding beam (*mawaribuchi*) for the tokonoma (left) and batten (*saobuchi*) for the ceiling (right). The precision and care with the smallest detail is complete—workmanship at its best.

洞庫と茶道口には紅がかった襖紙が張られている。床の間から斜めの壁にかけての横筋は、壁内の貫板の熱橋により、経年変化で土色が変わったもの。壁面の景色として意図され、デザインに組みこまれている

The *fusuma* panels on the cupboard (*doko*) and host's entrance (*sadoguchi*) are covered with paper with a pink tint. The horizontal bands on the walls in the tokonoma and along the diagonal wall are the result of discoloration due to aging of the walls. The effect on the landscape of the walls is an intended and incorporated element of the design.

にじり口脇の壁。障子の敷居、鴨居、戸当たりの枠で分割された明快な比例美。床柱の相手柱はコブシの皮つき丸太といわれ、寂びた風情の材である。暦の腰張りは継ぎ方にも感性が光る。有楽の時代の暦は残っておらず、寛永6年(1629年)のものが最古という

Wall with the *nijiriguchi* (left). Note the distinct proportional beauty achieved with the lines drawn by the sill for the shoji panel, the lintel, and the shoji panel stop. The untrimmed, rustic-looking *aitebashira* ("partner post") is thought to be magnolia. The pieces of the calendar wallpaper are joined with an eyecatching sensitivity. The calendars no longer include any from Uraku's time, the oldest being from the sixth year of the Kan'ei era (1629).

点前畳前の半畳より、茶道口を開けて水屋方向を見る。袖壁の曲線、中柱と床柱の間合い、斜めに立てた壁と三角形の鱗板。幾何学的な形態が響き合い、おもむきに富む奥行きがつくられている

View from the half mat space in front of the host's seat, looking in the direction of the *mizuya* (preparation room) with the host's entrance open. A symphony of geometrical forms—the arch of the wing wall, the spacing of the *tokobashira* corner post and the *nakabashira* central post, and the triangular *uroko-ita* board along the diagonal wall at the back—sets up a fine quality of depth in even such a small space.

庵通僊院 庭玉軒

17世紀前半
京都府京都市北区

Shinjuan Temple Teigyokuken Tea Room

Important Cultural Property (attached to Tsusen'in)
Completed: Early 17th century
Location: Kita ward, Kyoto, Kyoto prefecture

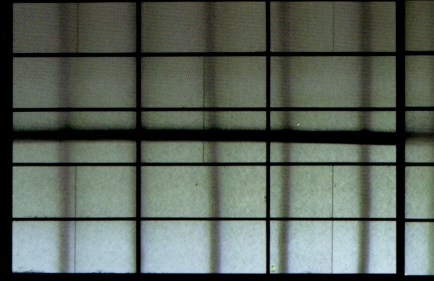

時代背景

　大徳寺の塔頭・真珠庵は、大徳寺第47世住持・一休宗純（1394-1481）の塔所として、1491（延徳3）年に建立された。真珠庵の本堂（重文・1638年）の北側に取りつく通僊院は、正親町天皇（1517-1593）から拝領した女御化粧殿を移建したものと伝えられる。茶室庭玉軒は、通僊院の北東隅に接して建てられており、茶人・金森宗和（1584-1656）の好みと伝えられてきた。この茶室の大きな特徴は、内坪と呼ばれる室内を土間にした構成である。露地を進むと潜り戸があり、その先が内坪となる。その内部は掛込み天井で覆われた1坪半ほどの空間で、飛石が打たれ、蹲踞や刀掛けが設けられている。茶席へは、庭から直接にじり口を上がるのではなく、内坪の空間を介して、そこに面した障子から入室するのである。この形式については、金森宗和が京屋敷に同じ内坪を備えた3畳台目を持っていたことが知られるが、[*10] ほかにも古い作例が伝えられており、千宗旦が利休の茶室を復古した「土間付き4畳半」、利休の「大坂屋敷の深3畳台目」や、さらにさかのぼって利休の師・武野紹鷗（1502-1555）の「紹鷗4畳半」などがあり、両者が付設した「脇坪ノ内」へと通じる。つまり、土間を備えた茶室のあり方は、草庵茶室の成立過程において、古式の流れに入るものであった。『山上宗二伝書』によると、利休の脇坪ノ内は幅が5尺ほどあり、全体で1坪半ほどの空間で、「脇ノ手水かまへ（構え）」と書きこまれ、坪ノ内に手水が設けられていたことがわかる。[*11] 興味深いことに、庭玉軒の内坪も、これとほぼ同じ大きさである。また、宗旦が復古した利休の「土間付き4畳半」は、やはり同じくらいの広さで、席への上がり口はにじりではなく、庭玉軒と同じ2枚障子であった。[*12] こういった共通性から、庭玉軒における内坪つきの構成は、利休が好んだ脇坪ノ内の系譜を汲んで成立したものであり、古式な草庵茶室の姿を今に想起させる遺構として見ることができる。そのように考えると、この茶室が金森宗和好みとして伝えられてきたのは、その祖父・金森長近（1524-1608）が利休の門人であったことも思い起こされ、何らかの縁を連想させるのである。

特徴と見どころ

　苔むす露地のなか、小ぶりな飛石の上を足元に気を配りながら伝って潜り戸を抜けると、そこは掛込み天井で覆われた三和土の空間、すなわち内坪となる。飛石は内坪のなかに入っても引きこまれており、外との連続感がつくられている。なかでは二方向に分かれて打たれており、まっすぐ足を運ぶと茶席へ、斜め左へ行くと蹲踞と刀掛けの棚へと導かれる。客はいったん斜めに進み、蹲踞で手と口を清め、もう一度同じ石を辿りもどってから席入りする。小さな空間のなか、飛石に導かれて身体的な距離感がつくられ、それとともに時間の感覚が引き延ばされて、席入りの心の準備が整えられる。

　内坪は南に向き、庇は短く、潜り戸の上には大きな連子窓があるため、午前中はたっぷりと光が入る。その光は茶席と内坪との境に立てこんだ障子で濾されて、室内を間接光でやわらかく照らす。内坪は、茶席に対して光庭のような機能も担っているのである。屋根には突上げ窓が開けられており、さらに蹲踞の前には手元周辺を照らす下地窓があって、1坪半ほどの小さな空間には三つの採光法が工夫されていることになる。

　茶席は2畳台目であるが、貴人口は低めの引違い障子とし、座敷への上がり口を大きく取ることで、内坪と茶席との結びつきが強められている。このため茶室内部にいても、あるいは内坪から茶室に入ろうとするときも、奥行きがつくられていて狭さを感じさせず、むしろ空間は伸びやかに感じられる。内坪という外と内とを取りもつ中間領域を巧みに取りこみ、豊かな光と空間の間合いをつくりだしている。

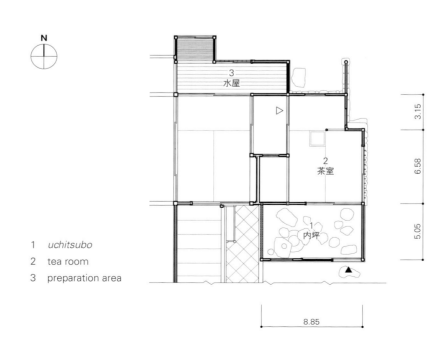

1　*uchitsubo*
2　tea room
3　preparation area

平面図　Floor plan

Historical Background

The Shinjuan subtemple of Daitokuji temple was built in 1491 in honor of Ikkyu Sojun (1394–1481), who had been Daitokuji's 47th abbot. Tsusen'in, the reception hall standing on the north side of the *hondo* main hall (1638; Important Cultural Property) of Shinjuan, is said to have formerly been the dressing hall (*kewaiden*) of a high-ranking court lady built for her by Emperor Ogimachi (1517–1593) and later moved to Shinjuan temple. The Teigyokuken tea room, built at the northeastern corner of Tsusen'in, is believed to have followed the taste of tea master Kanamori Sowa (1584–1656).

The distinctive feature of this tea room is its *uchitsubo*, the earthen-floored area at the entrance of the tea room. After passing through the *roji* garden, guests step through a small *kugurido* door into the *uchitsubo*, a space of one *tsubo* and a half (approx. 5 square meters) beneath the shelter of a sloping roof (*kakekomi tenjo*). The *tobiishi* stepping stones continue inside, leading to the stone washbasin and the sword rack stone. Instead of entering directly from the garden via a crawl-in entrance (*nijiriguchi*), guests step up from the *uchitsubo* space into the tea room through an entrance fitted with shoji panels. Another well-known instance of this style is Kanamori Sowa's tea room "with a *sanjo daime* (three-and-three-quarters tatami mat) room plus an *uchitsubo*" at his Kyoto residence. Among other old examples are the "four-and-a-half-mat room with earthen floor," Sen Sotan's reconstruction of Rikyu's tea room, and Rikyu's "fuka sanjo daime" ("deep" three and three-quarters tatami mats") at his Osaka residence. An even older example is Rikyu's teacher Takeno Joo's (1502–1555) "Joo Four-and-a-Half Tatami" tea room. The Teigyokuken *uchitsubo* can be linked to the "waki tsubo no uchi" attached to the tea rooms of Joo and Rikyu. In the formative process of rustic-style *wabi* tea rooms, structures with an earthen floor were of an early type.

According to the *Yamanoue Soji densho* (Record of Yamanoue Soji), Rikyu's "waki tsubo no uchi" is five *shaku* (151 centimeters) wide, an overall space of one *tsubo* and a half (approx. 5 square meters), with a *chozu* washbasin. Interestingly, that "tsubo no uchi" is about the same size as the Teigyokuken *uchitsubo*. Rikyu's "four-and-a-half-mat room with earthen floor" reconstructed by Sen Sotan was also about the same size and likewise had a pair of shoji panels for entering as at Teigyokuken, instead of a *nijiriguchi* crawl-in door. Given such similarities, we can say that the Teigyokuken with *uchitsubo* is of the "waki tsubo no uchi" lineage favored by Rikyu and reminiscent of an old *wabi*-style tea room. That the Teigyokuken is said to have been in the taste of Kanamori Sowa reminds us that his grandfather, Kanamori Nagachika (1524–1608), was a disciple of Rikyu—there may be a karmic tie linking them.

Characteristics and Highlights

Proceeding with care over the small stepping stones through the moss-covered garden, one stoops to pass through the *kugurido* entrance into the *uchitsubo*. The stepping stones are set so as to maintain continuity between outside and inside, and inside lead in two directions, straight ahead to enter the tea room, and diagonally to the left toward the washbasin and sword rack stone. The guest proceeds first to the left to cleanse hands and mouth at the washbasin, then retraces steps to enter the tea room. Within the small space, the spacing of the stones sets up a sense of prolonged physical distance that extends the passage of time and allows for the gathering of mental composure before entering the tea room.

The *uchitsubo* faces south, the eaves are short, and the wall over the *kugurido* has a large *renjimado*, bringing in plenty of light throughout the morning. The *uchitsubo* functions as a kind of light garden vis-à-vis the tea room, and the shoji panels between the *uchitsubo* and tea room filter the light, casting a soft indirect glow into the interior. With the *renjimado* in the upper wall, the skylight in the roof, and the *shitajimado* aperture in front of the washbasin, the small 5-square meter space is equipped with three different sources of natural light.

The tea room is small, consisting of two and three-quarters tatami mats (*nijo daime*), but the use of the *kiniguchi* entrance, set with slightly short sliding shoji panels to accommodate persons of high rank, enhances the link between the *uchitsubo* and tea room. The effect once inside, as well as when entering, is of a sense of depth. Rather than feeling cramped, it actually feels quite spacious. The *uchitsubo*'s intermediate space between inside and outside is skillfully incorporated, creating a rich mingling of light and space.

飛石に導かれて木戸の前へ。ここを潜り、内坪に入る。南面となり、連子窓、屋根には突上げ窓を開ける

The stepping stones lead to the wooden door of the tea room. Through the door is the *uchitsubo*. Note the bamboo-latticed *renjimado* window in the wall above the door and the cover of the skylight on the roof.

内坪。傾斜をつけた土間に小振りの飛石をやや高めに小さな歩幅で打ち、小空間に距離感をつくる。飛石には海、山、川の石を取り混ぜて配する。庭から内坪へは潜り戸から、席へは引違い障子の貴人口から入る

The *uchitsubo*. Within the quite small space, the sense of distance traveled is accentuated by the slope of the earthen floor, the height of the stepping stones, and their short spacing. The stones include those brought from the ocean, from the mountains, and from the riverbeds. The doorway from the garden is a low *kuguri-do* one stoops to enter, while the opening to the tea room (*kininguchi*) is fitted with shoji panels that slide past each other.

蹲踞の脇には手元を照らす下地窓、右には刀掛け石、その上方に刀掛け棚を吊る。竹の壁は左側が通用口になっていて、蹲踞に水を張るときに使われる動線となる

Next to the washbasin is a *shitajimado* window, shedding light on hands extended to wash. To the right is the sword-stowing stone. Guests would step up on this stone to place their sword on the rack above. The left side of the bamboo wall is a service access door from which water can be resupplied to the washbasin.

貴人口から点前座を見ると、色紙窓が情趣ある景をつくっている。ここには引違い障子が入り、にじって席入りする。色紙窓は北に向くが、椿の生垣からの照り返しで、午後からは緑を帯びた光を得る

The *shikishimado* ("shikishi card") window at the back of the room forms a tasteful scene viewed from the entrance. The entrance is fitted with shoji panels and entered on the knees. The *shikishimado* faces north, but from afternoon glows with green-tinged light reflecting off the camellia hedge outside.

点前座から貴人口の障子を外して内坪を見る。南の明るい光を内坪でいったん溜めて鎮めてから、茶席のなかへ浸透させる。中柱に曲木を使い、床框には手斧目を入れる。花明り窓を給仕口側につけた珍しいかたちである

The view from the host's seat toward the *uchitsubo*, with the shoji entrance panels removed. The bright light from the south that fills the *uchitsubo* is softened before it filters into the tea room. A curved log is used for the *nakabashira* central post and the crosspiece at the lower edge of the tokonoma shows rough gouging with an adze.

西翁院 澱看席

重要文化財
建立年代　17世紀後半
所在地　　京都府京都市左京区

Saioin Temple Yodomi-no-seki Tea Room

Important Cultural Property
Completed: Late 17th century
Location: Sakyo ward, Kyoto, Kyoto prefecture

時代背景

　金戒光明寺の塔頭・西翁院にある澱看席は、藤村庸軒(1613-1699)が手がけた茶室である。庸軒は千利休の孫・千宗旦(1578-1658)の門弟で、「宗旦四天王」の一人として知られる茶人であった。茶室の建設は1685(貞享2)年から1686(貞享3)年とされるが、一説に1668年(寛文8)年との伝承もある。西と南に開けた高台に立つことから、澱看席という名は、点前座の南の窓から遥か淀川まで遠望したことにちなむという。だが、江戸中期から後期の史料には「紫雲庵」や「反古庵」という名で記されており、庸軒の時代にどのように呼ばれていたかは定かではない。本堂の西北に茶室が取りつき、移建はなく、当時のままの姿をよく伝えていると考えられている。

　平3畳敷きで、点前座と客座との間に仕切り壁を立て、その壁に火灯口を開けたいわゆる「宗貞囲い」の茶室である。もう一つ、同じつくりに「道安囲い」があるが、これは炉の切り方の違いでそのように呼ぶ。この構えの由来については、古田織部(1543-1615)や千道安(1546-1607)などいくつかの説があるが、なかでも注目されるのは、千利休の作例二つが史料に伝えられていることである。[*13] いつ頃かはわからないが、空願という塗師のために利休が指図した茶室(宗貞囲い)と、医師で茶人の曲直瀬道山(1507-1595)とともにつくった茶室(道安囲い)である。また、利休自刃後、秀吉より赦されて千家が京都に再興されたのち(1594年・文禄3年か)、千宗旦は平3畳の「宗貞囲い」の茶室をそこに建てていたと伝えられている。[*14] このことから宗貞囲いの茶室は、利休の道統につながるものであったことをうかがわせる。

特徴と見どころ

　点前が始まる。道具がすべて運び出されるまで、亭主の姿は客から見えない。客は仕切り壁越しに亭主の気配だけを感じながら、火灯口が開くのを待つ。そうして亭主が姿を現わすとき、時間がその一瞬に凝集するかのような、強烈な印象がもたらされる。亭主の姿は丸く割り抜かれた火灯口に縁取られた「景」となり、そこがあたかも舞台と化したような見え方をする。亭主は背後の、澱看席の名の由来となった窓から射す光で照らされている。他方、この構えは茶を立てる場を次の間のごとく見せていることから、亭主の謙譲の気持ちを表わす構えともいわれる。制約、つまり壁で仕切り、客座からの視界を限定することで、侘びたおもむきが強められるとともに、侘びとは相矛盾するような舞台性をも帯びてくる。そんな逆説的な効果と両義性を持つのが、宗貞囲いの醍醐味である。

　仕切り壁は完全に仕切らず、中柱の先と上部を吹通しており、客座と点前座を隔てつつ連続した一室空間の感覚をつくる。3畳を融合するのが天井で、空間全体に片流れの総化粧屋根裏がかかる。草庵のデザインでは、天井の形式は上座、下座、亭主の座といった空間の格や目的を反映させ、高低の切りかえ、素材や意匠に変化をつけることが多いが、この茶室ではそのような決まりごとに拘泥していない。澱看席が持つおおらかな空気感は、この簡潔な天井のあり方によってもたらされている。

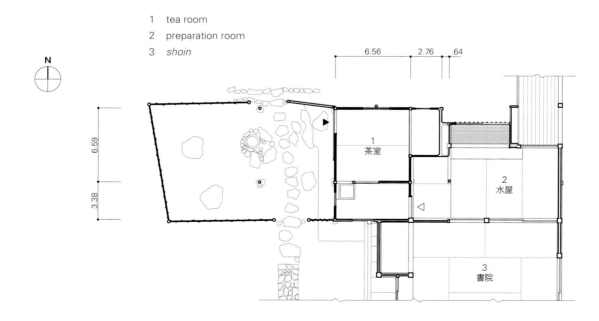

1　tea room
2　preparation room
3　shoin

平面図　Floor plan

Historical Background

The Yodomi-no-seki tea room in Saioin, a subtemple of Konkai Komyoji temple, was built by Fujimura Yoken (1613–1699), one of the four leading disciples of Rikyu's grandson Sen Sotan (1578–1658). Construction is said to have taken place in 1685–1686, but one theory dates it to 1668. The tea room stands on high ground with vistas to the west and south, and so the name Yodomi-no-seki (lit., "seat to view the Yodo river") is thought to come from the south window of the host's seat (*temaeza*), from which the Yodo river can be seen in the distance. Records from the middle and late Edo period call the tea room "Shiun'an" ("hermitage of purple clouds") or "Hogo'an" ("hermitage of discarded paper"). It is not known, however, what it was called during the time of Fujimura Yoken. Attached on the northwest side of the *hondo* (the main hall) of Saioin, the tea room is thought to have been there from the beginning, well-preserved in its original form.

The tea room is a *hirasanjo* (three mats aligned horizontally) with a partition between the host's seat and the guest's seat. A so-called "Sotei-gakoi" (Sotei enclosure), the partition has an arched opening (*katoguchi*). There is a similar structure termed "Doan-gakoi," which differs in the cut of the hearth. There are several theories as to who devised this kind of structure, one attributing it to Furuta Oribe (1543–1615) and another to Sen Doan (1546–1607). Two examples created by Rikyu are mentioned in historical records. When they were built is not known, but one is a tea room with Sotei-gakoi that Rikyu had made by a lacquerware craftsman named Kugan. The other is a tea room with Doan-gakoi built jointly by Rikyu and Manase Dosan (1507–1595), a doctor and tea master. Not long after Rikyu committed seppuku on the order of Toyotomi Hideyoshi, Hideyoshi pardoned the Sen family. After the family reestablished itself in Kyoto, probably in 1594, Sen Sotan is recorded as having built a *hirasanjo* tea room with Sotei-gakoi. Such records suggest that the tea room with Sotei-gakoi might be linked to Rikyu's lineage.

Characteristics and Highlights

The procedure of serving tea (*temae*) begins. But until all the utensils have been placed on the tatami, the host does not show himself to his guests. Aware of the host's movements behind the partition, the guests await the opening of the arched door. The moment when the door opens, then, is one that leaves a strong impression. Framed by the arched opening, the host's appearance forms a distinct "scene," as if the space were set as a kind of stage, lit up from behind by the glow through the window that gives the Yodomi-no-seki tea room its name. This layout presents the place where the tea is made as an adjoining room and is said to express the modesty of the host. By such constraint, that is, by use of a partition to limit what the guest can see, an ambiguous and paradoxical effect is produced that not only intensifies the feeling of *wabi* but also injects a dramatic element that is the antithesis of *wabi*. This is the attraction of the Sotei-gakoi.

The partition does not completely shut off the space of the host's seat, but is open beyond the *nakabashira* central post, creating a sense of a continuum of space between the guest's seat and the host's seat. The continuum is confirmed by the open ceiling covering the whole three-mat space, showing the bamboo rafters and battens. The ceiling design of the usual *soan*-style tea room is treated differently for the seat of the main guest, ordinary guests, and host, reflecting the purpose of the space below in differences of height and variations of materials and styles, but the Yodomi-no-seki is quite unrestrained by such conventions. The feeling of magnanimity that emerges from faithfulness to *wabi* taste in this tea room can be attributed to the simplicity of the ceiling.

点前座より火灯口越しに客座を見る
Looking from the host's seat through the arched door toward the guest's seat

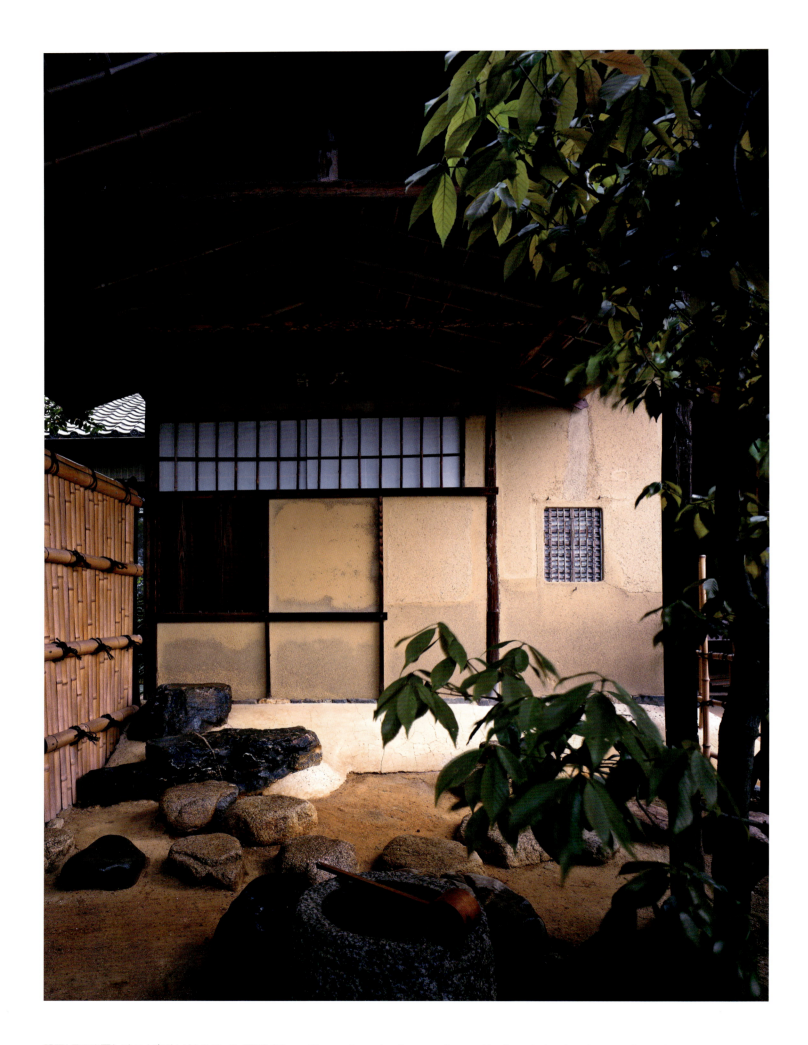

蹲踞と飛石を覆うように土庇がかけられている。西日をやわらげ、風雨から客人を守る配慮。亀腹（漆喰部分）の上に建てられており、にじり口前には高い沓脱石を置く

The awning extending over the washbasin and stepping stones softens strong sunlight from the west (foreground) and shelters guests from wind and rain. The tea room is built on a mounded, plaster-covered base called a *kamebara* (tortoise belly foundation), and the footwear-removing stone (*kutsunugi ishi*) is quite high.

にじり口を開けると、正面に床の間（4尺幅・121cm）がある。室床には墨蹟窓を開け、掛物を照らす。壁はスサ壁、床は板敷き、杉の丸太を使い、侘びに徹した床構え

Inside the *nijiriguchi* entrance, the tokonoma appears straight ahead. A *bokuseki*-style window in the outside wall of the tokonoma shines light onto the scroll. The walls are plastered with clay mixed with fiber, the floor made of wooden planks, and the corner post and the front crosspiece are cedar logs, giving the space a thoroughly rustic *wabi* look.

3畳のなか、宗貞囲いの構え、三方の壁に開けられた窓からの光、人の動きが加わって
じつに変化に富む空間となる。亭主の姿や動きは、火灯口を開けるまで客には見えない

Though confined to only three-mats, the Sotei-gakoi partition and light entering from windows on three sides, combined with human movement, make for a sense of space with considerable diversity. The sight and movements of the host are unseen until the arched door is opened.

点前座。藤村庸軒ゆかりの道具を置き合わせる。高台に立つため、かつては左の窓からは淀川の流れが、正面の風炉先窓からは嵯峨あたりまで見渡せたと伝えられる

Utensils associated with Fujimura Yoken at the host's seat (*temaeza*). As the tea room stands on high ground, the window at the left is said to have once looked out on a view with the Yodo river in the distance. The window beyond the hearth offered a vista open as far as Saga.

火灯口を開けると、一気に空間は広がる。茶を点てる場を半ば独立させ、次の間のように見せながらも、むしろ亭主の存在感は強められて、舞台性を帯びる。片流れ、総化粧屋根裏の簡明な天井が空間全体をまとめる

When the arched door is opened, the space suddenly expands. The division of the area where the tea is made into what appears to be a separate room enhances the presence of the host and lends a dramatic element to the scene. The open ceiling under the single slant of the roof unites the whole with clear and simple lines.

efecture

時代背景

　桂離宮は京都市の南西、桂川の西岸に位置し、総面積約7万m²、池を中心にして建てられた別荘建築である。桂は平安時代より貴族の別業（別荘）が建てられてきた地で、月の名所として知られる。『源氏物語』をはじめ、多くの詩歌においても参照され、古くより王朝文化の文脈が流れる場所であった。初代八条宮・智仁親王（1579-1629）がここを所領とし、別業を構える造営に着手したのは1615（元和元）年頃といわれ、1624（寛永元）年頃までには今日見る古書院の姿と、広い庭園を持つかたちへと発展していたと推定されている。1629（寛永6）年に智仁親王が亡くなったあとは放置されていたが、皇子の二代智忠親王（1619-1662）が受け継ぎ、1641（寛永18）年頃より池を含む庭の拡張整備工事と増改築に着手した。1649（慶安2）年までには古書院に接続して中書院が完成しており、その後、1661（寛文元）年から翌年にかけて新御殿が建てられ、御殿群は現在見る独特の雁行する形となった。新御殿は後水尾上皇（1596-1680）の行幸を仰ぐために建てられたが、その直前に智忠親王は逝去し、三代穏仁親王（1643-1665）が上皇を迎えた。以降、別荘として利用されたが、1881（明治14）年に宮家が断絶してからは宮内庁の管理となり、現在にいたる。

　桂離宮の成立を考える上で欠かせないのは、その基礎を築いた初代智仁親王が置かれた境涯と、政治的・文化的な背景である。智仁親王の幼少期から壮年期は、豊臣から徳川へと政権が変わる激動の時代であり、天皇の弟である親王の人生は、政権を牛耳る武家の思惑にたびたび巻きこまれた。その一方で、22歳で古今伝授を受けるほど和歌の世界に精通していた親王は、宮廷文化を代表する文化人であった。平安時代、藤原道長（966-1027）の桂殿があったとされ、『源氏物語』のモデルになったといわれる桂の地を所領にしたとき、ここに別業を建てる構想はすでに智仁親王のなかに宿っていたであろう。そこは月を愛で、池に舟を浮かべて詩や歌を詠み、風雅な王朝文化を復古し、実現する舞台としてあった。武家の支配下にあって、経済の安定と引きかえに、天皇や皇族が政治の実権から遠ざけられたという政治的な力学もそこには働いていたといえる。

　桂離宮は約半世紀をかけて整えられたものだが、二代智忠親王が造営に着手した頃は三代将軍・家光（1604-1651）の治世で、宮廷では後水尾上皇を中心に寛永文化が華開いた時代であった。後水尾上皇は智忠親王より20歳以上年長の従兄にあたり、親王は6歳のとき天皇の猶子（養子）となっている。後水尾サロンと呼ばれる当代一流の文化人の輪のなかに身を置いた親王は、とくに茶の湯の名人と伝えられており、茶を軸とする桂の拡張計画が導入された。親王は池を拡げ、そのまわりに茶亭を建て、露地をつくり、建物間を小径で結び、変化に富む庭をつくりあげた。後水尾上皇を迎えるために建てられた新御殿の座敷は、上皇の趣好に適うように普請したものと考えられ、江戸時代初期より好まれた数寄屋風書院の最高峰を今に伝えている。

特徴と見どころ

　桂離宮とは、月と水の建築である。建築と庭園が不可分のものとなり、洗練されたデザイン手法が散りばめられたこの別業の見どころは数限りなくあるが、建築をつくる側の視点からいえば、この別荘建築が持つ根本的な素晴らしさとは、明快なテーマの設定にある。ここは月を愛でるための建築であり、王朝風の舟遊びをするためにつくられた場所である。しかも、王朝的な文学的世界が二重構造となり、造営が動機づけられている。このテーマにもとづき、川から水を引き、造成工事をし、築山をつくり、池泉舟遊式庭園が整えられた。そして、月の方角と動きを読んで縁をしつらえ、天空に昇る月、水面に映る月を室内からも縁からも賞翫できるよう古書院が建てられた。さらには、その主題の上に、二代智忠親王が茶の湯の侘数寄の世界をフーガのように重ねて、風流の奥行きを拡げている。

　桂離宮には、松琴亭、賞花亭、笑意軒、月波楼の4つの茶亭が現在残るが、炉のほかにもかまどが付設されており、食事や湯茶などが用意できるようになっている。「膳組所」と呼ばれるこの機能的な設備は、従来のように水屋のような裏方空間としてあるのではなく、ここでは一つの建築的な見どころとして構成されている。たとえば、松琴亭では一の間前面の土庇の下、庭の景が美しく広がるパノラマのなか、それが風情を醸し出す一種の添景として組みこまれている。ここでは、鄙びた気分を楽しむ王朝的遊興の趣向が草庵の茶の湯と融合し、新しいもてなしのかたちが空間とともに創出されている。

Historical Background

Located on the west bank of the Katsura river in what is today the southwestern part of Kyoto, the Katsura Imperial Villa is a 70,000-square-meter pond and stroll garden with superb examples of seventeenth-century-style architecture. The Katsura area was long a noted spot for moon viewing in the Heian period (794–1184) and favored for the villas of court nobles, so it became a place closely associated with Heian court culture and mentioned in poetry and prose works of classical literature like *The Tale of Genji*.

Construction of the villa is believed to have begun around 1615 when the property passed into the hands of Prince Toshihito (1579–1629), founder of the Hachijo-no-miya family. By around 1624, work had progressed as far as completion of the Koshoin ("Old Shoin") reception hall, which remains today, and the design and layout of a spacious garden. After Toshihito died, the villa was neglected for a time, but Prince Toshitada (1619–1662) succeeded as second head of the family, and renovation and expansion got underway around 1641. By 1649 the Chushoin ("Middle Shoin") had been completed adjacent to the Koshoin and in 1661–1662 the Shingoten ("New Palace") was added, the cluster of three buildings forming a unique "flying geese formation". The Shingoten was constructed to accommodate the Retired Emperor Go-Mizunoo (1596–1680) during a planned visit, but right before the imperial visit Toshitada died, and it was his heir, Prince Yasuhito (1643–1665), who welcomed the ex-emperor. The property was used as a villa thereafter, but in 1881, when the Hachijo-no-miya family line died out, it was transferred to the management of what is now the Imperial Household Agency.

The way Katsura Imperial Villa came into being is inextricably bound up with the circumstances of the life of Prince Toshihito, who created its basic structure, and the political and cultural backdrop of his time. The period of his boyhood to middle age coincided with the turbulent transition from the rule of Toyotomi Hideyoshi (1537–1598) to the regime of Tokugawa Ieyasu (1542–1616). As the younger brother of the emperor, his fate was often at the mercy of powerful warrior class leaders and their strategies for controlling the court. Meanwhile, he became well known from a young age for his exceptional talent in waka poetry and was a leader of court culture. Having obtained the property in the Katsura area, where the powerful court noble Fujiwara no Michinaga (966–1027) had a villa in the Heian period that is said to have provided the model for the palace depicted in *The Tale of Genji*, Toshihito must already have had a plan to build a villa for himself. The area was an ideal setting for his yearning to restore the elegance of Heian court culture by holding moon viewing parties and floating boats on a pond from which to compose poetry. At work in the story of the Katsura villa were the political dynamics of the time, when the emperor and other members of the imperial family accepted distance from the center of power in exchange for economic stability under the rule of the warrior class.

Completion of the villa extended over about half a century. Second family head Toshitada's work in restoration and expansion coincided with the rule of third Tokugawa shogun Iemitsu (1604–1651). In the imperial court, it was the time of the flowering of the Kan'ei-era (1624–1644) culture fostered in the salons of the Retired Emperor Go-Mizunoo. While the reigning monarch, he had adopted Toshitada, who was then six years old, and Toshitada grew up to become a central member of the royal salon of leading literary figures. A noted tea master, he expanded the Katsura villa centered on his tea-ceremony inspired aesthetic. He enlarged the pond, built tea houses around it, made *roji* gardens, and connected the outbuildings with paths, creating a stroll garden rich in scenic variety. The *zashiki* reception room of the Shingoten (New Palace), built to accommodate the visit of by-then-retired Go-Mizunoo, which is thought to have been designed to suit the ex-emperor's taste, displays the highest level of *shoin* architecture in the *sukiya*-style that had been favored since the early Edo period.

Characteristics and Highlights

The villa's architecture is organized around the moon and water, and the buildings and garden are closely linked. Examples of refined design techniques abound, but from the perspective of an architect, probably what is the most fundamentally impressive is that it has a clearly defined theme. Everything is designed for enjoying the beauty of the moon and for the attendant courtly and literary pleasures to be pursued, such as composing poetry while on a boat floating in the pond. Water was diverted from the Katsura river, the topography of the garden was shaped, and the *tsukiyama* hillocks engineered to form a pond-and-stroll garden, all oriented to the moon-viewing theme. The Koshoin building is furnished with a main veranda situated in such a way, after careful reading of the position and movements of the moon, as to appreciate its progress through the heavens as well as savor its reflection on the water from the veranda vantage point. It is upon that theme that Prince Toshitada added a layer of elegance to the tea ceremony world of *wabi-suki* taste.

Four tea pavilions are preserved at the villa: Shokintei, Shokatei, Shoiken, and Gepparo. Among their facilities are not only floor hearths (*ro*) for making tea but also *kamado* cook stoves for preparing meals. The *zengumidokoro* areas (for the preparing of meals) were built not only for the service functions following the conventions of the *mizuya* preparation area but to be architecturally attractive. Under the eaves along the front of the Shokintei *ichi-no-ma* ("room one") with its beautiful panorama of the garden, for example, the *zengumidokoro* injects an element of rusticity in the whole. Here we see how the taste for courtly pastimes enjoyed in a "remote" setting was merged with the *soan*-style of tea ceremony to create the form for a new style of entertainment.

桂離宮のなかには4カ所の土橋がかかり、舟遊びの際には
ゆるやかな弧を描く橋の下を潜る趣向である

The earthen bridges spanning the pond at four places rise in a gentle arc, allowing comfortable passage for boating pleasures.

配置図　Site plan

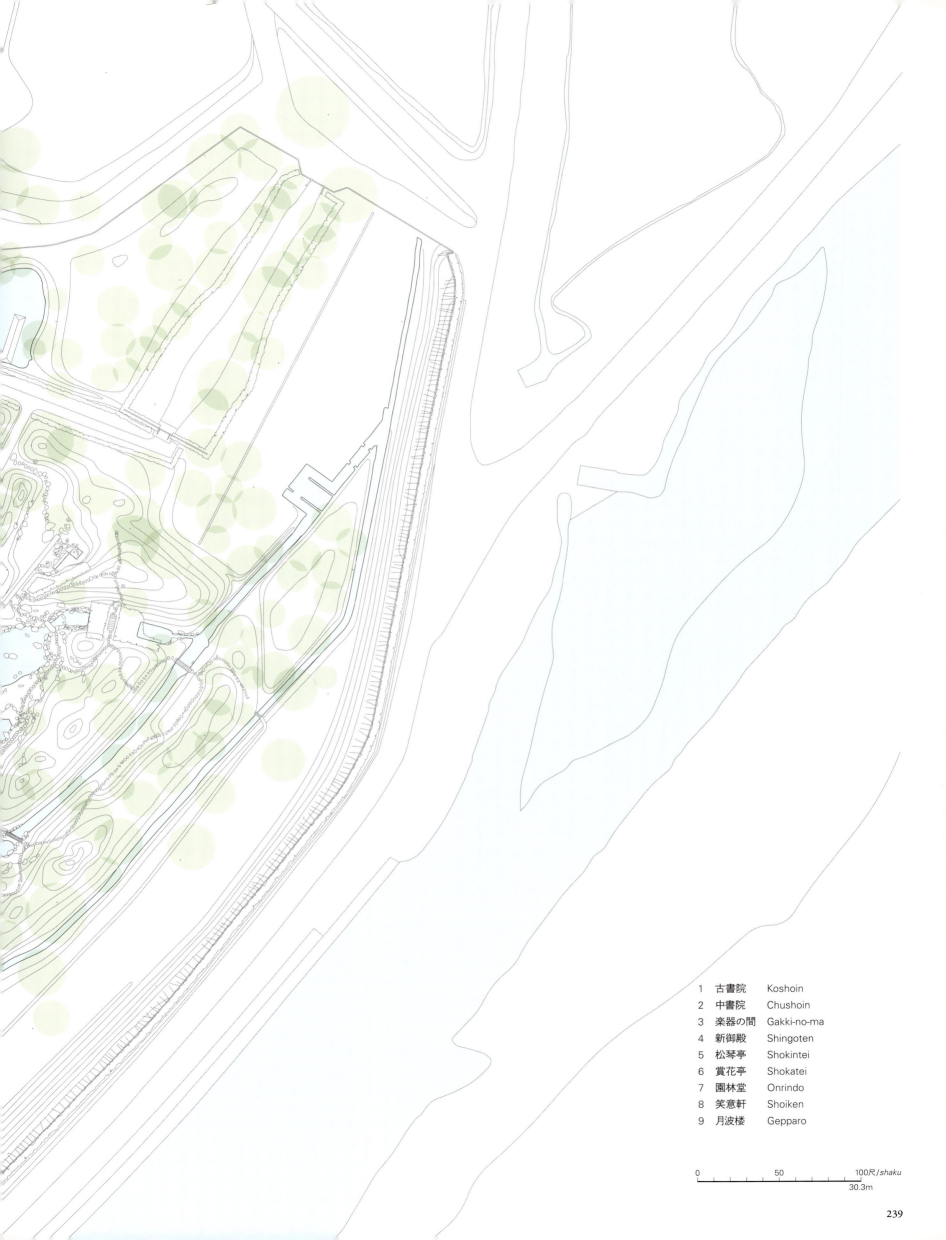

1	古書院	Koshoin
2	中書院	Chushoin
3	楽器の間	Gakki-no-ma
4	新御殿	Shingoten
5	松琴亭	Shokintei
6	賞花亭	Shokatei
7	園林堂	Onrindo
8	笑意軒	Shoiken
9	月波楼	Gepparo

舟に乗り、御殿に近づく。古書院は妻側を池に向ける。シンメトリーの明快な形を持ち
正面性の強いファサードが格調ある佇まいをつくる

Approaching the palace buildings by boat. The gable end of the Koshoin ("Old Shoin") faces the pond. It features a clearly symmetrical form, as a strong frontalism enhances the dignity of the facade.

水面から古書院の床までは約3mあり、舟で近づくにつれて建物が大きく見えてくる。
張り出す水際の曲線が優雅な遠近感をつくる

The floor of the Koshoin is three meters above the surface of the pond, so the building looms larger as one approaches. The spreading curve of the shoreline gives the scene an elegant depth of perspective.

5月の華やかな季節、南東側から見る御殿群。妻を正面とした古書院（右）に対し、中書院は棟の向きを矩折に接続し、楽器の間、新御殿へと連なる

The colorful month of May. The southeast side of the clustered palace buildings. In contrast to the Koshoin, whose gable faces front (right), the Chushoin ("Middle Shoin") presents its ridgeline in an L-shaped form connecting to the Gakki-no-ma ("Musical Instruments Room") and the Shingoten ("New Palace").

6月、新緑に囲まれた御殿群。古書院(右)に対し、中書院、新御殿と順次軒先を低めている。
池から眺めたとき、雁行形の美しいリズムが刻まれる

In June, the palace buildings surrounded by the bright greenery of early summer. Compared to the Koshoin (right), the eaves of the Chushoin and Shingoten are successively lower, setting up a pleasing flying-geese formation when seen from the pond.

池から古書院へと飛石を上っていく。縁の前には月見台(右手前)が付設されている。
右の囲いのなかには階段がつき、月明りが入るよう、大きな連子窓を開けている

Landing and climbing the stepping stones toward the Koshoin. Note the moon-viewing platform at the front of the veranda. Behind the enclosure at right are the steps up to the veranda; the wall has wide-spaced lattice bars to allow the light of the moon to enter.

古書院の縁まわり。部屋のなかからも月や庭がよく見えるように庇を少し高くしている。
縁から軒桁までの高さ約2.6m、壁上までの高さは約3m

The Koshoin veranda. The wall over the lintels is high, so as to raise the eaves upward, allowing the moon and garden to be enjoyed from within as well. The distance between the veranda and eave purlin is 2.6 meters. The floor to top-of-the-wall height is 3 meters.

新御殿。柿葺の屋根の下、軒の出が短いが、これは建てられた当初、中書院、新御殿は今のように明り障子を外まわりに入れず、吹放ちの縁であったためである。軒の出は中書院で約67cm（2.2尺）、新御殿で約85cm（2.8尺）

The Shingoten. The eaves beneath the cypress-shingled roof are short, and this is because, when first built, the Chushoin and Shingoten were not enclosed with shoji panels as they are today, but were open to their verandas. The Chushoin eaves extend 67 centimeters and those of the Shingoten 85 centimeters.

高床にしたのは、桂川の氾濫に備えるためと、夏の東風を通すためである。
中央は楽器の間で、中書院と新御殿を連結する。床高は、新御殿155cm
(5.1尺)、中書院185cm(6.1尺)、古書院170cm(5.6尺)

The floors are elevated, both to protect the buildings from the flooding of the Katsura river and to take advantage of the easterly breezes in summer. At center is the Gakki-no-ma tucked between the Chushoin (right) and Shingoten (left). The floor height for the Shingoten is 155 centimeters, for the Chushoin 185 centimeters and for the Koshoin 170 centimeters.

古書院には3カ所の飛石がつき、縁と庭とをつなげる。寂びた風情ある飛石が足取りを想起させる。川石のなか、上から3段目に平らな山石を挟んで区切りをつけ、印象を引き締めている

Stepping stones link the garden and the veranda in three places in the Koshoin. The worn and weathered rocks remind one of footprints. Among the river rocks, the placement of a mountain rock in the third step from the top injects a break in the pattern and sharpens the effect of their arrangement.

古書院、御輿寄前の石段と沓脱石。ここまで輿で乗り上げ、御殿に入室する。中高となった見事な沓脱石、そのまわりは小さな自然石の敷きつめで舗装されている

Stone steps and footwear-removing stone at the Okoshiyose formal entrance to the buildings. Here guests would alight from their palanquins. The beautiful footwear-removing stone is slightly convex and embedded in a pavement of small naturally shaped stones.

古書院、二の間より座敷の連なりを見る。二の間と一の間の間には筬欄間が入り、透けた組子が奥行きを見せる。襖という可動式の軽やかな間仕切りで、空間が奥へと展開していく

View from the *ni-no-ma* ("room two") at the Koshoin, showing the connections between the rooms. The closely spaced vertical bars filling the transoms (*osaranma*) between the *ni-no-ma* and the *ichi-no-ma* highlight the depth of the building. The space is divided by lightweight, moveable *fusuma* partitions, which can make the space seem to flow on and on into the depths of the building.

古書院、二の間。一方向からの明り障子を通した光が、襖の桐紋を華やかに輝かせる。この唐紙は胡粉地に雲母と黄土で型押ししたもの。障子を開けると、池の眺めが広がる

Facing southeast (toward the moon-viewing platform) in the Koshoin *ni-no-ma*, light streaming through the shoji panels shines brightly on the paulownia-leaf pattern on the *fusuma* doors. The paper covering the *fusuma* is made with a mixture of mica and ocher powder stencil printed onto a background layer of *gofun* (powdered shell) pigment. The shoji open onto the panorama of the pond.

部屋のなかから見る月と水月。月光は竹簀子縁に反射し室内を照らす。高床の位置から眺めるため、部屋のなかにいて庭が特別な距離感をもって見えてくる

The moon and its reflection on the water as seen from inside the Koshoin. Shining on the bamboo poles used to floor the moon-viewing veranda, moonlight illuminates the room. A raised floor gives a special sense of distance to one who views the garden from a vantage point within the building.

二代智忠親王が増築した中書院から、楽器の間、新御殿を見る。中書院と新御殿の床の高低差は30cmあり、その間にある楽器の間で段差が調節されている。中書院の襖絵は狩野三兄弟（探幽・尚信・安信）の筆といわれ、この絵は尚信による「竹林七賢図」と伝えられる

View from the Chushoin added by Prince Toshitada, looking toward the Gakki-no-ma and Shingoten. There is a difference of 30 centimeters between the floor height of the Chushoin and that of the Shingoten that is offset by the Gakki-no-ma between them. The *fusuma* paintings of the Chushoin are said to have been done by the three Kano brothers (Tan'yu, Naonobu, and Yasunobu) of the preeminent workshop of painters of the time. The painting shown here is thought to be the "Seven Sages of the Bamboo Grove" by Kano Naonobu.

中書院・一の間の大床と違棚。一の間の山水の画は探幽筆といわれる。古書院は、床柱以外はマツの角柱、天井廻り縁・竿縁はトガサワラが使われており、一方、中書院の柱は面皮つきのスギ、天井廻り縁・竿縁はモミが用いられ、古書院にくらべると数寄屋風の趣好が強い

The large tokonoma and staggered shelves in the *ichi-no-ma* room of the Chushoin. The landscapes on the walls and *fusuma* of the *ichi-no-ma* are said to be by Kano Tan'yu. The posts in the Chushoin are cedar, planed on four sides but with natural texture surfaces at the corners (*menkawatsuki*), and fir is used for the trimming around the ceiling and the ceiling battens. These features heighten the *sukiya* taste of the building in comparison with the Koshoin.

新御殿、上段つきの一の間と東側の入側縁。当初は障子が入らず、縁は吹放ちで
勾欄だけがまわり、より開放的な空間であった。高床のため、雨の跳ね返りがなく、
外側でも腰板なしの明り障子を立てこむことができる

The Shingoten, showing the *ichi-no-ma* with elevated area (*jodan*) and the interior veranda (*irigawa-en*) on the east side. Initially the veranda was surrounded only by the railing, giving the space an even more open feel. The height of the floor eliminates concern about backsplash from rain so that full-length shoji panels could be used without wood paneling on the lower part.

一の間、上段の付書院と櫛形の書院窓。窓上の羽目板はトチ、文机にはカラクワが使われている。文机下の背板はケンドン式で、外して風を通すことができる。上段框もトチで、美しい杢目を活かす

The *kushigata* ("comb-shaped") study window looking out on the garden from the elevated *tsukeshoin* study recess. The upper panel of the window is horse-chestnut (*tochi*) wood and the desktop is *karakuwa* (mulberry) wood. The backboard of the desk is inserted in drop-fit fashion so that it can be removed for better circulation of air (as here). The frame of the raised floor is also horse-chestnut wood.

櫛形窓と入側縁の明り障子の重なり。上質な光に満たされて、内部から膨らんでいくような不思議な空間となる。櫛形窓の石垣張の竪桟と、周囲の横桟の調和が美しい

Translucent shoji overlap where the study recess window opens on the interior veranda. Note the beautiful harmony between the horizontally oriented grid of the surrounding veranda and the vertically oriented grid of the shoji in the study papered in the *ishigakibari* style (vertical seams of the paper showing between the laths).

上段の間の桂棚。棚板と袋棚を矩折に組み合わせたデザイン。材の面取りと縦横の納まりに細やかな神経を行き届かせ、造りつけの家具として洗練をきわめた造形。画は狩野探幽筆

Decorative shelf (*katsuradana*) in the Jodan-no-ma. The shelves and cupboard are combined in an L-shaped design. Meticulous workmanship in the planing and joinery of the vertical and horizontal parts results in superbly refined works of built-in furnishing. The paintings are by Kano Tan'yu.

桂棚と格天井。棚は幾何学的な比例を駆使した美しい構成。タガヤサン、朱タン、キャラ、ベニイスなどの個性的な南洋材を含む18種類の材を巧みに組み合わせている

The *katsuradana* shelves and coffered ceiling. The shelves present a beautiful composition featuring geometrical proportions. The design skillfully incorporates eighteen different types of wood, including distinctive tropical trees, such as Bombay black wood (*tagayasan*).

格天井見上げ。ケヤキを板違いに張り、格縁は真塗。さまざまなデザイン要素が
駆使された上段の間を格天井が格調高く統合している

Looking up at the coffered ceiling. Zelkova (*keyaki*) boards are placed with the grain facing different directions and the batten ribs are painted with lacquer (*shinnuri*). The ceiling elegantly pulls together the diverse design elements on display in the Jodan-no-ma.

入側縁の外障子を外すと、柱だけを残して庭に浮かぶように空間は透ける。
この庭は鞠場と呼ばれており、二代智忠親王は蹴鞠の名人であった

When the shoji panels outside the interior veranda are removed, leaving only the posts, the building seems to be floating in space. This part of the garden is called the *mariba* ("ball field"); Prince Toshitada was famous for his skill at the courtly ball game of *kemari*.

松琴亭の屋根。右から茅葺の母屋、柿葺の茶室、二重棟の水屋。妻側の庇の出を深く取り、異素材、異なる形の屋根を巧みにまとめ上げている。扁額は初代智仁親王の兄、後陽成天皇の宸筆といわれる

The roof of the Shokintei tea house. From right, the thatched roof of the main structure, the thin wood shingle roofed tea room and the *mizuya* with its two-layered ridgeline. The gable eaves are deep, and the differently shaped roofs made of different materials are skillfully combined. The framed nameplate (*hengaku*) is said to be in the calligraphy of Emperor Go-Yozei, Prince Toshihito's elder brother.

松琴亭、北東面。縁のまわった数寄座敷（右）と草庵茶室の組み合わせ。荒磯に見立てた庭から白川石の橋を渡り、そこからが茶室の内露地の風情となる。茶室には土庇がかかり、連子窓の下ににじり口がある

The view from the northeast side of the Shokintei shows how it combines the *sukiya*-style reception room with veranda (right) with the *soan*-style tea room. From a part of the garden designed to evoke a wild seashore (*araiso*), one crosses the bridge made of Shirakawa stone (a granite) to enter the area styled in the manner of a tea *roji* garden. The eaves extend over an earthen area at the entrance (*tsuchibisashi*) where the *nijiriguchi* crawl-through entrance can be seen beneath the latticed window (*renjimado*).

松琴亭の一の間・床の間前から膳組所越しに北西を見る。茶の湯と開放的な酒宴の場を組み合わせ、粋をきわめたみやびな空間構成。左奥に月波楼が見え、その遠くに愛宕山がうっすらと見える。ここからの庭の眺めは、桂離宮のなかでも屈指のものであろう

View to the northwest from in front of the tokonoma in the Shokintei *ichi-no-ma*, seen through the meal preparation space (*zengumidokoro*). This vantage point offers perhaps one of the best views of the garden in the whole villa. The combination of tea ceremony taste and an open venue amenable to full enjoyment of food and drink make for a supremely tasteful and elegant spatial composition.

松琴亭・一の間の床の間。はなだ色の藍染紙と奉書を市松に張った斬新な意匠。
奥に茶室が見える。ひさご形の下地窓は、背面にある点前座の風炉先窓となる

The tokonoma in the Shokintei *ichi-no-ma* is lined with an innovative checkered pattern of high-quality *hosho* paper and light-indigo (*hanadairo*) paper. The tea room can be seen at the back (left). On the opposite side of the gourd-shaped *shitajimado* in the left alcove is the hearth before the host's seat in the tea room.

五月の中旬。中島から見る月波楼。楼の右手前に住吉の松があり、浮石とともに遠近感をつくる。屋根は柿葺の入母屋風とし、わずかにむくりをつけ、軽やかで瀟洒である

The Gepparo, seen from Nakajima Islet in the pond in mid-May. The famed Sumiyoshi pine spreads its branches before the pavilion, with the rocks in the pond heightening the depth perspective of the scene. The thin wood shingled hip-and-gable-style roof features a slightly humped contour that gives it a light and stylish look.

月波楼の内部。四隅からの隅梁と白竹の垂木で化粧屋根裏を支え、開放的で軽快なつくり。月波楼の名は白楽天の詩から取られ、満月が池に映ずる月影を楽しむための茶亭といわれる

Interior of the Gepparo. The light and open feel of the room is the result of a structure supported by beams rising from the four corners combined with pale-colored bamboo rafters. Gepparo ("Moon Waves Pavilion") is said to have been built to enjoy the reflection of the full moon on the pond; its name is associated with a poem by the Tang-dynasty poet Bai Juyi.

東に向き、満月を楽しむための竹簀子縁。奥には、亀の尾の刈込の向こうに紅葉山が見える。散り紅葉の唐紙が張られ、秋の茶屋としての風情が演出されている

Facing east is the bamboo veranda built for enjoying the full moon. Beyond the shrubbery is the hillock known for its maple leaves called Momijiyama. The *fusuma* (left) are decorated with paper printed with maple leaves in autumn, highlighting the mood of a cottage in the autumn.

十三夜の月が松琴亭の上に昇る。月波楼の縁から眺める　　The near full moon rises over the Shokintei tea house, as seen from the veranda of the Gepparo.

孤篷庵 忘筌

重要文化財
建立年代　18世紀
所在地　　京都府京都市北区

Kohoan Temple Bosen Tea Room

Important Cultural Property
Completed: 18th century
Location: Kita ward, Kyoto, Kyoto prefecture

時代背景

　孤篷庵は大徳寺の塔頭で、1612（慶長17）年、小堀遠州（1579–1647）が自らの菩提所として建立した。当初は大徳寺塔頭・龍光院内にあったが、その後、現在地に移り、1643（寛永20）年には方丈、書院などが完成し、伽藍が整えられた。忘筌の間は、方丈内の北西角につくられた書院風の茶室で、遠州最晩年の作となる。孤篷庵は1793（寛政5）年に火災に遭い、主要建物を焼失したが、松江藩主・松平不昧（1751–1818）や近衛家の援助を得て再興された。方丈（重文）は大徳寺山内雲林院の客殿を1797（寛政9）年に移築したもので、忘筌については遠州時代の起こし絵にもとづき、このときに焼失前の状態に再建された。

　遠州は近江出身の武将で、父の時代より豊臣家、のちに徳川家に仕え、また、古田織部を師に茶の湯の道をきわめた茶人であった。早くから建築造園に才を発揮し、徳川家康の伏見城を皮切りに、城、禁裏や女御御所などの作事奉行として武家・公家の両方から重用された。また、徳川将軍家の茶道師範を勤め、武家全盛の時代にあって、身分社会から求められる茶の湯の格式化に対応し、利休以来の草庵における侘茶のかたちと、武家にふさわしい書院の茶のあり方とを一体化した。自らのために作意した忘筌は、その探求の到達点といわれる茶室である。

特徴と見どころ

　美しい西日を浴びつつ、琵琶湖に浮かぶ小舟に見立てたかのようなこの茶室には、近江に生まれた遠州の望郷の思いや原風景、光の体験が投影されているのかもしれない。庭と空間を不可分のものとして構成し、導かれた繊細な光の表現。その卓抜した構成は、今も新鮮さを失わない。

　忘筌は西に向いており、遠州は西日を着想の源泉に、この空間を構想した。それは独特の縁先に凝縮されている。落縁先に中敷居を入れ、上部のみに明り障子を立てて下は吹放す。西からの強い直射光は上方の障子で受けとめ、光を和らげてから室内に導いている。胡粉の砂摺りで天井を白くし、光を受けて、座敷は明るく瀟洒な雰囲気となる。夕方のひととき、落縁先の手水鉢「露結」の水面に反射した光が白い天井に映りこみ、丸い鏡が動くようにしてきらきらと輝く。一方、点前座の脇に開けた明り障子の外は坪庭になっていて、点前座を朝の光で照らす。

　12畳敷きに張付壁の1間床を備え、ヒノキの角柱に内法長押をめぐらせた書院風の座敷が忘筌の基本のつくりとなる。ここが茶室であることをさりげなく示すのは、床脇の明り障子を入れた地窓と、その脇の方立柱のあたりに漂う和らいだ風情である。この方立柱のみ丸みをつけたクリ材を使い、草庵風の点前座の構えがつくられている。

　点前畳は床の間と並べて配されており、これは遠州が好んだ構えで、座敷のなかで亭主が座る場所がいちばんの席となる。そこからは吹放した障子の下、内露地を凝縮したかのような手水鉢と寄せ灯籠の景が絶妙な遠近感をもって目に入ってくる。だが、その奥に広がる「八景の庭」まで見通せるかといえばそうではなく、明り障子と灯籠うしろの生垣でゆるやかに遮られたかたちで、庭の光と背後の広がりの気配だけが感じられる構成になっている。

　この座敷には、じつに五通りもの動線が組みこまれている。亭主と客の動線は交差せず、両者は座敷にて対面することになる。しかも、どの入口からも、そこを開けた瞬間にはっとするような眺めや奥行きがつくられている。孤篷庵の建物全体のなかで見ると、縁伝いに長い動線がつくられていて、忘筌はその中軸のようなかたちで組みこまれており、それは茶室でありながら、閉じられた一室ではないという側面も持っている。特筆すべきは、客の席入りに二通りあることで、一つは、方丈の西側に沿って飛石伝いに庭から忘筌の縁を上がって入る方法、もう一つは、忘筌の南につながる座敷の広縁から縁伝いに入る方法である。前者は忘筌の中敷居を潜るかたちになることから、「舟入り」によくたとえられる。飛石伝いの席入りは草庵の露地に見立てたアプローチ、縁伝いの席入りは書院の茶のアプローチとなり、おもむきの異なる二つのかたちがここに組み立てられている。

Historical Background

Kobori Enshu (1579–1647) built Kohoan, a subtemple of Kyoto's Daitokuji, in 1612 as his own family temple. Kohoan was originally located on the grounds of Ryokoin, another Daitokuji subtemple; three decades later it was moved to where it now stands and in 1643, the *hojo* abbot's quarters and *shoin* reception hall were completed. Enshu had the *shoin*-style Bosen tea room attached to the northwestern corner of the *hojo* in his closing years. Kohoan suffered a fire in 1793 and its major buildings burned down including the *hojo*. The compound was restored with the assistance of the Matsue domain lord Matsudaira Fumai (1751–1818) and the Konoe Family. In 1797 the guest hall (*kyakuden*) of Unrinin, another Daitokuji subtemple, was moved to Kohoan to become the new *hojo*. At that time the Bosen tea room was rebuilt in its pre-fire, original form based on folding paper models (*okoshi-e*) made in Enshu's time.

Born in Omi province, Enshu was a leading warrior general who first served the Toyotomi family and later the Tokugawa shogunate. He was also a noted tea master who had trained under Furuta Oribe (1543–1615). From early on he exhibited talent in architecture and landscape gardening and was esteemed by both warriors and court nobles as the shogunal *sakuji bugyo* (construction magistrate). He took charge of rebuilding the Fushimi castle for Tokugawa Ieyasu as well as other castles, the emperor's palace, and high-ranking court ladies' residences. He served as a tea ceremony teacher for the Tokugawa shoguns and developed the formalities of tea ceremony as demanded by a class-based society in the golden age of samurai culture. He sought to integrate Rikyu's *wabi* taste in tea ceremony in the "thatched hut" (*soan*) style with a *shoin*-style of tea suitable for the warrior class. The Bosen tea room intended for his own use is said to represent the height of his pursuit of that ideal.

Characteristics and Highlights

This tea room, built as if it were a boat floating on a lake in the glow of the western sun, may have been the projection of Enshu's memories and nostalgia for the countryside where he grew up near Lake Biwa in Omi province. Featuring finely tuned expressions of light and shadow, the designs of the building and garden are inextricably entwined. Even now, the building's superb layout retains its impressive freshness.

The Bosen tea room faces west, as the origin of Enshu's design is oriented to western sunlight, and encapsulated in the distinctive treatment of the veranda. A raised sill (*nakajikii*) has been installed midway between the posts on the edge of the outer veranda (one step lower than the inner veranda) with translucent shoji panels in the upper part and the lower part entirely open. The strong light of the western sun shines through the garden and is softened by the shoji panels before entering the room. The ceiling boards, painted with white *gofun* pigment, reflect the light, giving the room a bright and elegant atmosphere. For a time in the evening, a white circle of light reflected off the water brimming in the "Roketsu" ("Dew Forming") washbasin beside the outer veranda, shimmers brightly on the ceiling. In the morning, light from the *tsuboniwa* "pocket" garden at the back of the tea room filters through the translucent shoji to light up the host's seat.

The basic layout of the Bosen tea room is a twelve-mat room. The one-mat tokonoma has a *fusuma*-like wall (*haritsuke-kabe*). The room is in the *shoin* style, with non-penetrating tie beams between squared cypress posts. The hint that this is a tea room is the translucent shoji in the side window at the host's seat and the tranquil atmosphere around the *hodatebashira* beside the window. This post only is of chestnut wood in a rounded shape, hinting of the conventions of the *soan*-style host's seat.

The host's seat is aligned with the tokonoma, an arrangement preferred by Enshu that gives it precedence in the room. From there, he would have been able to savor the depth of perspective achieved by the water basin close to the veranda and the *yosedoro* stone lantern further out, as seen through the open space under the shoji panels. The view of the "Garden of the Eight Views" beyond would not have been seen, being gently separated by the shoji panels and the hedge behind the lantern in a composition that only hints of the light and open space of the wider garden.

This tea room has no fewer than five lines of access. The lines of movement of the host and guests do not mingle; the host and guests only face each other within the room. But from any of the five entrances, the view upon entering has been contrived for depth and scenic beauty. Looking at the layout of the Kohoan building as a whole, we can see the long lines of movement along the verandas with the Bosen tea room incorporated into its core. While it is a tea room, it is not just one enclosed room. There are two paths along which guests would enter, one following along the west side of the *hojo* following a line of stepping stones before stepping up onto the outer veranda, and the other passing along the inner veranda from the room on the south side of Bosen. In the case of the former, the guests would enter the room passing under the *nakajikii,* which is sometimes likened to "getting on the boat." The route via the stepping stones is a *mitate* likeness of the approach to a *soan*-style tea garden, while the entrance via the inner veranda is the *shoin*-style approach. So the building incorporates two different styles into its setting.

玄関。方丈の南東隅に取りつき、縁から上がる。貴賓のアプローチとして格式を重んじ、妻側には唐破風をつけ、平天井を張り、床には平瓦を敷く

The main entrance of the temple is at the southeast corner of the *hojo*, via the veranda. To enhance the formality of the approach for high-ranking guests, the gable is given an undulating bargeboard (*karahafu*) and a flat ceiling, and the entrance floor is paved with flat tile.

玄関を南側から見る。門戸から方丈の縁まで6mほどの短い距離のなかにも景をつくりだす

View from the south side of the entrance approach. Even in the short 6-meter distance from the gate to the *hojo* veranda, the scenery is carefully composed.

忘筌の奥に広がる八景の庭。緑のニュアンスを重ねて庭の奥行きがつくられている。水の流れに見立てた土と苔や木々との滑らかな連なりは、まさに汀の景を想起させる。松には丁寧に手が入れられており、初々しい芽吹きの姿を見せる

The "Garden of Eight Views" opens out beyond the Bosen tea room. Nuanced layers of greenery create a sense of depth. The earth laid as substitute for water and the smooth overlapping of moss, shrubbery, and trees faithfully evokes a waterside scene. Glowing with tender loving care, the pines are vigorous with the new growth of spring.

庇の下、一直線に打たれた飛石を伝い、中敷居を潜って忘筌に席入りする、いわゆる舟入りのかたち。中敷居の高さは約140cm (4.6尺)。すだれと障子で西日を遮る

A straight line of stepping stones passes under the eaves, and guests enter the Bosen tea room by passing under the middle sill (*nakajikii*), as if getting on board a boat. The height of the *nakajikii* is 140 centimeters from the ground. The hanging *sudare* blinds and shoji panels screen the glare of the western sun.

点前座からの眺め。巧みな遠近感。那智黒石を敷き、丸みのある川石を一つ添えて生垣で囲い、手水鉢・露結と寄せ灯籠を据えて内露地とする。穏やかに遮りつつ透かし、背後には八景の庭の拡がりが光とともに感じられる

忘筌の間。書院風の端整な座敷に、数寄屋の表現手法を巧みに融合する。胡粉の砂摺り天井は縁側に射しこむ光の照り返しを受けて、部屋全体を穏やかに明るくする

The Bosen tea room is in the simple and elegant *shoin* style skillfully incorporating elements from *sukiya* architecture. The *gofun* pigment painted on the sand-rubbed ceiling boards (*sunazuri tenjo*), was intended to reflect the light entering from the veranda and gently illuminate the room.

1 formal entrance
2 veranda
3 *hojo*
4 Bosen tea room
5 preparation room
6 *tsuboniwa*

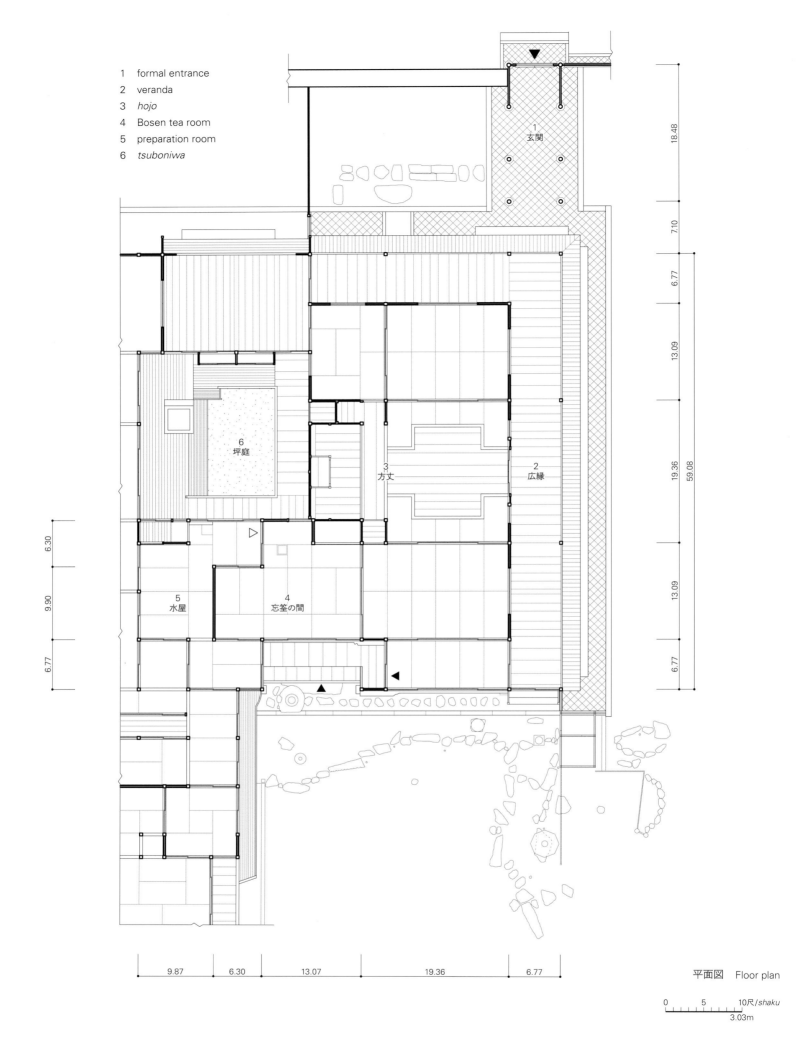

平面図　Floor plan

（右）点前座。床の間の脇壁下半分に井桁を組み、上部を透かし、下部に唐紙を張った瀟洒な構え。点前座左の丸面柱はクリ材で、草庵茶室の中柱を想わせる。床・古備前三角花入、唐物丸壺の茶入に富田金襴の仕覆、唐物ぐり盆・内朱、水指・真塗手桶・余三作、茶碗・彫三島、茶杓・片桐石州作

(Right) Host's seat. The lower half of the side of the tokonoma is fitted with a frame with the upper part open and the lower part covered with an elegant collage of figured papers. The rounded post at the back is a reminder of the *soan*-style *nakabashira*.

卓越した縁の構成。縁伝いに席入りするアプローチ(左)と、庭から中敷居を潜って席入りするアプローチの二通りが想定されている

The superb veranda design allows for two ways of approaching the tea room—along the stepping stones and under the *nakajikii* middle sill or along the inner veranda.

三溪園 聴秋閣

重要文化財
建立年代　17世紀前半
所在地　神奈川県横浜市中区

Sankeien Garden Choshukaku Tea Pavilion

Important Cultural Property
Completed: Early 17th century
Location: Naka ward, Yokohama, Kanagawa prefecture

時代背景

　聴秋閣は、1922（大正11）年、近代の数寄者・原三溪（富太郎・1868 - 1939）が、古建築を蒐集してつくった横浜の庭園・三溪園に移築した数寄屋風の楼閣建築である。この建物の来歴については諸説あるが、古くより佐久間将監真勝（1588 - 1642）の作と伝えられてきた。佐久間将監は江戸城本丸の造営などを指揮した作事奉行で、小堀遠州とは同業の同時代人であり、両者ともに茶人、建築に異才を発揮した点で共通する。聴秋閣の成立については、1623（元和9）年、徳川家光上洛に際して命を受けた将監が、二条城内にこの建物を普請したと伝えられてきた。その後、家光の乳母・春日局に下賜され、江戸の稲葉家（孫の正則邸）に移され、その邸内に三笠閣という名であったという。1881（明治14）年には牛込の二条公爵邸へ、40年後には三溪園へ移され、聴秋閣の名が与えられた。ただし、創建は二条城内ではなく江戸城西の丸の吹上御苑、あるいは同・山里の庭園にあったとする異説もある。いずれにせよ、三溪園へは3回目の移築ということになるだろう。

　聴秋閣は軽やかな望楼を載せた檜皮葺の建物で、内部は書院造を基調としつつも部材寸法が細く、天井高は低く、全体に小振りなつくりとし、庭に開いた茶亭の雰囲気を持つ。寛永期（1624 - 1644）に描かれたといわれる「江戸図屏風」（国立歴史民俗博物館蔵）には、有力大名の下屋敷内庭園の諸所に数寄屋風楼閣が描かれており、庭間に茶屋風の建物を持つことが、公家の別業のみならず、武家の間でも盛んに行われていたことがわかる。それは当主自らが楽しむ建物であるとともに、おそらく将軍の御成などにも備えた施設であり、くつろいだ雰囲気のなかにも、崩しすぎない格式の風が求められたと考えられる。

特徴と見どころ

　まず、動的な屋根の構成である。内部に応じて三つの屋根を重ね合わせており、どこから眺めるかによって外観の印象は変化に富む。正面は北東側で、1階の檜皮葺の屋根に小さな寄棟の望楼を軽快に載せる。それが西にまわって見ると、1階の一部が45度に欠けており、その上に入母屋の妻をつけて屋根に変化を持たせている。これは内部にある斜めの付書院に呼応したものだが、創建当初の庭から眺めたとき、この角度の外観が興趣ある庭の点景となるように計画されたためだろう。これは内部についても同様で、窓の外に何か特別な景色があったからこそ斜めの付書院という着想が導かれたはずで、それを書院の窓から眺めるとともに、部屋の景として取りこむ意図であったろう。

　入口は杢板を四半敷に敷きつめた土間とする。土間はL字形で部屋の中央部分に入りこみ、これを扇の要のようにして、右から上座、付書院、床の間、点前座、相伴席へと広がる珍しい構成となる。これは、舟着き場から舟入りのようにして席に入る趣向であろうか。土間から畳敷きへ上がる蹴上げは22cmで、移行は滑らかである。境には低い勾欄がついており、その高さに合わせるようにして上座の障子の腰も低く抑え、障子を開けたときの外の縁勾欄も低い。斜めの付書院の卓板も低くそろえ、床の間との境にはミニチュアのような禅宗様の擬宝珠勾欄がつく。つまり、西側の書院窓や明り障子を開けると、屋形船の欄干越しに水の景を楽しむような組み立てである。そのように考えると、外からもこの軽快な建築が舟屋形のように見えてくる。当初は水辺に建てられていたのかもしれない。

　点前座は風炉先を壁で仕切り、上座に対して奥まった茶立所風の構えとする。風炉先の壁の下は木瓜形に吹抜き、低い竪格子を入れ、壁の上部寄りに下地窓を開けた珍しい構成である。吹抜けた木瓜形のみやびな意匠と、斜めの付書院との組み合わせは、たがいに個性の強いものでありながら絶妙な関係で釣り合い、この空間を特徴づけている。

　2階は二面に縁勾欄をまわし、肘掛け窓をつくっている。ここからの眺めは、望楼ならではの開放感が堪能できる。庭と一体になった数寄の楼閣として、外からは庭の点景として眺められる対象となり、内からは庭を俯瞰する視点を提供している。

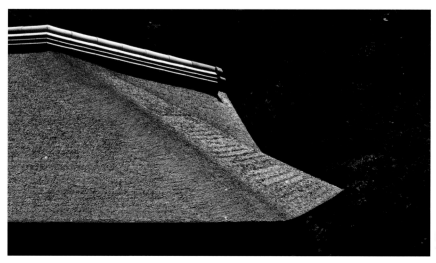

変化に富む屋根の形
The lively forms of the roof

Historical Background

Choshukaku is a *sukiya*-style tea pavilion relocated in 1922 to the Sankeien Garden built by Hara Tomitaro (tea name Sankei; 1868–1939) to bring together a number of old buildings he had collected. Theories vary about the origin of Choshukaku ("listening-to-autumn" pavilion), but its construction has long been attributed to Sakuma Shogen (or Sanekatsu; 1588–1642), the shogunal *sakuji bugyo* (construction magistrate) who led in the construction of the Edo castle donjon and other buildings. A contemporary and also a *sakuji bugyo* was Kobori Enshu. Both were tea masters and also demonstrated extraordinary talent in architecture. Regarding how Choshukaku came into being, records indicate that Shogen was ordered to build the original structure within the compound of Nijo castle in Kyoto in preparation for a visit by third Tokugawa shogun Iemitsu (1604–1651). The pavilion was later granted to Kasuga no Tsubone, Iemitsu's wet nurse, and moved to the premises of the residence of her grandson Inaba Masanori in Edo. There it was called Mikasakaku ("three hat" pavilion). In 1881 it was moved to the residence of the Nijo family in Ushigome, and four decades later to the Sankeien Garden, at which time it was given the name Choshukaku. Other accounts say it was first built at the Fukiage Palace in the *nishi-no-maru* (west compound) of Edo castle or at the Yamazato garden of the *nishi-no-maru*. In any case, the building was relocated three times.

Roofed with cypress bark shingles, the pavilion is topped with a light and chic-looking lookout tower. The interior is basically *shoin-zukuri*, but built with slender members and given a low ceiling, so is overall small in scale. It has the air of a teahouse open to the garden. The *Edo-zu byobu* (Edo Folding Screen Paintings; in the collection of the National Museum of Japanese History), believed to have been produced in the Kan'ei era (1624–1644), shows *sukiya*-style pavilions here and there in the gardens of *shimoyashiki* (suburban) residences of major daimyo in Edo. This indicates that having a teahouse-style building in a garden was quite common not only among court nobles but leading members of the warrior class. It would have been used for enjoyment by the household head but also as a facility to accommodate the visit of the shogun or serve on other important occasions—a place probably required to have both an easy, relaxed atmosphere and some elements of formality.

Characteristics and Highlights

Foremost is the "three-hat" roof composition, made up of different shaped roofs in accordance with the nature of the interior. The impression of the exterior is thus delightfully varied no matter from what the direction one is looking. The front is the northeast side, where the small lookout tower sits on the one-story cypress-bark roof. From the west, we can see that part of the ground floor is cut off at a 45-degree angle and the roof is modified with a small gable in the hipped roof. This roof structure follows the diagonal line of the *shoin* recess of the interior, and must have been designed this way because the appearance with this angle presented an interesting sight as seen from the garden where the building originally stood.

The entrance is in earthen-floor style but is floored with squares of wood in a diagonal checkerboard pattern. The L-shaped entrance protrudes into the center of the room, acting like the pivot, with a rather unusual arrangement of the main guest's seat (*kamiza*) to the right and the *tsukeshoin* at the back right. Straight ahead is the tokonoma on the right and the host's seat on the left, and the accompanying guest (*shoban*) seat is at the left of the entrance. The arrangement may be intended to evoke the feeling of a "dock," from which one enters the teahouse as if boarding a boat, complete with low railings at the sides. The skirting of the shoji in the *kamiza* matches the height of the railing; the railing outside, visible when the shoji is open, is likewise scaled to match. The height of the diagonally set sill board of the *shoin* recess, too, is kept in harmony with the low railings, and a miniature Zenshuyo-style decorative railing (*giboshi koran*) marks the boundary with the tokonoma. In other words, the furnishings are contrived in such a way that, when the *shoin* recess window and shoji panels on the west side are thrown open, the surrounding scenery can be enjoyed as if gazing out over the railings of a *yakatabune* pleasure boat. Once we look at the tea house in this way, the exterior of the building, too—with its lightweight lines—comes to resemble the shape of a boat. Perhaps its original location was, in fact, on the edge of a body of water.

The host's seat has a partition wall behind the hearth and is designed in *chatatedokoro* ("tea-brewing place")-fashion somewhat hidden vis-à-vis the *kamiza* seat. The design of the partition is quite unusual, with lower part cut out in curves of the classic *mokko* shape, a low grill with vertical bars, and in the upper part of the wall a *shitaji*-style window. Two very assertive design elements—the wall cutout with its elegant curves and the *shoin* recess with its striking angle—are combined with perfect balance, giving this space its distinctive character.

The second floor has rail-encircled verandas on both the southeast side and the front or northeast side and windows with sills at elbow height (when seated on the floor). The view from this room can be enjoyed as is only possible from this kind of lookout-tower vantage point. As a *sukiya*-style pavilion designed specifically with the garden in mind, the building from outside presents a beautiful sight in the overall landscape of the garden and provides inside a vantage point for enjoying a bird's-eye view of the garden.

北東側・正面。水の流れを渡って入室する。主室となる上の間、奥まった次の間(左)、望楼と、三つの屋根をかける。擬宝珠のついた低い縁勾欄(右)の内は上座に当たる

Front on the northeast side. Entrance is across a stream via stepping stones. Three roofs cover the *kami-no-ma* main room, the *tsugi-no-ma* inner room (left) and the lookout tower. The *kamiza* guest seat is inside the shoji with the veranda encircled by a railing with decorative *giboshi*-topped posts.

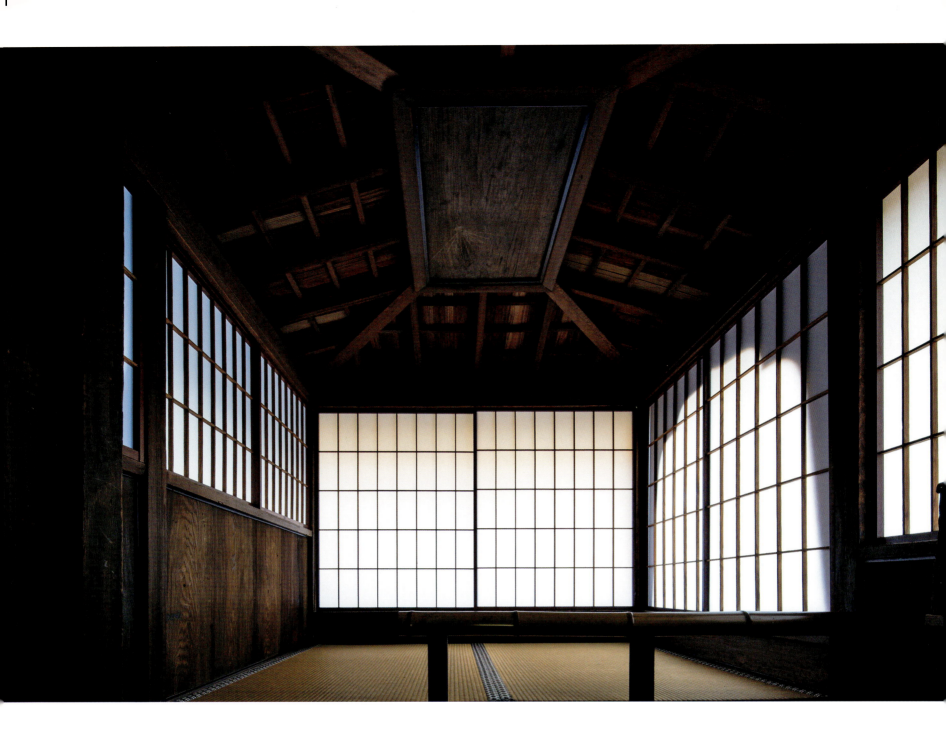

（上）望楼内部。台目畳2畳敷きの座敷。中央を鏡天井とし、周囲を化粧屋根裏とする。上階に火灯窓を開けるのは金閣以来の流れで、楼閣建築の源流が禅宗建築であることを示唆する

(Above) Interior of the lookout tower room. The room is floored with two *daime* (three-quarter sized) tatami. The center of the ceiling has a smooth board (*kagami tenjo*) and surrounding it the ceiling is open with the rafters visible. The bell-shape *katomado* window became the fashion for the upper stories of pavilions from the time of the Kinkaku Pavilion (Rokuonji) onward, suggesting how the roots of this sort of pavilion architecture must lie in Zenshuyo architecture.

（右上）北側からの眺め。障子を開け放つと、緑のなか、舟のように浮かぶ。斜めの付書院上に入母屋の妻を掲げた変化に富む屋根の形。望楼には二方向に勾欄をつける

(Upper right) View from the north side. When the shoji are all opened, the building floats in the greenery like a boat on the water. Note the idiosyncratic rooflines, with a gable raised in the hip roof over the diagonal wall of the *shoin* recess. The lookout tower has railings on two sides.

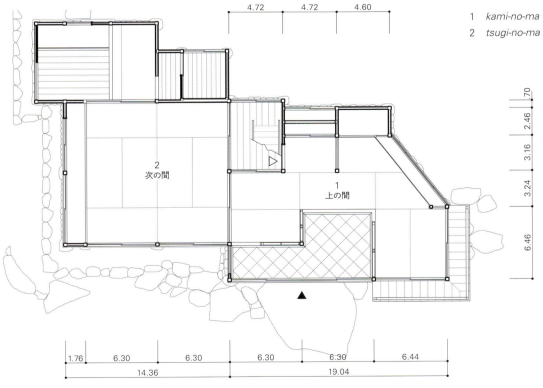

1　kami-no-ma
2　tsugi-no-ma

1階平面図　First floor plan

2階平面図　Second floor plan

土間から上の間を見渡す。長押をまわした書院造ではあるが、木割が細く、全体に低く抑えている。竿縁の天井高204cm(6.75尺)、鴨居下168cm(5.54尺)、小壁高さ23cm(7.5寸)、長押見付け79mm(2.6寸)、鴨居見付け33mm(1.1寸)、廻り縁見付け27mm(9分)

Looking across the kami-no-ma from the entrance level. The shoin-zukuri structure features nageshi (non-penetrating tie beams), but the size of members is slender, and the board-and-batten ceiling is relatively low at 204 centimeters. The railings, skirting of the shoji panels, and height of the tsukeshoin study recess are quite low.

玄関の踏みこみ土間。約1尺(30.3cm)角の板を四半敷に割りつける。板はスギと思われ、腐りにくい根木を使い、大理石の石目のような杢目を出して目違いに張る洒落たデザイン

This is the entrance way, entered with footwear on. Boards about 1 *shaku* (30.3 centimeters) square are embedded in the diagonal-row (*shihanjiki*) pattern. The boards are thought to be cedar, using the wood near the root that is resistant to rot. The pieces are laid in a checkerboard (slanted at a 45-degree angle) created by turning the direction of the grain for a quite stylish effect.

土間の天井は、外に近い方のみ掛込み天井とし、上がり口の方は、内部の竿縁天井と高さを変えずに下がり小壁をつけ、3本吹寄せの意匠とする。奥には一段下がって8畳の次の間がつく

The ceiling over the entrance floor (*doma*) is a slant ceiling near the entrance, and over the area where one steps up into the room the ceiling is board and batten with a shallow box wall decorated inside with three lattice bars. At the back, one step down, is the attached eight-mat *tsugi-no-ma* room.

亭主は階段の裏を潜って席入りする。そのため茶道口は極端に低い。木瓜形の刳り抜きからは斜めの付書院が見える。土間上の天井にめぐらせた下がり壁が、空間に区切りをつけている

The host's entrance is under the staircase, which means that the entrance is quite low. The diagonal line of the *shoin* recess can be seen through the cut-out of the partition wall. The *sagarikabe* walls hanging from the ceiling over the entrance punctuate the space.

西日に染まる上の間。点前座まわりの型破りな構成、大胆な斜めの付書院と床の間。
変則的な平面をすべて破綻なく巧みにまとめあげた手腕は見事

Western sun shines into the *kami-no-ma*. The seamless integration of an unconventional presentation of the host's seat, the tokonoma, and the bold diagonal line of the *shoin* into a harmonious whole hints at the work of a master designer.

江沼神社 長流亭

重要文化財
建立年代　1709年
所在地　　石川県加賀市

Enuma Shrine Choryu-tei Pavilion

Important Cultural Property
Completed: 1709
Location: Kaga, Ishikawa prefecture

時代背景

　江沼神社の長流亭は、福井県との県境に近い加賀市大聖寺に位置する。ここは加賀藩二代藩主・前田利常（1594－1658）が隠居の際、三男・利治（1618－1660）に与えた地で、支藩（大聖寺藩）として10万石を有する城下町であった。錦城山の東麓には藩邸が構えられていたが、1693(元禄6)年に大火で殿舎を失い、1709(宝永6)年に三代藩主・前田利直（1672－1711）が修築した。長流亭はこのときに藩邸の庭園内に建てられた亭である。町の東西を流れる大聖寺川のほとりに立ち、かつては川端御亭の名で呼ばれた。二つの6畳半の座敷、その周囲に畳敷きの入側縁をめぐらせ、柿葺の寄棟屋根を被せた簡潔なつくりである。当時の藩邸や庭園の様子は詳らかではないが、利直はその最晩年に、庭の北西端に立つこの水辺の亭で客とともに川の景を楽しみ、茶の湯でもてなし、ときに川に下りて舟遊びをする拠点としてここを使ったのであろう。若い頃より江戸の暮らしが長かったこの藩主にとって、大聖寺川の水景は郷里の想いと深く結びついたものであったに違いない。

特徴と見どころ

　長流亭は夏の光が美しい亭である。夏は川向うから朝日が上ってきて、水面に反射した光が縁に入射する。縁は四周にめぐらされており、座敷へは縁越しに光を導き入れる仕組みである。上の間と縁との境は明り障子と書院窓とし、障子で濾された間接光で内部は満たされる。座敷は直接外に開かないので、付書院には透かし彫りの欄間を入れたり、その脇壁を木瓜形に割り抜いたりして、光と風を入れ、景を透かしている。軒の出が短いのは、桂離宮の中書院・新御殿のように、もしかしたら当初は入側縁は縁座敷ではなく、板敷きの吹放ちであったからかもしれない。現在の外観も軽快で美しいが、建具や壁の入っていない、より開放的な夏の亭の佇まいを思い描くのである。

Historical Background

Enuma Shrine's Choryu-tei pavilion and garden is located in the Daishoji area of the city of Kaga, near the border with Fukui prefecture. When Maeda Toshitsune (1594–1658), second lord of the Edo period Kaga domain, retired he gave the area to his third son Toshiharu (1618–1660). The Daishoji branch domain was established under the Kaga domain with Toshiharu as its first lord. The domain residence was built at the eastern foot of Mt. Kinjo, but in 1693, a great fire reduced all its buildings to ashes. In 1709, third Daishoji domain lord Maeda Toshinao (1672–1711) rebuilt the residence, and the Choryu-tei pavilion, which was constructed on the grounds of the garden, dates from that time. Located at the edge of the Daishoji river running east and west through the town, Choryu-tei (once called Kawabata Ochin or "Riverside Pavilion"), is a simple structure consisting of two six-and-half-tatami rooms surrounded by a tatami-floored interior veranda (*irigawa-en*), covered by a hipped roof of thin wood shingles. What the domain residence and the gardens originally looked like is not known, but it is most likely that Toshinao used this waterfront pavilion at the northwestern corner of the garden as a hub of activity in his closing years, enjoying the beautiful river scene with his guests, entertaining them with tea ceremony hospitality, and sometimes enjoying the pleasures of boating on the river. For this lord, who had spent many long years living in Edo since he was young, the landscape of his homeland along the Daishoji river must have been a place of particular nostalgia.

Characteristics and Highlights

Choryu-tei is at its best in the strong sunlight of summer. In summer, the sun rises at a point beyond the opposite shore of the river, and light reflected off the river shines into the veranda. The interior veranda runs around all four sides, so light enters the inner chambers through the verandas. The boundary between the *kami-no-ma* ("upper room") and the veranda is demarcated by shoji panels and window in the study recess (*shoin-mado*); light filtered through shoji fills the interior with indirect light. The inner rooms do not open directly on the outside, but light, breeze, and glimpses of the scenery enter through the finely worked transom of the *tsukeshoin*, the decorative *mokko*-shaped windows at the sides of the *tsukeshoin*, and other openings. The eaves are rather short, so it may be that the veranda was originally not interior but an open, board-floored veranda. The appearance of the building from outside is beautifully light, and we can easily imagine it as an airy summer pavilion unencumbered by enclosing shoji or walls.

直線的でシャープな印象の柿葺・寄棟造の屋根。軒の出が72cmと、建物の大きさにしては短い。障子の外の突上げ戸を撥ね上げて全開する

The thin wood shingles and hipped roof project sharp, linear lines. The eaves extend only 72 centimeters, making them rather short for the size of the building. The veranda opens to the outside when the top-hinged shutters outside the shoji are raised.

古くは道路の通る南西側(右)にも川が流れ、三角州に立っていた。
建物の四方に建具を立て、開放的な夏向きの亭

The building once stood on a delta with another stream flowing along the southwest side (right), where a road now runs. With all its shutters raised, the building makes a fine pavilion for summer open to the breezes.

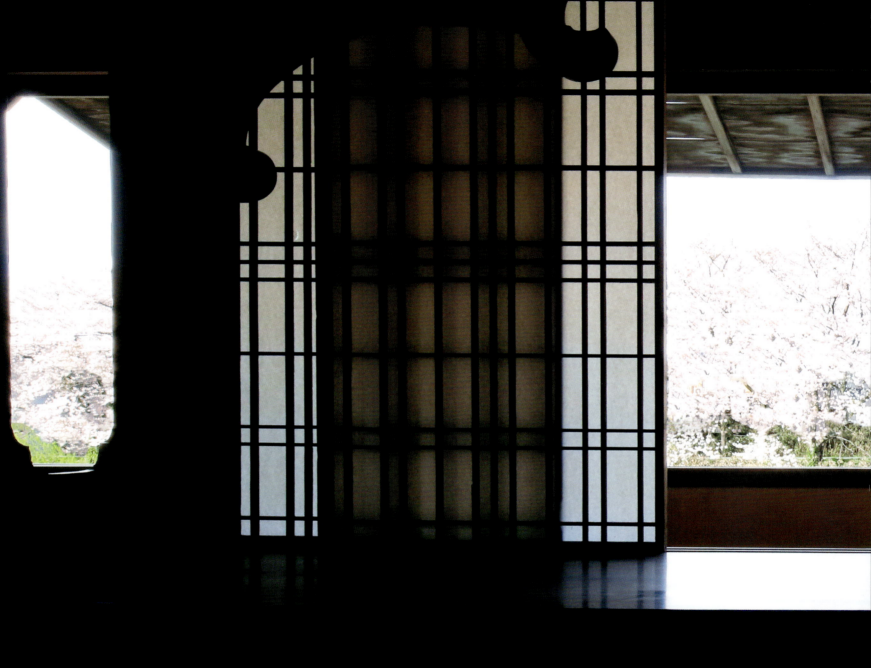

には蕨手のついた火灯窓、脇には木瓜形の透かし窓が入り、外の景を縁取る

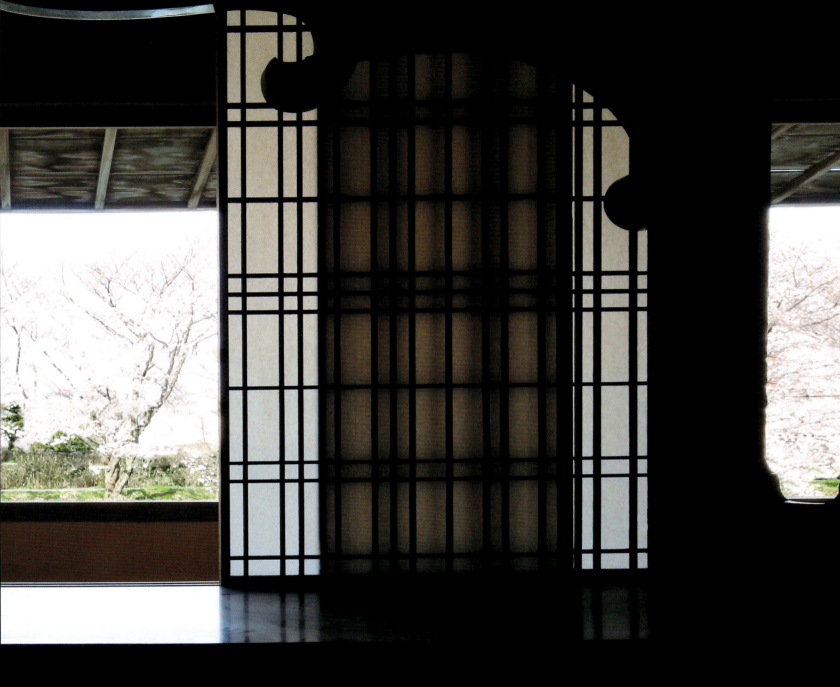

The *katomado* window of the *tsukeshoin* study recess is decorated with fern-frond (*warabite*) curves, and the *mokko*-shaped windows at the sides frame scenes of the landscape beyond.

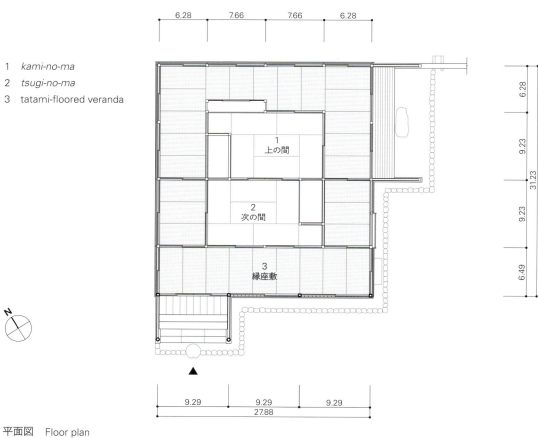

1 kami-no-ma
2 tsugi-no-ma
3 tatami-floored veranda

平面図　Floor plan

（上）玄関の桟唐戸を開けると正面に帯板戸があり、そこから縁を伝って上の間に入室する

(Above) Inside the *sankarado* paneled doors at the entrance is an *obi-ita* (belted panel) door opening on the veranda that leads inside to the *kami-no-ma*.

（右）四周にめぐらされた畳敷きの入側縁から眼下に流れる川の景を楽しむ。夏の朝、爽やかな光と空気に満たされる

(Right) Pleasant views of the river flowing immediately outside unfold beyond the tatami-floored interior veranda encircling the building. On a summer morning, refreshing light and air fills the space.

角屋

重要文化財
建立年代　17世紀−18世紀
所在地　　京都府京都市下京区

Sumiya *Ageya* House

Important Cultural Property
Completed: 17th–18th century
Location: Shimogyo ward, Kyoto, Kyoto prefecture

時代背景

　京都市内の南西、通称・島原こと西新屋敷は、江戸時代に揚屋文化が栄えた場所であった。揚屋とは、芸能や文芸に秀でた太夫を置屋から呼び、歌舞音曲や和歌俳諧などの宴を催すための施設であり、そこは名流の文化人が集った社交場であった。島原は1641(寛永18)年に創設された公許の花街で、全盛期であった元禄期(1688‐1704)には揚屋が20軒以上立ち並び、身分の違いを越えて、町衆、公家、武士との交流の場を築いた。その舞台となったのが、趣向を凝らし、華美を競い、江戸時代の技術と粋を結集して生まれた揚屋建築であり、なかでも角屋はその最高峰として知られる。現在は揚屋としては機能していないが、大規模に整備された質の高い揚屋建築として保存されている唯一の例となる。

　角屋の初代は、島原の前身の六条三筋町から揚屋を営み、二代目の時代には1641(寛永18)年に島原の地に移り、現在の建物の中心部分が建設された。その後、延宝年間(1673‐1681)に敷地を拡張、さらに1787(天明7)年に敷地を拡張したときに大規模な普請が行われ、ほぼ現在の姿に整えられた。延床面積は約792坪(2,618㎡)、主屋は2階建て、表棟(東側)と奥棟(西側)で構成され、広庭や坪庭を備え、3棟の土蔵と2棟の茶室が立つ。敷地東側の通りに面して立つ表棟は細身の出格子で覆われ、長さは31mにおよぶ。格子で閉じられたそのなかには、饗宴にふさわしい華麗な空間が、江戸時代の町人文化の遺香を漂わせつつ今も息づいている。

特徴と見どころ

　角屋には、数寄の遊び心あふれる部屋が大小取り交ぜて数多くある。それぞれの部屋にはテーマがあり、それにちなんでデザインが考案され、空間に物語性が吹きこまれている。そのとき天井のデザインは、たとえば「扇の間」や「檜垣の間」に見られるように、テーマをまとめる要となっている。あるいは、紅や青の鮮やかな壁、みやびな襖絵、凝りに凝った明り障子など、空間を装飾しつつ仕切る装置が、ひとときの夢に遊び興じるための劇場性を高めている。なかでも大広間は饗宴の晴れ舞台となるが、そこは床の間・書院・違棚を備え、対面の場としての書院造の格調を引き出しつつも、形式にとらわれない斬新な表現が追求されて、もてなしの空間へと変換される。ここに江戸時代も後期に入り、書院造と数寄屋造をこなしきった町人文化の成熟と活力を見ることができる。

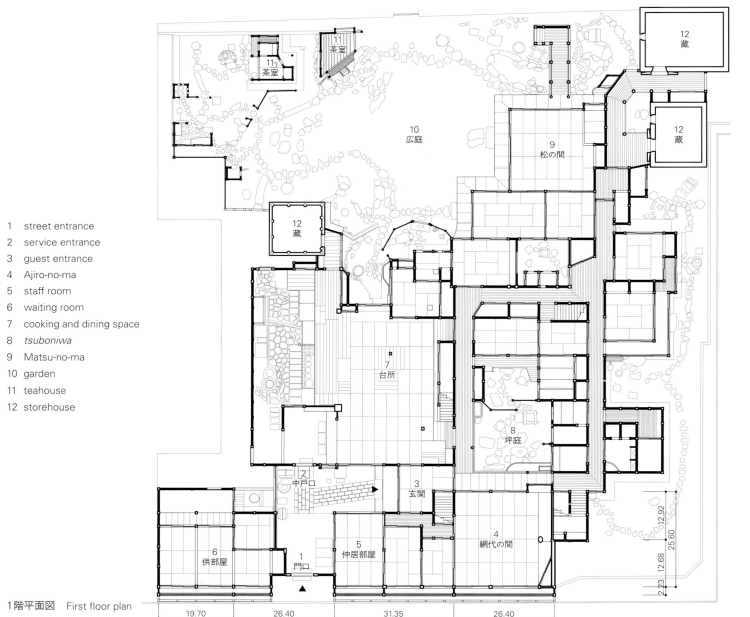

1　street entrance
2　service entrance
3　guest entrance
4　Ajiro-no-ma
5　staff room
6　waiting room
7　cooking and dining space
8　*tsuboniwa*
9　Matsu-no-ma
10　garden
11　teahouse
12　storehouse

1階平面図　First floor plan

Historical Background

The Nishi Shin'yashiki area in the southwestern part of Kyoto, formerly called Shimabara, is known for the flowering of "*ageya* culture" in the Edo period. The *ageya* were a type of banquet hall found in the licensed entertainment district to which high-ranking *tayu* (premiere geisha) were sent from their *okiya* houses to serve clients with dancing, singing, and music as well as *waka* poetry. They served as salons where distinguished men of culture gathered and mingled, transcending the rigid class lines dividing aristocrat, samurai, and townsman at the time. The Shimabara district was established in 1641 and was home to more than 20 *ageya* in its heyday during the Genroku era (1688–1704). The stages upon which this cultural ferment unfolded were *ageya* houses that vied for originality and splendor, drawing on the refined taste and advanced craftsmanship that had developed during the Edo period. The Sumiya House is known as one of the best of such buildings. No longer used as an *ageya*, it is the only extant example of *ageya* architecture of high quality.

The first head of the Sumiya opened an *ageya* in Rokujo Misuji-cho, where the entertainment district was located prior to being moved to Shimabara. The second head moved the business to Shimabara in 1641, where the core part of the building we see today was first constructed. In the latter half of the seventeenth century the facilities were expanded. At the time of the further expansion of the grounds in 1787 the building part was enlarged, creating the complex nearly as we see it today. Built on an area of 2,618 square meters, Sumiya consists of the two-story main building, the front building (east) and back building (west), with a garden, a *tsuboniwa* (small enclosed garden), three storehouses, and two teahouses. The front building faces the street on the east side of the compound and is covered with a latticework facade that extends a full 31 meters. Within this lattice-enclosed compound we find the gorgeous spaces provided by the *ageya* for banquets and entertainment where the discerning taste and vibrant atmosphere of Edo-period urban culture still lingers.

Characteristics and Highlights

The Sumiya is equipped with a fine variety of large and small rooms whose furnishings brim with the subtle elegance cultivated by connoisseurs of *suki*, which was an aesthetic incorporating the playful and unconventional into highly refined tastes. Each room has a theme around which its furnishings are designed, imbuing the space with a kind of narrative. The design of the ceiling serves as the pivot of the theme, as can be seen in the Ogi-no-ma (Room of Fans) and the Higaki-no-ma (Room of Cypress Fences). Brightly colored red or blue walls, elegant *fusuma* panel paintings, shoji panels with frames for their translucent panes of great ingenuity and intricacy, and other devices that served to both decorate and partition the space dramatize the fleeting entertainment provided by *ageya* hospitality. In the large banquet room that would have been the scene of grand parties, for example, the space is transformed for the pursuit of enjoyment not only with the fixtures (tokonoma, *shoin*, staggered shelves, etc.) of *shoin-zukuri* elegance standard in places where people would gather, but supplied with innovative designs unconfined by the criteria of conventional arts. In this building we can observe the maturity and vigor of late Edo-period townsman's culture with its masterful mingling of *shoin* and *sukiya* architectural styles.

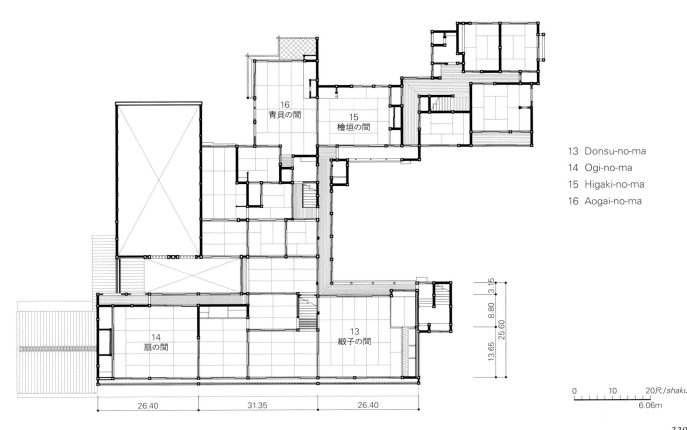

2階平面図　Second floor plan

13 Donsu-no-ma
14 Ogi-no-ma
15 Higaki-no-ma
16 Aogai-no-ma

門口を一歩入ると、もてなしの空間を予感させる華やかな佇まい。ここは中戸口で、台所に通じる内用の玄関となる。客用の玄関は矩折となった敷石の先にある。家紋の入った海老茶色の暖簾の上には柿葺の庇が差しかけられ、その上に端反りの冠木、櫛形窓の構成

An elegant atmosphere one step inside the street entrance hints at the world of entertainment that lies within. Here is the service entrance (with the curtain), called the *nakatoguchi*, which leads to the kitchen. The paving stones extending to the right lead to the main guest entrance. Above the wood shingle-covered roof sheltering the reddish-born *noren* curtain emblazoned with the house crest is a *kabuki* crossbar with tapered ends and two *kushigata* (comb-shaped) windows.

正月飾りをした玄関。斜めにアプローチし、奥行きをつくっている。沓脱石、その先には式台がつき、籠で乗りつけられる。切石畳の両側には那智黒石を敷きつめ、紅色との対比がしっとりとした雰囲気をつくる

Traditional New Year's decorations festoon the main guest entrance. The approach is slightly angled, giving an impression of depth. Above the footwear-removing stone is a *shikidai* platform where the palanquins bearing important guests would be put down. The area around the cut-stone paved approach is filled with Nachi black stones, contrasting with the red of the building to create a quiet, graceful atmosphere.

緞子の間。23畳。大壁に付書院、床、違棚をしつらえる。立湧・吹寄せ・立菱の組子が空間に響く。亀甲紋の棚の地板や千筋紋の落し掛けには、かつて朱漆が塗りこまれていた

The Donsu-no-ma (Room of Brocades) is 23 mats in size with a *tsukeshoin*, a tokonoma and staggered shelves set against the long wall. The patterns of shoji mullions set in *tatewaku* (rising steam) waves, *fukiyose* ("scattered by the wind"), and *tatebishi* (diamond) designs echo through the room. The tortoise-shell-motif-inlaid shelf and the *otoshigake* lintel with the creased ("thousand-lined") pattern were formerly finished with red lacquer.

檜垣の間。吹寄せの横桟に縦の波線が交わる優美な明り障子は、見飽きることのない抽象画のようである。波桟は幅広板からの刳り出し。自由な発想が、障子の桟一つにも吹きこまれている。それは角屋というもてなしの舞台があるからこそ成立するデザインである

The Higaki-no-ma (Room of Cypress Fences). The "scattered" (*fukiyose*) lines of the horizontal mullions combined with wavy-lined verticals give the elegant shoji partition the ceaselessly interesting quality of an abstract painting. The wavy verticals are strong, having been carved to that shape from a broad piece of wood. One can feel the lively, free-ranging imagination of the craftsmen even in the crosspieces of the shoji panels, and these are designs that found their element precisely because they were made for an elegant banquet house like Sumiya.

青貝の間の明り障子。扇形や団扇形の大胆な窓を配した遊び心あふれる意匠、その下には松皮菱文の繊細な組子が入る。角屋の障子はどれも美しく、部屋ごとに組子に変化をつけ、個性をつくる。ここにも粋の追求がある

The shoji of the Aogai-no-ma (Room of Mother-of-Pearl) parade bold folding-fan-shaped, round-fan-shaped, and other delightful patterns in their upper parts with panels of finely set pine-bark-diamond (*matsukawabishi*) mullions in their lower parts. The Sumiya's shoji are all beautiful explorations of the *iki* aesthetic of the chic and stylish, with unique and original designs for each different room.

檜垣の間。天井、欄間、障子の腰を檜垣のモチーフで統一する。洒落た天井はイチイ（アララギ）材。柱は2本とも個性の強い天然の絞り丸太で、これ以上ありえないほど部屋の雰囲気に合った材の選択である

The Higaki-no-ma (Room of Cypress Fences) ceiling, transoms, and shoji panels all repeat the braided-net-like fence motif. The chic ceiling is made of yew (*ichii* or *araragi*). The two posts at the front of the room are well-polished *shibori-maruta* featuring natural undulations of the wood that could not have been chosen more suitably to fit the atmosphere of the room.

扇の間。21畳敷き。天井には、客であった一流の絵師や歌人が筆をふるった
扇がリズミカルに貼られ、当時の隆盛ぶりを物語る。小壁には群青を入れた
浅葱土を塗り、青が鮮やか。襖を開くと浄瑠璃の高座が現れる

The Ogi-no-ma (Room of Fans) is 21 mats in size. Fan shapes, painted by the top-class painters and poets who were guests of the Sumiya, are pasted in a rollicking pattern over the entire ceiling, hinting at the lively atmosphere of the *ageya*'s heyday. The short wall above the lintels, plastered with *asagi-tsuchi* (blue colored clay) mixed with ultramarine pigment, makes a striking sight. The *fusuma* open to reveal a stage for seating *joruri* singers.

旧閑谷学校

特別史跡
国宝・重要文化財
建立年代　17世紀後半−18世紀初頭
所在地　　岡山県備前市

Former Shizutani School

Special Historic Site
National Treasure; Important Cultural Property
Completed: Late 17th–early 18th century
Location: Bizen, Okayama prefecture

石塀。1701年に完成。全長765mにおよび、校地と外とを画する　　The stone wall encircling the school grounds, completed in 1701; runs for 765 meters.

時代背景

　江戸時代、徳川政権により政情が安定すると、教育への関心が高まり、藩校（藩士子弟のための学校）をはじめ、郷校（庶民子弟のための学校）、私塾や寺子屋など、さまざまな種類・規模の学問所が各地で開かれた。教育は支配階層である武家のみならず、商家、農家の子弟の間にも広がりを見せ、社会の発展の原動力となった。なかでも旧閑谷学校は、好学の大名として名高い備前岡山藩主・池田光政（1609－1682）が創立したもので、藩営による庶民教育の草分けといわれる。

　岡山城から北東におよそ30km、旧閑谷学校は標高200mほどの丘陵に囲まれた小盆地に立つ。学校の創始は、1666（寛文6）年、光政が父と祖父の改葬地を選定するにあたり、側近の津田永忠（1640－1707）の案内でこの地を視察したことに始まる。光政は「山水清閑、宜しく読書講学すべき地」とこの地を称賛し、墓地ではなく、学問所の建設を永忠に命じた。

　閑谷学校の教育は、光政が奨励した儒学を柱とした。1670（寛文10）年には仮学舎が建てられ、その後、講堂、孔子を祀る聖堂が建造され、現在の配置や建物の基礎がつくられた。1682（天和2）年に光政は逝去するが、臨終の際に永忠を呼び、この学校を永久に存続させるように、と遺言したことから、永忠の采配のもとでさらなる施設の拡充が図られた。1684（貞享元）年には新聖堂（重文）、1686（貞享3）年には光政の霊を祀る「芳烈祠」（重文・明治8年に閑谷神社と改称）が建設され、1701（元禄14）年には、備前焼瓦を葺いた講堂（国宝）と、校地を区切る石塀（重文）が完成した。創建当初（1673年）の講堂は茅葺で、その後、瓦葺に改築（1677年）されたが、永忠は1684年（貞享元）年頃、学校の近隣に窯を築造して備前焼瓦の生産を開始し、講堂をはじめとする東側の建物群を備前焼瓦に葺きかえて屋根を強化した。

　丘の南斜面を活かした校地の区画は東西に長く、東側には聖廟をはじめとする備前焼本瓦葺の儀礼的な建物群、西側には、防火目的で土盛りされた火除山を挟んで、常時学習し、生活する茅葺の学房学舎が配置されていた。1847（弘化4）年、学房より出火し、西側の建物の多くを焼失したが、東側は火除山を築いた消防計画が功を奏して延焼を免れ、当初の景観をそのままに伝えている。

特徴と見どころ

　創設以来350年近くを経た今も、ここは学びの聖地と呼ぶのにふさわしい場所である。初代藩主が掲げた庶民階層にも広く教育を施す理想、さらに、それを永久に存続させようとした信念。その精神性と気概を、静かな威厳を湛えた建築を通して知ることができる。

　当地の建築の基本方針は、恒久性への希求であろう。まず、それを象徴するのが、校地を一周する石塀である。石を切りこみはぎ式と呼ばれる眠り目地できっちりと積み上げ、上端はかまぼこ形に嵌めこんで仕上げており、備前焼の屋根とともに閑谷学校の独特の景観を形づくっている。これは、草木の根が石積のなかではびこらないようにする対策であろう。この塀のなかには、泥を洗い落とした同じ石質の割栗石が詰められており、土気の侵入を防いでいるという。だから、わざわざこのようなかたちの切石積としたのである。しかも、手間暇のかかるビシャン叩き仕上げを765m。この石塀だけを見ても、建設の指揮を執った津田永忠の並外れた情熱と気骨が感じられる。

　建物に関しても、素材や技術が長期的視野に立って定められている。備前焼の屋根は強く、美しい。講堂・聖廟・閑谷神社の屋根は、垂木の上に野地板などの下地板を三重に張り重ね、留土を使用せずに瓦を葺き、さらに瓦座に備前焼の細い排水管を入れて雨漏りに備えた入念なつくりという。[*15] いうまでもなく、講堂内の拭漆仕上げも、美しさとともに材の保護を兼ねたものである。

　講堂に隣接する小斎（1677年・重文）は、藩主が生徒の学習の様子を見学したときに使われた座所である。ここで光政は、講堂から聞こえてくる生徒の声に耳を傾けたのであろうか。藩主が抱いたこの学び舎への深い慈愛を思わせる建物で、無駄なディテールを省き、簡潔ながらもプロポーションの美しい数寄屋造となっている。

Historical Background

With political stability established under the rule of the Tokugawa shogunate in the first half of the seventeenth century, interest in education swelled and many schools of different types and sizes appeared around the country—*hanko* (domain schools for samurai children), *kyoko* (public schools for commoners' children), *shijuku* (private academies), *terakoya* (small popular schools). The schooling provided education not only to the children of the ruling samurai class but also of merchants and farmers, and became a driving force for development in society. The former Shizutani School was a pioneer in domain-supported education of commoners, a project to which founder Ikeda Mitsumasa (1609–1682), first lord of the Okayama domain, was personally devoted.

Located some 30 kilometers northeast of Okayama castle, the school lies in a small basin surrounded by low hills. Its curriculum centered on Confucian learning, which Mitsumasa particularly encouraged. The temporary school building put up in 1670 and the lecture hall and temple of Confucius later added formed the basis of the layout and buildings we see today. At his deathbed in 1682, Mitsumasa summoned his aide Tsuda Nagatada (1640–1707) and ordered him to assure that the school would continue to exist far into the future. Under Tsuda's leadership the school's facilities were further expanded, with a new Confucian temple (Important Cultural Property) built in 1684 and the Horetsushi, a shrine dedicated to Mitsumasa (Important Cultural Property; renamed Shizutani Shrine in 1875) completed in 1686. In 1701 the lecture hall roofed with Bizen-ware tiles (National Treasure) and the stone wall (Important Cultural Property) demarcating the grounds of the school were completed. The lecture hall originally had a thatched roof, later replaced with tile, but after Tsuda built a Bizen tile-making kiln near the school around 1684, the roofing of the buildings on the eastern side of the grounds was changed to Bizen-ware tiling.

The school grounds stretch from east to west, with the Bizen-ware-roofed ceremonial buildings on the eastern side, and the thatch-roofed buildings where the students studied and lived on the western side. The eastern and western sides were separated by a mound—called Hiyoke-yama ("Fire Protection Hill") to prevent fire from spreading. In 1847 a fire broke out in a school building and destroyed most of the western-side buildings. Thanks to the "fire protection" mound, the eastern-side buildings remain to this day virtually intact.

Characteristics and Highlights

Even today, after the passage of 350 years, the former Shizutani School retains its aura of a mecca of learning. The quiet dignity of its architecture bespeaks the spirit and fortitude of an institution dedicated to the ideal of domain-supported education widely open to the common people and the founder's commitment to continuity.

The basic posture of architecture here is the pursuit of durability, and the first symbol of that endeavor is the wall encircling the grounds. Along with the Bizen-ware-roofed buildings behind it, the wall, built with rocks hewn to fit together seamlessly by the *nemuri-meji* (closed seam) technique, and with its top rounded off, is part of the distinctive landscape of the school. The technique was probably adopted so as to prevent weeds and shrubs from taking root between the stones. It is said that the inside of the stones in the wall are packed with fine, carefully washed gravel of the same type of stone in such a way as to keep soil from seeping in. This explains why the wall is shaped the way it is and why it is still in good repair. Moreover, its entire 765 meters is painstakingly finished with bushhammer treatment (*bishan-tataki*). The wall alone is testimony to Tsuda Nagatada's extraordinary dedication and attention to detail in supervising the construction.

Long-term perspective was also clearly decisive in the selection of materials and construction techniques for the buildings. The Bizen-ware-tiled roofs are strong as well as beautiful. A three-layer base of rafters and sheathing supports the roofs of the lecture hall, Confucian temple, and Shizutani shrine. The tiles are applied to the roof without use of clay to hold them in place, and below the tiles slender drain pipes of Bizen ware are meticulously inserted to prevent rain from leaking in. The lacquer-finished floor in the lecture hall interior not only makes a beautiful sight but contributes to the preservation of the flooring.

The Shosai rest house (Important Cultural Property, completed 1677) adjacent to the lecture hall is a facility said to have been used by the domain lord when he would visit to observe the students in their studies. We can imagine Mitsumasa seated here, listening to the voices of the students going through their lessons in the adjacent lecture hall. It is building that evokes the deep love of the first domain lord for this place of learning he had founded. It is a work of beautifully proportioned *sukiya-zukuri* architecture, simple and stripped of all unnecessary details.

山に囲まれた小盆地のなか、丘陵の南面に校地が整備されている。右に聖廟の建築群、中央には公門を前に構えて講堂、小斎、習芸斎、飲室など、国宝・重文の建物群が立ち並ぶ

At the edge of a small basin sheltered by hills at the back, the school grounds stretch along the southern hillside. To the right are the Confucian temple and associated buildings, and in the center and left are the main gate and behind it the lecture hall, the Shosai (Lord's Rest House), the Shugeisai (Learning Arts Hall), and other buildings.

講堂内部。拭漆の床に火灯窓のシルエット。
毎月6回（1と6のつく日）、『論語』などの『四書』の講釈が行われていた

小斎。1677年の建立。藩主が臨学したときの休憩所で、講堂に接続して立つ。簡潔な数寄屋造である。3寸(約9cm)角の細い柱、細い垂木、薄くシャープな軒反りを持つ柿葺の屋根。棟には備前焼瓦を載せる

The Shosai was built in 1677 as a place to accommodate the domain lord when he would visit the school. Built in a very spare *sukiya* style, it has slender posts 9 centimeters square, slender rafters, and a thin-wooden shingled roof with thin, slightly upturned eaves. The ridge is topped with Bizen-ware tiles.

奥より小斎の妻側、付属の浴室、塀を見る。それぞれの屋根の形、薄さ、リズミカルな重なりが魅力。入母屋の妻面は漆喰で塗籠にして火に備えている。この妻の仕上げは小斎に限らず、当地の建築群の特徴となっている

At the back is the gable of the Shosai and in the foreground the bathhouse and enclosing wall. The shapes, slender lines, and rhythmical overlapping of the rooflines are eyecatching. The *nurigome* plastering of the gable ends are a fire-prevention measure. The gable finishing seen here is not unique to the Shosai but a feature of all the school buildings.

閑谷神社の練塀から聖廟を見る。右の建物は儒教の祖・孔子を祀る大成殿、左は拝殿にあたる中庭(ちゅうてい)。備前瓦は高温焼き締めにより、釉薬を塗らなくても水漏れせず堅牢となる。土に鉄分が多く、焼成ムラが独特の質感をつくりだす

Roofs of the Confucian temple compound from the plastered wall (*neribei*) in the Shizutani shrine. The building on the right is the Taiseiden dedicated to Confucius. To the left of it is the Chutei worship building. Bizen tiles are unglazed and fired at extremely high heat, making them hard, strong, and impervious to rain even without being glazed. The clay contains large amounts of iron and the unevenness of the firing gives them a distinctive variation of color and texture.

飲室（重文）。教師と生徒の休憩室。中央には花崗岩を刳り抜いてつくった約1m四方の炉縁が入る。火の用心から薪の使用は禁じられ、炭が使われた。柱の見込みが深く、メリハリのある陰影を大きな白壁につけている

Dining hall and rest lounge for teachers and students. In the center is a 1-meter square fireplace made by chipping out the center of a single block of granite. As a precaution against fire, charcoal was used in place of firewood. The posts protrude quite a bit from the plaster walls, casting an interesting rhythm of shadows.

文庫(重文)。堅牢で耐火に優れた土蔵造。重要な書物を所蔵していた。外壁は白漆喰で塗り固め、上部に炎返しがまわる。漆喰屋根の上に、備前焼瓦を葺いた置屋根を被せる

Important books were kept in this sturdy and fireproof earthen-walled storehouse (*kura*). The walls are mud daubed, and finished with white plaster; they flair outward at the top to turn back any flames that might lick toward the roof. On top is a separately added roof (*okiyane*) covered with strong Bizen-ware tiles.

吉村家住宅

重要文化財
建立年代　主屋：17世紀前半　表門：1798年
所在地　　大阪府羽曳野市

Yoshimura House

Important Cultural Property
Completed: Main Building early 17th century, Front Gate 1798
Location: Habikino, Osaka prefecture

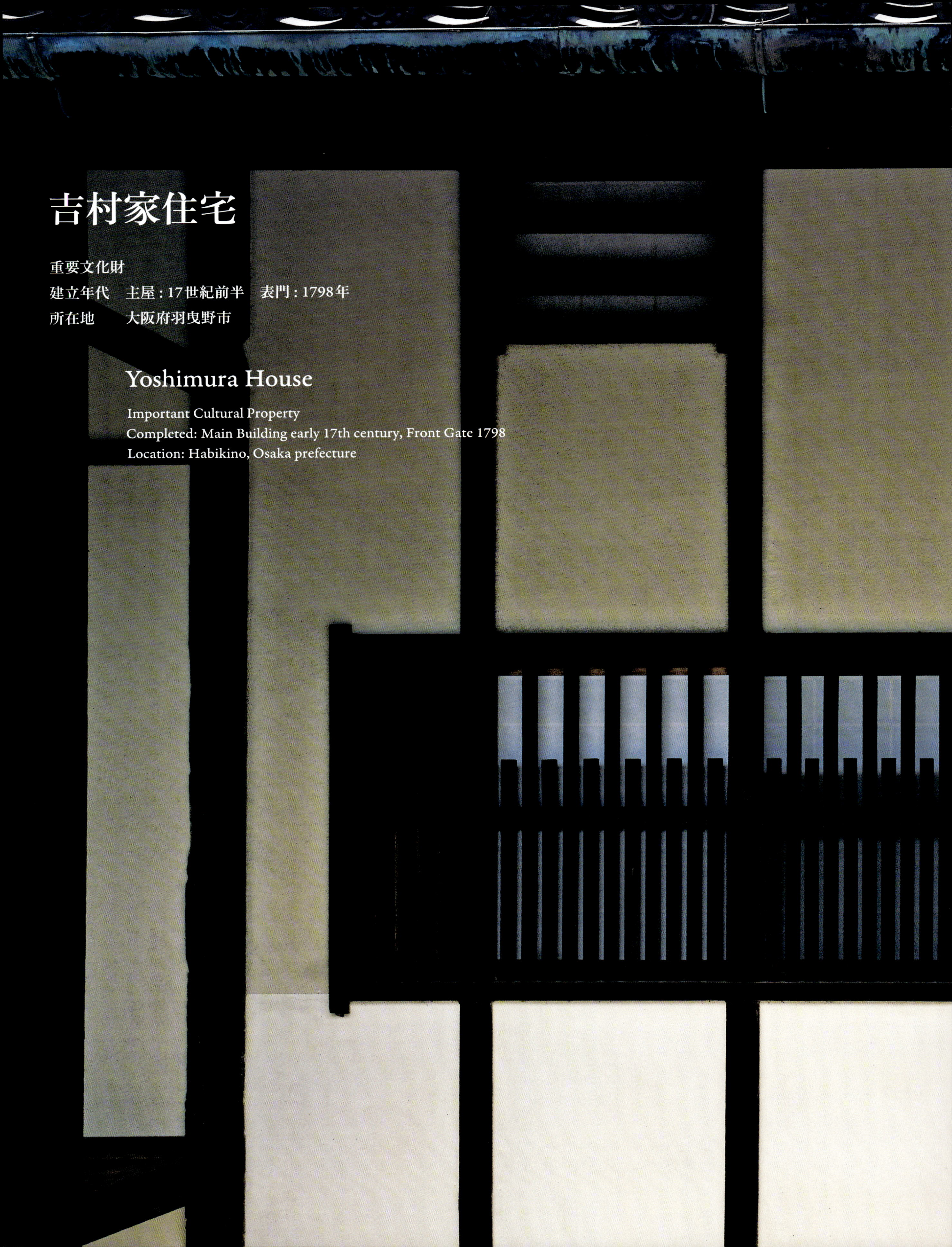

時代背景

　吉村家住宅は、南河内（大阪府南東部）の羽曳野市島泉に位置する豪農の住居である。当家は古くからこの地に住み、1594（文禄3）年には検地帳に「庄屋」と記される地主階級であったことが知られ、また、1729（享保14）年の時点では「大庄屋」として18カ村を管轄していた記録が残る。大坂夏の陣（1615年）の兵火で罹災し、その後まもなく再建されたと伝えられるのが主屋の居室部分であり、西側の客座敷はやや遅れて増築されたと考えられている。

　18世紀末に大きな改造が行われており、このとき屋根は茅葺の入母屋造から現在の大和棟（高塀造）に改められ、また、19世紀初めには土間まわりなどが改造された。1951（昭和26）年には、ほぼ3年をかけて解体修理が行われ、居室とそれに続く客室部が17世紀の平面にほぼ復原されたが、大和棟の屋根などは改造時（18世紀末）のかたちが踏襲されている。

特徴と見どころ

　民家において、外から見たとき、町屋の魅力が格子であるのに対し、農家の魅力は屋根である。自然や田畑の広がる環境にあって、その土地をつかさどる庄屋の住居は、屋根が第一のテーマとなり、家格や力を象徴するものとなる。おもに大和から河内に見られる大和棟こと高塀造は18世紀に入ってから発生し、庄屋以上の階層の農家にしか用いられない屋根形式であった。なかでも、吉村家住宅の大和棟の造形美は随一を誇る。外から見ると、屋根の占める比率が大きく、茅葺屋根部分の高さは壁面とほぼ同じほどある。また、建物の全長（桁行）が約41mもあるため、屋根に迫力がある上、大和棟が変化に富んだ見え方をつくっている。そもそもこの形式は理にも適うもので、茅葺の屋根の下は断熱効果が高いために冬は暖かく、夏は涼しく、火を扱う釜屋を覆う瓦葺の落屋根は防火性が高い。また、高塀造の名の由来となった主屋妻側の漆喰壁は、釜屋煙出しからの火に備えた防火壁となる。

　屋敷構えは高い家格にふさわしく、通りには長屋門を持ち、その西に土蔵と制札場（法令などを民衆に伝える高札所）が連なる。門を入ると正面に主屋が立つが、その間には中庭を挟む。この庭は村の行事や共同作業などに使われた庭で、大庄屋として機能するためになくてはならない緩衝的な空間であっただろう。

　主屋は大きく三つの部分に分けられ、中央に家族の居室部、西側に客室部、東側に釜屋と納屋を備えた土間の内庭がある。全体の面積では、土間部分が全体の約4割を占めている。土間内は差鴨居を用い、牛梁と桁をかけた広々とした空間である。大きな屋根の下、限られた採光により、土間のなかは薄闇のなかに陰影の濃淡がつくられている。ここには現代の住居が喪失した空間の深みがあり、懐かしさとともに安堵感を喚起する場所である。

　家族の居住部分のほかに、別個に式台と玄関の間を設けた客座敷がある。さらにその奥（西側）には、役人などを接待するための付書院を持つ奥座敷や風呂を備えており、庄屋が担った役割ならではの間取りや機能、部屋のつくりが見られる。土間や中庭も含め、ここは村を率いた大庄屋の生活と生産の場であり、村人たちだけでなく、さまざまな階層の人々が交わる場であった。

付書院を備えた応接用の奥座敷
Formal reception room (*okuzashiki*)

Historical Background

A wealthy farmer family's house of the Edo period, the Yoshimura house is located in the Shimaizumi area of Habikino, southeastern Osaka prefecture. The family had lived in the area for centuries, and a 1594 land survey register (*kenchicho*) indicates that it was of the landowning class—recording it as a "shoya" (village headman). Another document of 1729 lists the family as a "great *shoya*" with eighteen villages under its jurisdiction. The family home was destroyed in a fire that occurred at the time of the Tokugawa shogun's summer siege of the Osaka castle in 1615. It was rebuilt soon afterward, old records say, but it was probably the living quarters (the main building) that was rebuilt then, while the guest room (*kyaku zashiki*) is thought to have been added on its west side a little later. Large-scale remodeling was done to the house toward the end of the eighteenth century, and at that time, the roof changed from a thatched hip-and-gable roof to the *yamato-mune* style roof we see today. A thatched gable roof covers the main part (*omoya*) of the dwelling with plastered gable walls (*takahe*), and a tiled roof extends over the kitchen area. In the early nineteenth century, some remodeling was done including the earthen-floored area (*doma*). Starting in 1951, the house underwent a three-year dismantling and repair project. With a few exceptions including the *yamato-mune* roof that was maintained from the eighteenth-century remodel, the living quarters and the attached guest area were restored to nearly their original seventeenth-century forms.

Characteristics and Highlights

The exterior charm of folk architecture may be the latticework in the case of town houses, but for farmhouses, it is above all the roof that makes the most compelling sight. In the rural landscape of woods and fields, it was the roof that was the major theme of the dwelling of a local headman who shouldered responsibility for the local community. It symbolized the status and strength of its occupant. The *yamato-mune* style of roof (also called *takahe-zukuri* after the distinctive gables), found mainly in the area from the Yamato (Nara) basin to the Kawachi area of eastern Osaka, emerged after the beginning of the eighteenth century and was used in farmhouses of only *shoya* or higher status families. The Yoshimura house roof is an outstanding example of the *yamato-mune* beauty of form. Seen from outside, the height of the thatched roof over the main part of the house is about the same as the height of the walls. Also, since the house is a full 41 meters long, the massive roof lends it strength and the *yamato-mune* style variety of form. It is a style that ingeniously accords with practical good sense: a thatch roof more effectively insulates against both winter's cold and summer's heat, making the dwelling more comfortable, while a lower, fire-resistant tile roof covers the kitchen (*kamaya*) where fires are stoked. The plaster-covered wall of the gable in the main roof adjoining the *kamaya*, which gives the *takahe-zukuri* style its name, is also a measure against fire.

The frontage of the Yoshimura compound, as befits a family of high standing, has a *nagayamon* front gate and west of it, along the large earth and plastered wall is the public notice board where various decrees, edicts, and announcements would be posted to inform citizens of what was expected of them. Inside the gate, the main house lies directly ahead across a broad yard. This yard was used for village events and community work projects and was surely a buffer zone indispensable in the performance of the *shoya*'s responsibilities.

The main house is divided into roughly three parts. The center part holds the family living quarters and the western part was used for entertaining or accommodating guests. The eastern end is the *uchiniwa*, the interior earthen-floored work space housing the cookstove (*kamado*) and storeroom (*naya*). The earthen-floored area accounts for about 40 percent of the whole house. The *doma* interior is a vast open space built with penetrating head jambs, purlins, and massive *ushibari* longitudinal beams. Beneath the great roof with few openings to let in exterior light, the *doma* is a dimly lit realm of shifting shadows. This is a sort of space lost in modern dwellings; it inspires a sense of nostalgia as well as comforting shelter.

Separate from the family living quarters are guest rooms with a separate entrance platform (*shikidai*) and entry hall. In addition, further back in the building on the west side is a set of inner reception rooms (*okuzashiki* with a *tsukeshoin*) where the family head would entertain officials from the domain lord and a guest bath. The layout, function and structure of the rooms testify to the role played by a *shoya* household in the community. Together with the earthen-floored area and the outer courtyard, this compound was the scene of life and productivity of a powerful village leader standing at the head of the village. It was no doubt the arena of exchange among people of all walks of life.

（上）長屋門より主屋の釜屋の瓦屋根を見る。門庇の竹の化粧垂木は1、2、3本の吹寄せとする。釜屋のなかは台所で、煙出しがつく。妻は漆喰で固めて防火構造としている

(Above) View from under the *nagayamon* gate toward the roof over the *kamaya* part of the main house. The bamboo rafters are clustered in groups of one, two, and three, giving the open ceiling an attractive look. The cupola covers the flue releasing smoke from the kitchen fires of the *kamaya* below, so the adjacent gable of the main house is covered with plaster to protect against the danger of flying sparks.

（右）主屋の大和棟を見る。勾配違いの瓦屋根が立体感を強調する。茅葺の妻側に本瓦を葺き、妻は白漆喰壁とし、釜屋は一段低い瓦葺の落屋根とする

(Right) View of the *yamato-mune* design of the main roof. The gable end of the thatch roof is clad with several rows of tile. The gable end has a white plaster wall, and the roof of the *kamaya* part of the house is a step lower. The disparity in the angles of the tiled parts of the roof accentuates the sense of three-dimensionality.

長屋門から斜めにアプローチがつき、主屋へといたる。広い中庭は、
大庄屋の暮らしになくてはならない空間であった

The entrance to the house lies at a diagonal from the *nagayamon* gate. The Yoshimura headmen were responsible for several villages so quite a large inner courtyard was needed.

大きな茅葺の下、本瓦葺の長い軒庇が釜屋（右）まで続く。茅葺は、夏は涼しく、冬は暖かい。軒下は柱を塗りこめない真壁造。日本の古民家のなかでも、もっとも美しい柱割りの構成がここにある

Under the massive thatch roof, the *hongawara*-tiled eaves extends all the way along the house to the *kamaya* (right). The thatch roof makes for warmth in winter and cool in summer inside the house. Beneath the eaves we can see the *shinkabe-zukuri*, or plastered wall with the posts left exposed. Among Japanese folk houses, this is one of the most beautiful examples of column spacing to be found.

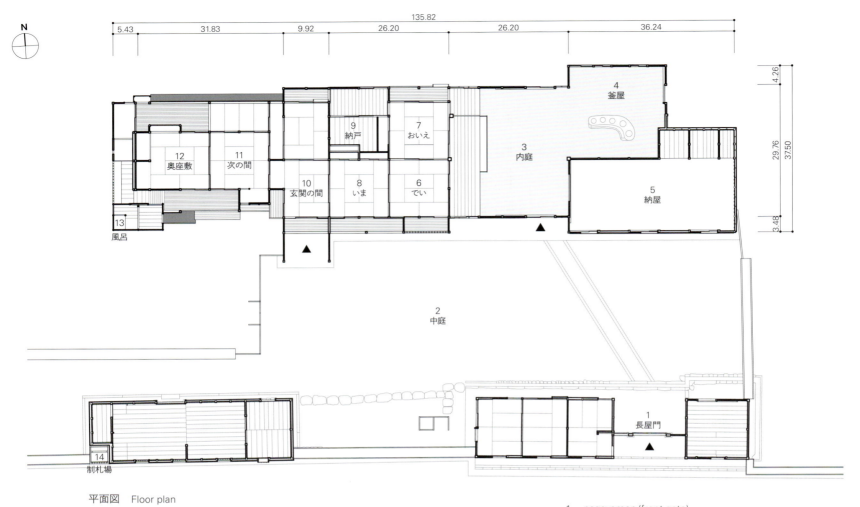

平面図　Floor plan

1 *nagayamon* (front gate)
2 courtyard
3 *doma* (inner court)
4 *kamaya* (kitchen)
5 storeroom
6 front room (*dei*)
7 family room (*oie*)
8 sitting room
9 storeroom
10 entry hall
11 anteroom
12 formal reception room
13 guest bath
14 public notice board

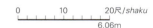

通りから長屋門を見る
Street view, looking toward the thatch-roofed *nagayamon* gate.

(右)土間は約110㎡の大きな空間で、そのなかには黒い漆喰塗のかまどを備えた35㎡ほどの釜屋がある。換気は高い天井の上昇気流を利用し、煙出しから排出する

(Right) In the spacious earthen-floored (*doma*) workspace, about 110 square meters in size, the kitchen equipped with a black-plastered cookstove (*kamado*) occupied about 35 square meters. Smoke from the cookfires is drawn upward and out through the flue in the roof by air currents created by the high ceiling.

巨材によるダイナミックな空間。約8mの牛梁がかかる。
割り竹による簀子天井、左には使用人用の吊部屋がある

Massive beams, including *ushibari* longitudinal beams some eight meters long, orchestrate a dynamic space. Note the slatted ceiling made of split bamboo and at the left the loft that served as sleeping quarters for the servants.

吉島家住宅

重要文化財
建立年代　1907年
所在地　　岐阜県高山市

Yoshijima House

Important Cultural Property
Completed: 1907
Location: Takayama, Gifu prefecture

時代背景

　高山は、飛騨の山懐に抱かれた城下町である。武将・金森長近が1585(天正13)年頃より城を築いて都市の基盤を整備し、1692(元禄5)年以降は幕府の直轄領であった。吉島家は江戸後期より生糸や繭の売買、金融、酒造などを生業として栄えた商家で、四代目・吉島斐之(1837-1915)が現在の吉島家住宅の前身となる建物を新築したのは、1876(明治9)年のことであった。その前年、高山の町は大火に見舞われ、吉島家も土蔵のみを残して類焼したのである。しかし、これは家作制限を受けずに普請する好機でもあった。江戸時代、町人の住居には軒高の制限、材料の制限、前庭の禁止などの規制が課されており、幕府に何度も上納金を献上するほどの富を築いたとしても、町人は望むような普請を許されなかったからである。ヒノキ、マキ、サワラ、ネズ、ヒバは幕府によって「禁令の五木」と指定されてきたが、明治維新による幕府の崩壊でその枷はなくなり、人々は財力に見合うかたちで、規模、材料、意匠を自由に選択できる時代となった。

　当家の建物は、やはり重文指定を受けている明治期の民家・日下部家住宅(1879年竣工)と隣り合って立つ。かつては扶持人町であったという静かな通り沿いに、抑制の効いた両家のファサードが続き、端正な町並を形成している。都市のなかにあって、町屋の美学は格子である。格子は通りへの防御を固めつつ、町並に参画する表の顔をつくる。吉島家は1905(明治38)年にふたたびもらい火をし、正面の「みせ」1階と2階部分、蔵のみを残して焼けたが、1907(明治40)年から翌年にかけて再建された。また、1923年(大正12)年から2年間をかけて、吹抜け部分の一部変更、廊下や水まわり部分などに手を入れている。

特徴と見どころ

　高山の町家は南北に流れる宮川に沿って立つが、吉島家住宅は東に面するファサードの長さが26mであるのに対し、かつて裏手の方は宮川のほとりまで達し、63mの奥行きを持っていた。本来、この住宅は二つの部分——重文指定を受けている東側半分(表側)の本屋部分と、西側半分の蔵部分——から構成されていた。本屋部分は一部2階建てで、吹抜けとなった1階部分は接客部分と居室部分からなる。そのなかで、接客部分は土間と接し、居室部分は庭に接する平面計画である。一方、西側半分(裏手)には本蔵、上手蔵、現存しないが、酒蔵、米蔵、材木蔵、漬物蔵が立ち並んでいた。蔵は土蔵造で、裏庭を挟みながらそれぞれ独立して建てられていたが、さらにその上には大屋根がかかり、いくつかの蔵が一つ屋根の下にまとめられ、その棟高は本屋より高い10mほどもあったという。木造の本屋は、裏側に控えた白漆喰による蔵の集合体と均衡を保つようにしてあったわけで、商売・生活・生産の機能は表と裏の空間が一体となり、十全に満たされるつくりとなっていた。ちなみに材木蔵には、焼失に備えて仮屋1軒分の材木が貯蔵されていたという。

　本屋では、柱、梁、束、差鴨居によって立体的に構築された豪快な吹抜け空間のなか、人が交わる接客空間と、プライベートな生活空間が"同居"する。部屋間にはそれぞれの目的に合った建具を入れ、閉めると固有の領域がつくられる。一方、建具を開けると、全体が等質なシングルスペースのようになる。人の手で障子や格子戸を動かすことにより、空間が伸び縮みし、場面が変わっていく。「建具は小さな建築」とは、七代目現当主の言葉であるが、建具の魅力にあふれたこの空間で生まれ育った人だからこそ、実感できる空間体験であろう。

　この民家は、光が抜群に美しい。南側の高窓から入るやわらかな光は、大きな吹抜け空間全体を明るくし、磨き抜かれた木組みの艶を際立たせる。さらに、前庭、光庭、奥庭を効果的に配してあり、それを取り巻く空間には新鮮な外気を取りこみ、適切な光を与えている。今でも忘れられないのは、光庭に降り注ぐ夕立の光景であり、その激しい雨音である。それを土間に座って眺めていたのであるが、家のなかに大雨が降っている——そんな不思議な感覚であった。この家には、日々の生活を通して、空間との無限の対話があるように感じられる。

並び立つ吉島家住宅(手前)と日下部家住宅
Street view of the Kusakabe House and the Yoshijima House (foreground)

Historical Background

Takayama, the location of the Yoshijima House, is a castle town nestled in the Hida mountains of central Honshu island. The castle built there around 1585 by the local warlord Kanamori Nagachika laid the foundations for development of the town and surrounding domain. From 1692 until the end of the Edo period (1615–1867), the town was placed under the direct control of the Tokugawa shogunate. The Yoshijima were merchants who prospered from around the late Edo period from various businesses, including the buying and selling of silk and silkworm cocoons, money lending, and sake brewing. In 1876, Yoshijima Ayayuki (1837–1915), fourth head of the family, built the new dwelling that was the precursor of the present-day Yoshijima house. The previous year, a great fire had swept the town of Takayama, burning down all the Yoshijima family buildings except their storehouses. It was a good chance to rebuild, since, with the ending of the shogunate in 1868, the many restrictions that had been imposed on house (*minka*) building were no longer in effect. During the Edo period, regulations limited the height of eaves and the quality of materials that could be used, banned front yards, and so forth, and even townsmen who had amassed wealth were not permitted to build a house the way they liked. Townspeople were barred from building with quality woods like cypress (*hinoki*), podocarp (*maki*), cypress (*sawara*), juniper (*nezu*), and conifer (*hiba*). Once those fetters were removed, people could decide the dimensions, materials, and decoration of their dwellings as they wished and according to their financial resources.

The Yoshijima House stands next to another *minka* of the same era, the Kusakabe House (completed in 1879), which is also a nationally designated Important Cultural Property. The restrained facades of the two houses line the quiet street, contributing to a fine townscape. The aesthetic of *machiya* townhouses lies in their latticework facades. The latticework serves not only to protect the house against the activity in the street but also to show the face of the house as a participant in the townscape. In 1905 the Yoshijima House was burned down again, catching fire from a neighboring house, with only the first and second floors facing the street and the storehouses surviving. The house was rebuilt in 1907–1908. Over the two years starting in 1923 partial changes were made to the high, open ceiling space; the corridors and the kitchen, bathroom, and other areas where water is used were renovated.

Characteristics and Highlights

The Yoshijima compound lies along the Miyagawa river, which runs north and south through the city of Takayama. The compound faces east, its front facade running 26 meters along the street, and once extended 63 meters to the banks of the Miyagawa at the back. The compound consisted of two parts, the eastern or front half with the main house (now designated an Important Cultural Property) and the western half was the site of the family storehouses. Part of the main house is two stories. The single-story part, which is open to the roof, includes both public space for receiving customers and private dwelling space, with the public space facing the *doma* earthen-floored area at the entrance and the private space facing the inner courtyard. The layout also shows the storehouses at the back or western side of the compound. The main storehouse (*hongura*) and upper storehouse (*kamitegura*) remain, but the sake brewery (*sakagura*), rice storehouse (*komegura*), lumber storage (*zaimokugura*), and pickle house (*tsukemonogura*) are no longer extant. The storehouses were all independent structures built in the *dozo-zukuri* or orthodox storehouse style with wooden structure frames covered with thick mud walls, and a number of the storehouses were spanned by large roofs, some 10 meters high, even higher than the main house. The main house remaining today was part of a complex of structures built together and in balance with the white plastered storehouses at the back of the compound in a style that unified the inner and outer functions of sales, living, and production into one, highly compact space.

In the main house, the front area features part that is left open for the luxurious exposure of posts, beams, struts, and lintels where the customer meeting area and the private dwelling areas merge. The rooms are divided with *tategu* panels—moveable fixtures made with board, shoji grids covered with paper, lattices, and combinations of all three—as suited to the purpose. When closed, they create realms of space for specific purposes. When the *tategu* are opened or removed, space is united and homogenized. And so it is that space can be made to expand or contract and scenes can be changed with but the light-handed movement of panels or lattice slats. The remark of the current and seventh head of the Yoshijima family, that "*tategu* are themselves architecture on a small scale," surely reflects the experience of space of someone who has grown up in space replete with the marvelous benefits of *tategu*.

One of the outstanding features of this house is the beauty of the light within it. The soft light that enters through the high windows on the south side illuminates the entire space under the open roof, showing off the highly polished structure of posts and beams to exquisite effect. In the front courtyard (*nakaniwa*), light court, and inner courtyard, openings have been made appropriately around them to bring in fresh air and a suitable amount of light. I will never forget one evening in the house, when I was there during an evening shower and heard the roaring sound of rain. I happened to be sitting in the back *doma* when the rain began, and had the curious sensation that the rain was coming down right inside the house. Living in such a house would be like having an endless conversation with space.

土間から見る約8mの吹抜けと部屋の連なり。
鴨居から下はさまざまな建具を立てこんで空間を仕切る

View of eight-meter high open ceiling and succession of adjoining rooms. A variety of types of partitioning is used to divide the space below the lintels.

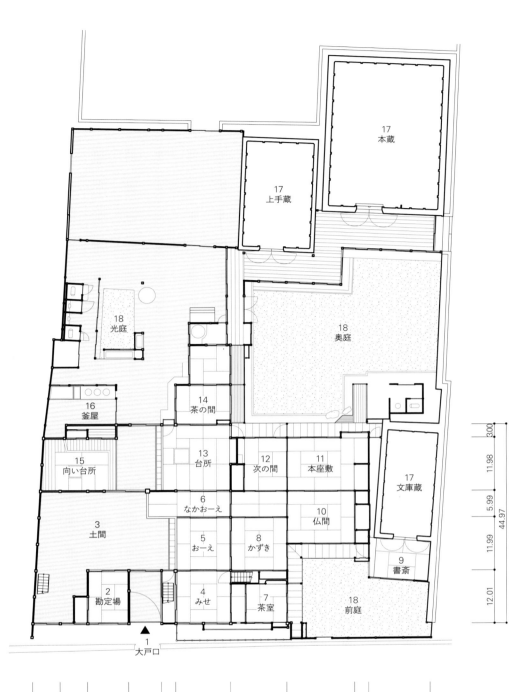

1 entrance
2 accounting office
3 *doma*
4 shop
5 reception room (*oe*)
6 reception room (*nakaoe*)
7 tea room
8 dressing room (*kazuki*)
9 study
10 Buddhist altar room
11 formal reception room
12 anteroom
13 family dining room
14 sitting room (*cha-no-ma*)
15 servants dining room
16 kitchen
17 storehouse
18 courtyard

1階平面図　First floor plan

(右)大黒柱から奥はプライベート空間。そこに南の高窓から直射光が落ちてくる。大黒柱の脇には、今は大坂格子が入るが、かつては格子が入らず、写真のように開放感があった

(Right) View from the entrance *doma*, the centrally located *daikokubashira* post marks the boundary between public and private space in the house. Outside light shines into the room through high windows on the south side.

高山は積雪の多い地域で、梁と束は屋根の重みを均等に下へ伝える。
柱はヒノキ、梁は曲げに強いアカマツを使い、木の特徴を活かす

Takayama is a region of heavy snows. The complex of struts and beams helps distribute the weight of the roof equally to the posts. Utilizing the inherent qualities of timber, the posts are cypress and the beams red pine (*akamatsu*), which resists warping.

土間から入口を見返す。土間は家のなかでも半公共的な空間で、多くの人が出入りし、接客応対をした

View toward the entrance from the earthen-floored area (*doma*). The *doma* is a semi-public space in these houses, where people were constantly coming and going. Visitors were received here.

上階から見る建具の連なり。吊り束で障子を立て、奥への視線をゆるやかに遮る。格子の奥は台所(食事室)・茶の間と続くプライベート空間。左の連子は無双で、格子をぴったりと閉ざすこともできる

The view from the upper floor shows the variety of partitions used in the house. The shoji panel set beneath the hanging strut gently shields the inner parts of the house from view. Beyond the lattice lies the private quarters with the dining room and family sitting room (cha-no-ma). The lattice on the lefthand side is a "muso-renji" lattice with a sliding panel that closes the slats, completely closing off the view.

町屋の表情は格子がつくる。通りに面する東側は、部屋の性質に応じてさまざまな格子で覆われている

Lattices define the face of a *machiya* house. In the case of the Yoshijima House, the east side, which faces the street, has various kinds of lattices differing in accordance with the type of room behind.

主要建造物データ　Data of the Buildings
*本書に掲載する主要建造物のみ記す

円覚寺 舎利殿（国宝）
所在地　　神奈川県鎌倉市山ノ内
建立年代　14世紀–15世紀（室町時代）
規模形式　桁行3間・梁行3間・一重裳階付・入母屋造・柿葺

東福寺 三門・禅堂（国宝・重要文化財）
所在地　　京都府京都市東山区本町
〈三門〉国宝
建立年代　15世紀初頭（室町時代前期）
規模形式　5間3戸2階二重門・入母屋造・本瓦葺・両山廊付・
　　　　　各切妻造・本瓦葺
〈禅堂〉重要文化財
建立年代　15世紀（室町時代前期）
規模形式　桁行7間・梁行4間・一重裳階付・切妻造・本瓦葺

鹿苑寺 金閣
所在地　　京都府京都市北区金閣寺町
建立年代　1398年（室町時代前期）・1955年再建（昭和時代）
規模形式　1・2階：桁行11.7m・梁行8.5m
　　　　　3階：桁行5.5m・梁行5.5m
　　　　　漱清：桁行4.1m・梁行2.2m・三重・宝形造・柿葺

慈照寺 銀閣・東求堂（国宝）
所在地　　京都府京都市左京区銀閣寺町
〈銀閣〉
建立年代　1489年上棟（室町時代後期）
規模形式　東面および西面7.9m・北面6.9m・南面5.9m・
　　　　　二重・宝形造・柿葺
〈東求堂〉
建立年代　1485年（室町時代後期）
規模形式　桁行6.9m・梁行6.9m・一重・入母屋造・檜皮葺

相國寺 鐘楼（京都府指定有形文化財）
所在地　　京都府京都市上京区
建立年代　1843年（江戸時代末期）
規模形式　桁行3間・梁行2間・袴腰付・入母屋造・本瓦葺

龍安寺 方丈庭園（史跡・特別名勝）
所在地　　京都府京都市右京区龍安寺御陵ノ下町
作庭年代　15世紀末–16世紀（室町時代後期）
規模形式　枯山水・南北9.3m・東西23m

園城寺光浄院 客殿（国宝）
所在地　　滋賀県大津市園城寺町
建立年代　1601年（桃山時代）
規模形式　桁行7間・梁行6間・一重・入母屋造・妻入・
　　　　　正面軒唐破風付・柿葺
　　　　　中門：桁行1間・梁行1間・一重・切妻造・柿葺

高台寺 霊屋（重要文化財）
所在地　　京都府京都市東山区下河原通八坂鳥居前下る下河原町
建立年代　16世紀末–17世紀初頭（桃山時代）
規模形式　桁行4間・梁行3間・一重・宝形造・正面向拝1間・
　　　　　唐破風付・檜皮葺

姫路城 天守（国宝）*
所在地　　兵庫県姫路市本町
建立年代　17世紀初頭（桃山時代）
規模形式　大天守：五重6階・地下1階付・本瓦葺
　　　　　東小天守：三重3階・地下1階付・本瓦葺
　　　　　西小天守：三重3階・地下2階付・本瓦葺
　　　　　乾小天守：三重4階・地下1階付・本瓦葺

妙喜庵 待庵（国宝）
所在地　　京都府乙訓郡大山崎町
建立年代　16世紀末（桃山時代）
規模形式　茶室2畳・次の間1畳板畳付・勝手の間より成る・一重・
　　　　　切妻造・柿葺・土庇付

有楽苑 如庵（国宝）
所在地　　愛知県犬山市御門先（名鉄犬山ホテル敷地内）
建立年代　1618年頃（江戸時代初期）
規模形式　茶室2畳半台目・水屋の間3畳・廊下の間より成る・
　　　　　一重・入母屋造・柿葺

大徳寺真珠庵通僊院 庭玉軒（重要文化財）
所在地　　京都府京都市北区紫野大徳寺町
建立年代　17世紀前半（江戸時代前期）
規模形式　茶室2畳台目・水屋の間・土間より成る・杮葺

西翁院 澱看席（重要文化財）
所在地　　京都府京都市左京区黒谷町
建立年代　17世紀後半（江戸時代中期）
規模形式　茶室3畳および勝手口脇袋棚より成る・一重・切妻造・杮葺・
　　　　　正面土庇付・切妻造・杉皮葺

桂離宮 書院＊
所在地　　京都府京都市西京区桂御園
建立年代　17世紀（江戸時代前期）
規模形式　古書院：桁行15.8m・梁行10.9m・入母屋造杮葺・
　　　　　　　　　西側面一部桟瓦葺
　　　　　中書院：桁行9.0m・梁行9.0m・南面入母屋造・杮葺
　　　　　楽器の間：桁行6.9m・梁行5.0m・南面寄棟造・北面切妻造・
　　　　　　　　　　東・南面杮葺・西面桟瓦葺
　　　　　新御殿：桁行13.8m・梁行14.1m・南面入母屋造・
　　　　　　　　　北面切妻造・杮葺

大徳寺孤篷庵 忘筌（重要文化財）
所在地　　京都府京都市北区紫野大徳寺町
建立年代　18世紀（江戸時代後期）
規模形式　桁行4間・梁行3間・一重・切妻造・桟瓦葺

三溪園 聴秋閣（重要文化財）
所在地　　神奈川県横浜市中区本牧三之谷
建立年代　17世紀前半（江戸時代前期）
規模形式　1階：上の間・次の間
　　　　　2階：2畳および階段室より成る
　　　　　二重・上重寄棟造・下重入母屋造・檜皮葺

江沼神社 長流亭（重要文化財）
所在地　　石川県加賀市大聖寺八間道
建立年代　1709年（江戸時代中期）
規模形式　桁行9.5m・梁行8.4m・南面玄関・東面土庇付・一重・
　　　　　寄棟造・杮葺

角屋　緞子の間・檜垣の間・扇の間・青貝の間（重要文化財）＊
所在地　　京都府京都市下京区西新屋敷揚屋町
建立年代　17世紀-18世紀（江戸時代前期-中期）
規模形式　緞子の間23畳・檜垣の間14畳・扇の間21畳・
　　　　　青貝の間17畳半

旧閑谷学校（国宝・重要文化財）＊
所在地　　岡山県備前市閑谷
〈講堂〉国宝
建立年代　1701年（江戸時代中期）
規模形式　桁行19.4m・梁行15.6m・一重・入母屋造・本瓦葺
〈小斎〉重要文化財
建立年代　1677年（江戸時代中期）
規模形式　桁行8.8m・梁行5.6m・一重・入母屋造・杮葺
〈習芸斎および飲室〉重要文化財
建立年代　1701年（江戸時代中期）
規模形式　桁行13.7m・梁行6.9m・一重・入母屋造・本瓦葺
〈文庫〉重要文化財
建立年代　1677年（江戸時代中期）
規模形式　土蔵造・桁行9.7m・梁行3.9m・2階建・切妻造・
　　　　　東西庇付・本瓦葺
〈石塀〉重要文化財
建立年代　1701年（江戸時代中期）
規模形式　石築塀・敷地一周・折曲り延長764.9m

吉村家住宅（重要文化財）＊
所在地　　大阪府羽曳野市島泉
〈主屋〉
建立年代　17世紀前半（江戸時代前期）
規模形式　桁行41.2m・梁行11.4m・切妻造段違・東端入母屋造・
　　　　　茅および本瓦葺・四面庇付・本瓦・杮および桟瓦葺・
　　　　　玄関附属・杮葺
〈表門〉
建立年代　1798年（江戸時代後期）
規模形式　長屋門・桁行18.0m・梁行4.0m・入母屋造・茅葺

吉島家住宅（重要文化財）＊
所在地　　岐阜県高山市大新町
建立年代　1907年（明治時代）
規模形式　主屋：桁行16.7m・梁行13.6m・北面突出部 桁行5.4m・
　　　　　梁行7.3m・一部2階・切妻造段違・桟瓦葺

注　Notes

*1　玉村竹二「文献上より見たる円覚寺舎利殿」『国宝円覚寺舎利殿―修理調査特別報告書―』
　　神奈川県教育委員会　1970年
*2　芳賀幸四郎『東山文化の研究』河出書房　1945年　pp. 458–467
*3　吉永義信「東求堂の再検討」（造園雑誌10・2）日本造園学会　1943年
　　〈https://www.jstage.jst.go.jp/article/jila1934/10/2/10_2_22/_pdf〉（参照2016-11-13）
*4　田中正大「竜安寺方丈前庭之図」（建築史研究・38）建築史研究会編　1972年
*5　京都府教育庁文化財保護課『重要文化財高台寺霊屋修理工事報告書』1956年、および、
　　日高薫「高台寺霊屋蒔絵考」（国華・1192）国華社　1995年
*6　中村昌生「妙喜庵待庵」参考『日本建築史基礎資料集成』（20・茶室）中央公論美術出版　1974年
*7　堀口捨己『利休の茶室』（復刻版）鹿島出版会　1990年　pp. 394–397
*8　中村昌生監「妙喜庵茶室 待庵」『国宝・重文の茶室』世界文化社　1997年　p. 10
*9　堀口捨己「織田有楽の茶室如庵」『茶室研究』（復刻版）鹿島出版会　1990年　pp. 114–115
*10　「松屋會記」（正保5年3月25日）千宗室編『茶道古典全集』（9）淡交社　1956年　p. 443
*11　「山上宗二伝書」中村昌生編著『数寄屋古典集成1 利休の秘法』小学館　1987年　p. 23, p. 25
*12　千宗左・千宗室・千宗守監修・中村昌生編「利休の屋敷と茶室」参考『利休大事典』淡交社　1989年
*13　「草人木」千宗室編『茶道古典全集』（3）淡交社　1956年　p. 201, p. 205
*14　「松屋會記 久重茶會記」（慶長13年2月25日）千宗室編『茶道古典全集』（9）淡交社　1956年　pp. 232–233
*15　巖津政右衛門『閑谷学校』（岡山文庫37）日本文教出版　1971年　p. 73, p. 110

主要参考文献　References

［全般］
伊藤延男編『禅宗建築』（日本の美術126）至文堂　1975年
太田博太郎『新訂 図説日本住宅史』彰国社　1971年
太田博太郎『書院造』（日本美術史叢書5）東京大学出版会　1966年
太田博太郎・川上 貢編『日本建築史基礎資料集成』（16・書院1）中央公論美術出版　1971年
太田博太郎・中村昌生編『日本建築史基礎資料集成』（20・茶室）中央公論美術出版　1974年
太田博太郎『原色日本の美術』（10・禅寺と石庭）小学館　1990年
岡田 譲『床の間と床飾り』（日本の美術152）至文堂　1979年
川上 貢『日本中世住宅の研究』（新訂）中央公論美術出版　2002年
川上 貢編『室町建築』（日本の美術199）至文堂　1982年
川上 貢・ほか編『日本美術全集』（13・禅宗の美術）学研　1994年
服部文雄編『僧房・方丈・庫裏』（日本の美術161）至文堂　1979年
平井 聖編『桃山建築』（日本の美術200）至文堂　1983年
文化庁監・伊藤延男・ほか編『文化財講座 日本の建築』（3・中世2）第一法規出版　1977年
文化庁監・伊藤延男・ほか編『文化財講座 日本の建築』（4・近世1）第一法規出版　1976年
堀口捨己『庭と空間構成の伝統』（縮刷版）鹿島研究所出版会　1977年
堀口捨己『書院造りと数寄屋造りの研究』鹿島出版会　1978年
堀口捨己『茶室研究』（復刻版）鹿島出版会　1990年
中川 武編『日本建築みどころ事典』東京堂出版　1990年
中村昌生監『国宝・重文の茶室』世界文化社　1997年
森 蘊編『庭園とその建物』（日本の美術34）至文堂　1966年
横山 正『数寄屋逍遥―茶室と庭の古典案内―』彰国社　1996年

［各建造物］

大岡 實・ほか『国宝円覚寺舎利殿―修理調査特別報告書―』神奈川県教育委員会 1970年
大岡 信・福島俊翁『東福寺』（古都巡礼 京都18）淡交社 1977年
京都府教育庁指導部文化財保護課編『国宝東福寺三門修理工事報告書』京都府教育委員会 1978年
関野 克編『金閣と銀閣』（日本の美術153）至文堂 1979年
柴田秋介・ほか『鹿苑寺金閣』（日本の庭園美2）集英社 1989年
芳賀幸四郎『東山文化の研究』河出書房 1945年
『国宝慈照寺東求堂修理工事報告書』京都府教育委員会 1965年
キーン，ドナルド『足利義政―日本美の発見―』（角地幸男訳）中央公論新社 2003年
京都府教育委員会『国宝慈照寺銀閣修理工事報告書』京都府教育庁指導部文化財保護課 2010年
重森三玲・ほか『日本庭園史大系』（5・室町の庭1）社会思想社 1973年
有馬頼底・ほか『相國寺』（古都巡礼 京都2）淡交社 1976年
西村 貞『庭と茶室』（講談社アート・ブックス）講談社 1956年
中根金作「竜安寺の池庭の遺構と石庭の作庭年代について」（造園雑誌21・4）日本造園学会 1958年
重森三玲・ほか『日本庭園史大系』（7・室町の庭3）社会思想社 1971年
吉川 需編『枯山水の庭』（日本の美術61）至文堂 1971年
重森三玲『枯山水』中央公論新社 2008年
内藤 昌編『城と館』（復原日本大観1）世界文化社 1988年
内藤 昌編著『ビジュアル版 城の日本史』角川書店 1995年
堀口捨己『利休の茶室』（復刻版）鹿島出版会 1990年
中村昌生『待庵―侘数寄の世界―』淡交社 1993年
齋藤 裕「茶室のエッセンス1–11」（茶の湯332–339）茶の湯同好会 2001–2002年
小脇源治郎編『國寶建造物如庵竝露地移築工事報告』小脇源治郎 1943年
名古屋鉄道『国宝如庵・重要文化財旧正伝院書院 移築修理工事報告書』名古屋鉄道 1972年
中村昌生「如庵の再生」（伝統と創造のノート1・日本美術工芸）日本美術工芸社 1973年
内藤 昌『新桂離宮論』（SD選書12）鹿島出版会 1967年
内藤 昌・西川 孟『桂離宮』講談社インターナショナル 1977年
斎藤英俊編『近世宮廷の美術―桂／修学院と京都御所―』（日本美術全集19）学習研究社 1979年
石元泰博・磯崎新・熊倉功夫・佐藤理『桂離宮―空間と形―』岩波書店 1983年
和辻哲郎『桂離宮―様式の背後を探る―』中公文庫 1991年
佐藤 理『―昭和・平成の大修復全記録―桂離宮の建築』木耳社 1999年
熊倉功夫『後水尾天皇』中公文庫 2010年
『重要文化財孤篷庵本堂・忘筌及び書院修理工事報告書』京都府教育委員会 1965年
『重要文化財 旧東慶寺仏殿・月華殿・旧燈明寺三重塔・聴秋閣 修理工事報告書』
　三溪園重要文化財建造物修理実施委員会 1956年
文化財建造物保存技術協会編『重要文化財 江沼神社長流亭修理工事報告書』
　重要文化財江沼神社長流亭修理委員会 1978年
『重要文化財 角屋修理工事報告書』京都府教育委員会 1971年
内藤 昌・西川 孟『角屋―図版刷』中央公論社 1983年
巖津政右衛門『閑谷学校』（岡山文庫37）日本文教出版 1971年
閑谷学校創学330年記念事業実行委員会・ほか編『閑谷学校資料館図録』
　特別史跡旧閑谷学校顕彰保存会 2000年
『重要文化財 吉村家住宅修理工事報告書』重要文化財吉村家住宅修理委員会 1970年
工藤圭章編『農家Ⅲ』（日本の民家3）学習研究社 1981年
宮本長二郎編『民家と町並 近畿』（日本の美術288）至文堂 1990年
伊藤ていじ・畑亮夫・ほか『重要文化財 吉島家住宅』毎日新聞社 1984年
吉島忠男『吉島家住宅』私家版 1999年

| 謝辞 | Acknowledgements |

ご協力に深く感謝申し上げます
(敬称略)

林屋晴三
有馬賴底
熊倉功夫

円覚寺
東福寺
鹿苑寺
慈照寺
相國寺
龍安寺
園城寺
高台寺
姫路フィルムコミッション
妙喜庵
名鉄犬山ホテル／有楽苑 如庵
大徳寺 真珠庵
金戒光明寺 西翁院
宮内庁京都事務所
大徳寺 孤篷庵
三溪園保勝会
江沼神社
角屋保存会
特別史跡旧閑谷学校顕彰保存会
吉村堯／吉村家住宅
吉島忠男／吉島家住宅
(掲載順)

写真提供　鹿苑寺 蔵 p. 72, p. 73, p. 78, p. 79

翻訳　リン・E・リッグス
　　　武智 學

図面制作・画像オペレーション　丸谷晴道（齋藤裕建築研究所）
レイアウト・デザインデータ制作　勝田亜加里（デザイン実験室）

プリンティング・ディレクション　勝又紀智（図書印刷）

Seizo Hayashiya
Raitei Arima
Isao Kumakura
(Honorific titles are omitted.)

Engakuji
Tofukuji
Rokuonji
Jishoji
Shokokuji
Ryoanji
Onjoji
Kodaiji
Himeji Film Commission
Myokian
Meitetsu Inuyama Hotel/Urakuen Jo-an
Daitokuji Shinjuan
Konkai-Komyoji Saioin
Imperial Household Agency Kyoto Office
Daitokuji Kohoan
Sankeien Garden
Enuma Shrine
Sumiya
Preservation Association in honor of "Special historic spot: Former Shizutani School"
Takashi Yoshimura/Yoshimura House
Tadao Yoshijima/Yoshijima House

Photograph credits:
　All photographs ©Yutaka Saito except the mentioned below.
　p. 72, p. 73, p. 78, p. 79 : Courtesy Rokuonji

Translation: Lynne E. Riggs
　　　　　　Manabu Takechi

Drawing and image processing:
　Harumichi Maruya (Yutaka Saito Architect & Associates)
Page layout and design data processing:
　Akari Katsuta (Design Laboratory)

Printing direction:
　Noritoshi Katsumata (TOSHO Printing)

著者紹介　About the Author

©Nacása & Partners

齋藤　裕　建築家

1947年	北海道小樽市生まれ
	独学で建築を学ぶ
1970年	齋藤裕建築研究所を設立
1986年	日本建築家協会新人賞を「るるるる阿房」で受賞
1992年	吉田五十八賞を「好日居」で受賞
1993年	東京アートディレクターズクラブ・原弘賞を『ルイス・バラガンの建築』で受賞
1998年	日本建築学会・北海道建築賞を「曼月居」で受賞
2000年	日本建築学会・学会賞および作品選奨を「曼月居」で受賞

建築作品集に、『齋藤裕の建築』(TOTO出版　1998年)、
『現代の建築家シリーズ 齋藤裕』(鹿島出版会　1994年)がある。
また、写真を媒介として建築空間を探求し、写真集を出版する。
既刊写真集に、
『ルイス・バラガンの建築』(TOTO出版　1992年／メキシコ・ノリエガ出版　1994年／
TOTO出版・改訂版　1996年)、
『フェリックス・キャンデラの世界』(TOTO出版　1995年)、
『建築の詩人　カルロ・スカルパ』(TOTO出版　1997年)、
『カーサ・バラガン』(TOTO出版　2002年)、
『ルイス・カーンの全住宅：1940-1974年』(TOTO出版　2003年)、
『ヴィラ・マイレア／アルヴァ・アールト』(TOTO出版　2005年)、
『AALTO: 10 Selected Houses アールトの住宅』(TOTO出版　2008年)、
『日本建築の形 I』(TOTO出版　2016年)がある。
そのほかに、エッセイ集『STRONG』(住まいの図書館出版局　1991年)、
対談集『建築のエッセンス』(A. D. A. EDITA Tokyo　2000年)が出版されている。

Yutaka Saito　Architect

1947	Born in Otaru City, Hokkaido, Japan.
	Studied architecture independently.
1970	Founded Yutaka Saito Architect & Associates.
1986	Won the Japan Institute of Architects Prize of the Best Young Architect of the year for "Rurururu Abo."
1992	Won the Isoya Yoshida Prize for "Kojitsu-kyo."
1993	Won the Tokyo Art Directors Club Hiromu Hara Prize for *Luis Barragan*.
1998	Won the Hokkaido Architectural Prize of the Architectural Institute of Japan for "Mangetsu-kyo."
2000	Won the Architectural Institute of Japan Award for "Mangetsu-kyo." Won the 2000 Selected Architectural Design Award of the Architectural Institute of Japan for "Mangetsu-kyo."

The collection of his architectural works has been published:
Gendai no kenchikuka shirizu Saito Yutaka [Contemporary Architect: Yutaka Saito] (Kajima Shuppankai, 1994), and *Yutaka Saito: Architect* (TOTO Publishing, 1998).
Along with his architectural practice, he has begun to photograph architecture as part of his study of space and published photographic books including;
Luis Barragan (TOTO Publishing, 1992, revised edition, 1996; Noriega Editores, 1994),
Felix Candela (TOTO Publishing, 1995), *Casa Barragan* (TOTO Publishing, 2002),
Louis I. Kahn Houses (TOTO Publishing, 2003), *Villa Mairea/Alvar Aalto* (TOTO Publishing, 2005), *Aalto: 10 Selected Houses* (TOTO Publishing, 2008) and *The Essence of Japanese Architecture I* (TOTO Publishing, 2016).
He is author of books entitled *STRONG* (Sumai-no-Toshokan Shuppannkyoku, 1991) and *The Essence of Architecture* (A. D. A. EDITA Tokyo, 2000).

日本建築の形 II

2017年4月17日　初版第1刷発行

著・写真	齋藤 裕
発行者	加藤 徹
発行所	TOTO出版（TOTO株式会社）

〒107-0062　東京都港区南青山1-24-3
TOTO乃木坂ビル 2F
[営業]TEL: 03-3402-7138　FAX: 03-3402-7187
[編集]TEL: 03-3497-1010
URL: http://www.toto.co.jp/publishing/

編集	三輪直美
デザイン	工藤強勝
印刷・製本	図書印刷株式会社

落丁本・乱丁本はお取り替えいたします。
本書のコピー・スキャン・デジタル化等の無断複製行為を禁じます。
本書を代行業者等の第三者に依頼してスキャンやデジタル化することは、
たとえ個人や家庭内での利用であっても著作権上認められておりません。
定価はカバーに示してあります。

©2017 Yutaka Saito

Printed in Japan
ISBN978-4-88706-363-1